Weapons of Mass Deception

JOURNALISM AND POLITICAL COMMUNICATION UNBOUND

Journalism and Political Communication Unbound seeks to be a high-profile book series that reaches far beyond the academy to an interested public of policymakers, journalists, public intellectuals, and citizens eager to make sense of contemporary politics and media. "Unbound" in the series title has multiple meanings: It refers to the unbinding of borders between the fields of communication, political communication, and journalism, as well as related disciplines such as political science, sociology, and science and technology studies; it highlights the ways traditional frameworks for scholarship have disintegrated in the wake of changing digital technologies and new social, political, economic, and cultural dynamics; and it reflects the unbinding of media in a hybrid world of flows across mediums.

Other books in the series:

Journalism Research That Matters
Valérie Bélair-Gagnon and Nikki Usher

Voices for Transgender Equality: Making Change in the Networked Public Sphere
Thomas J. Billard

Reckoning: Journalism's Limits and Possibilities
Candis Callison and Mary Lynn Young

News After Trump: Journalism's Crisis of Relevance in a Changed Media Culture
Matt Carlson, Sue Robinson, and Seth C. Lewis

Press Freedom and the (Crooked) Path Toward Democracy: Lessons from Journalists in East Africa
Meghan Sobel Cohen and Karen McIntyre Hopkinson

Data-Driven Campaigning and Political Parties: Five Advanced Democracies Compared
Katharine Dommett, Glenn Kefford, and Simon Kruschinski

Borderland: Decolonizing the Words of War
Chrisanthi Giotis

Not Your Parents' Politics: Understanding Young People's Political Expression on Social Media
Neta Kligler-Vilenchik and Ioana Literat

Movement Media: In Pursuit of Solidarity
Rachel Kuo

The Politics of Force: Media and the Construction of Police Brutality
Regina G. Lawrence

Connective Action and the Rise of the Far-Right: Platforms, Politics, and the Crisis of Democracy
Steven Livingston and Michael Miller

Authoritarian Journalism: Controlling the News in Post-Conflict Rwanda
Ruth Moon

Apocalyptic Authoritarianism: Climate Crisis, Media, and Power
Hanna E. Morris

Imagined Audiences: How Journalists Perceive and Pursue the Public
Jacob L. Nelson

Pop Culture, Politics, and the News: Entertainment Journalism in the Polarized Media Landscape
Joel Penney

The Invented State: Policy Misperceptions in the American Public
Emily Thorson

Democracy Lives in Darkness: How and Why People Keep Their Politics a Secret
Emily Van Duyn

Media and January 6th
Khadijah Costley White, Daniel Kreiss, Shannon C. McGregor, and Rebekah Tromble

Building Theory in Political Communication: The Politics-Media-Politics Approach
Gadi Wolfsfeld, Tamir Sheafer, and Scott Althaus

Capturing News, Capturing Democracy: Trump and the Voice of America
Kate Wright, Martin Scott, and Mel Bunce

Weapons of Mass Deception

How Right-Wing Media Wage Information Warfare and Undermine American Democracy

Yunkang Yang

OXFORD
UNIVERSITY PRESS

Oxford University Press is a department of the University of Oxford.
It furthers the university's objective of excellence in research, scholarship,
and education by publishing worldwide. Oxford is a registered trade mark of
Oxford University Press in the UK and in certain other countries.

Published in the United States of America by Oxford University Press
198 Madison Avenue, New York, NY 10016, United States of America.

Library of Congress Cataloging-in-Publication Data
Names: Yang, Yunkang, 1989- author
Title: Weapons of mass deception : how right-wing media wage information
warfare and undermine American democracy / Yunkang Yang.
Description: New York, NY : Oxford University Press, 2025. |
Series: Journalism and political communication unbound |
Includes bibliographical references and index.
Identifiers: LCCN 2025023496 (print) | LCCN 2025023497 (ebook) |
ISBN 9780197820308 paperback | ISBN 9780197820292 hardback |
ISBN 9780197820315 epub | ISBN 9780197820339
Subjects: LCSH: Mass media—Political aspects—United States |
Disinformation—United States | Conservatism in the press—United States |
Press and propaganda—United States | Truthfulness and falsehood in mass media |
Rich people—Political activity—United States
Classification: LCC P95.82.U6 Y36 2025 (print) | LCC P95.82.U6 (ebook)
LC record available at https://lccn.loc.gov/2025023496
LC ebook record available at https://lccn.loc.gov/2025023497

DOI: 10.1093/9780197820339.001.0001

Paperback printed by Marquis Book Printing, Canada
Hardback printed by Lightning Source, Inc., United States of America

The manufacturer's authorized representative in the EU for product safety is
Oxford University Press España S.A., Parque Empresarial San Fernando de Henares,
Avenida de Castilla, 2 – 28830 Madrid (www.oup.es/en or product.safety@oup.com).
OUP España S.A. also acts as importer into Spain of products made by the manufacturer.

For my parents, 云霞 *and* 杨立刚

CONTENTS

LIST OF FIGURES

LIST OF TABLES

ACKNOWLEDGEMENTS

THIS BOOK WOULD NOT HAVE been possible without the support of my dissertation committee chair, W. Lance Bennett. In the wake of the 2016 U.S. election, Lance sparked my interest in the subject of right-wing media and provided invaluable guidance throughout the research process. It was truly a privilege to learn from his scholarship. I am deeply grateful to Lance not only for his inspirational mentorship, but also for being my strongest advocate throughout these years.

My dissertation evolved into a book manuscript during my time as a postdoctoral research scientist at the Institute for Data, Democracy & Politics at George Washington University. I am deeply indebted to Matthew Hindman, my postdoctoral mentor, for his guidance throughout the book's development. Matt's insights into framing and structuring the manuscript helped shape its narrative, and his advice on the intricacies of academic publishing was indispensable for me to navigate this process. Beyond his intellectual support, Matt generously took the time to provide line edits on my writing, sharpening my arguments, and elevating the clarity of my prose. Matt's mentorship offers a model of generosity and kindness that I will carry forward in my career.

I owe a debt of gratitude to Steven Livingston, who became an integral part of this project's intellectual development at its early stage. His guidance and insights were indispensable in shaping the project during its formative years. Steve's mentorship also extended beyond the page. He welcomed me into the intellectual community he helped build, celebrated my success along the way, and, during my time as a post-doctoral research scientist at the institute he founded, made me feel supported during the isolating period of the Covid-19 pandemic. It is truly my honor to have Steve as my mentor and friend.

The book also benefited from the support of my dissertation committee members—Matthew Powers, Kirsten Foot, Adrienne Russell, and Emma Spiro—all of whom read the dissertation with care and provided thoughtful feedback. I feel deeply fortunate to have had their guidance and encouragement.

I have been fortunate to present portions of my book at numerous academic conferences, workshops, and talks, including the American Political Science Association Annual Meeting in 2018, the University of Southern California's Annenberg School for Communication and Journalism in 2019, the Weizenbaum Institute in 2023, and the University of North Carolina Chapel Hill's Center for Information, Technology, and Public Life in 2024. At these events and many others, I received invaluable support and feedback from colleagues and peers. I am grateful to Josephine Lukito, Tan Zhao, Qian He, Hsiao Yuan, Sabine Lang, Shannon McGregor, Tressie McMillan Cottom, Kate Starbird, Mike Ananny, Regina Lawrence, T. J. Billard, Scott Althaus, David Karpf, Young Mie Kim, A. J. Bauer, Curd Knüpfer, Rebekah Tromble, Ethan Porter, and Janny W. Fritzen for their encouragement. I also thank the John S. and James L. Knight Foundation for their generous support of the book's research.

My colleagues at Texas A&M University have been immensely supportive through the final stages of writing and revisions. I would like to thank Hart Blanton, Jennifer Mercieca, Tang Lu, Bryce Henson, Jennifer Lueck, and Antonio C. La Pastina for their advice as I transitioned to the role of assistant professor.

I would like to express my gratitude to my editors at Oxford University Press. I am thankful to Daniel Kreiss and Nik Usher for their insightful feedback, which enhanced the clarity of the manuscript. I also appreciate Angela Chnapko and Andrea Smith for their stewardship of the review and production process. It is truly a privilege to work with such dedicated editors.

Finally, I want to thank Ryan Skorupski. Ryan's independent mind has been a constant source of perspective, offering me clarity and helping me stay centered. His friendship has been a true gift.

Yunkang Yang
Houston, 2025

INTRODUCTION

AROUND 2 P.M. ON JANUARY 6, 2021, a mob overwhelmed police and stormed the U.S. Capitol. Carrying weapons and shouting "Hang Mike Pence," the rioters arrived at the House chamber to see lawmakers still fleeing—just yards away—on the other side of a barricaded glass-paneled wooden door. Screaming obscenities, the rioters smashed the glass. A woman in the mob jumped up and pushed herself through a broken window.

A shot rang out, and the woman fell back. Blood poured from her mouth, covering half of her face. She twitched for a few seconds and then died.

The woman was Ashli Babbitt, a 35-year-old from San Diego. Babbitt had explained on Twitter that she came to D.C. because she "knew" the election had been stolen. On November 10, she retweeted claims of massive voter fraud broadcast by Tucker Carlson on Fox News. On November 16 and December 14, she echoed claims from Rush Limbaugh and One America News (OAN) that electronic voting machines had switched votes to Biden. On December 19, she retweeted Newsmax's assertion that "the Kraken"—a dog whistle for the ultimate weapon to overturn the election results—was coming.

Babbitt wrote her last tweet on January 5, the day before her life came to a violent end. "Nothing will stop us. They can try and try and try but the storm is here and it is descending upon DC in less than 24 hours . . . dark to light."

Weapons of Mass Deception. Yunkang Yang, Oxford University Press. © Yunkang Yang (2025).
DOI: 10.1093/9780197820339.003.0001

Babbitt was right about one thing: "nothing will stop us." Many right-wing media outlets continued to question the legitimacy of the 2020 election in the wake of the insurrection, even though some of their owners and hosts privately expressed disbelief about election fraud claims.[1] Since 2021, poll after poll has shown that most Republican voters still refuse to see Joe Biden as the legitimate winner of the 2020 election.[2] In 2022, 179 Republicans who denied or cast doubt on the 2020 election were elected to the 118th Congress.[3] Then, in 2024, American voters reelected Donald Trump as the 47th president—a twice-impeached, convicted felon who had not only summoned a mob to overturn the will of the people but also declared, half-jokingly, that he would be a dictator on day one.

How did the peaceful transfer of power, the hallmark of American democracy, almost end in a violent attack? Why do most Republican voters, when their candidate loses, no longer believe the results of a free and fair election? And what, if anything, can we do about it?

As Babbitt's case suggests, any answer to these questions must begin with an examination of Fox News, Breitbart, and other right-wing media that told millions of Americans the "Big Lie" that the 2020 election was rigged.[4] Democracy is only as strong as its citizens' faith in it. Preserving American democracy requires scholars, regulators, and the public to have a deeper understanding of these organizations: how they operate, what they publish, and how they coordinate.

Weapons of Mass Deception is thus a book about right-wing media and its critical—and widely misunderstood—role in American politics.

It draws upon vastly more data than any previous study of right-wing media: the full text of approximately 4 million online stories from 30 of the largest right-wing TV and digital outlets from January 2017 to December 2020, along with approximately 8 billion Facebook interactions regarding these stories. It couples this mega-scale analysis of right-wing media content with a deep dive into the media's organizational patterns and practices, sifting through internal emails, Federal Election Commission (FEC) filings, legal documents, and private communications among right-wing media employees.

The book's evidence forces us to question some of our most basic assumptions about right-wing media. For example, do right-wing media outlets truly behave like partisan news organizations that just put a spin on news favorable to their own party? Or do they instead behave like full-fledged political organizations, mobilizing resources and selecting tactics in pursuit of tangible political objectives? Do right-wing media always operate in the interest of the GOP—functioning in effect as a party press? Or do they pursue the interests of their owners and allied political elites—even when doing so damages the Republican party? Do they always echo and amplify each other—functioning as what scholars described as an "echo chamber" or "network propaganda"?[5] Or do they clash with each other when they pursue different political agendas?

Rethinking Right-Wing Media

Social scientists have generally viewed right-wing media in two ways. The first sees them as partisan news organizations that frame and select news through a partisan, ideological lens. Fox News, for example, is viewed as a biased news outlet, the right-wing counterpart to MSNBC. This approach has placed right-wing media's ideological bias at the center of academic inquiry. While media scholars have compared Fox's biased coverage to that of other news organizations,[6] political scientists and economists have used field experiments and survey instruments to evaluate the effect of Fox's bias.[7] Their findings often highlight the following: Fox exhibits a consistent conservative bias in its news coverage and could have a measurable effect on shaping people's attitudes and behavior.

To be sure, right-wing media outlets exhibit significant bias in how they select and frame news. But bias is far from the whole story.[8] In their book *Network Propaganda*, Harvard researcher Yochai Benkler, Robert Faris, and Hal Roberts offered a second perspective. They argued that right-wing media should be considered as mainly market-driven propaganda outlets that repeat and amplify each other's falsehoods.[9] According to their analysis, right-wing media propaganda is primarily an audience strategy aimed at profiting from the White, Christian market segment on the political right.[10] In essence, *Network Propaganda* suggests that the primary reason why right-wing media spread lies is because these falsehoods, designed to appeal to the audiences' identity, are lucrative.

My book offers a third way of thinking about right-wing media. The main story of the book unfolds in two parts. In Part I, I argue that many right-wing media outlets function as political organizations. This is not only evident in their overt political organizing activities, such as fundraising and voter outreach, but also in their routine partisan reporting that can help achieve political objectives.

In Part II, I demonstrate that while different right-wing media outlets often engage in ideological conflict, they can also coalesce into a powerful political machine—marked by a striking level of coherence and goal-orientation—capable of convincing millions of Americans that the 2020 election was stolen. While Part I delves into the political logic of right-wing media at the individual outlet level, Part II brings this analysis to the network level—exploring how this logic manifests through the interactions among right-wing media outlets and their relationship with the Republican Party.

The Book's Story

Part I: Right-Wing Media as Political Organizations

Political organizations are formal entities that articulate political issues, recruit participants, coordinate tasks, determine the timing of actions, and select methods and tactics.[11] These elements, as political scientists Bruce Bimber, Cynthia Stohl, and Andrew Flanagin argued, are present in research on many traditional political organizations. They can be understood as performing three general functions: resource mobilization, tactics selection, and the achievement of political goals. For example, political parties mobilize voters and run campaigns to win elections, social movement organizations mobilize protesters and engage in street theater to raise social awareness, and interest groups mobilize legislative resources and engage in lobbying to achieve policy goals.

On the surface, it may seem counterintuitive to compare right-wing media to political organizations. After all, OAN hires "reporters" who attended White House briefings, Fox boasts state-of-the-art television studios, and Breitbart positions itself as an international news organization with bureaus in multiple countries. However, upon closer examination of their actions during critical moments in America' political history, I find that many right-wing media outlets effectively operated like political organizations. They mobilized resources, selected tactics, and pursued tangible political outcomes.

For example, during the 2016 election, the *National Enquirer* paid a porn star $150,000 to bury a story about Donald Trump's extramarital affairs; during the 2018 election, multiple Fox personalities physically campaigned for Donald Trump in his rallies;[12] in the 2020 election, Breitbart emailed its subscribers to solicit funds for Republican candidates; following the January 6 insurrection, OAN ran a prominent front-page story titled "OAN Call to Action: How to Donate to Lawmakers Who Stayed True to President Trump," linking to fundraising sites for Republicans who voted to overturn the 2020 election results.[13] These activities, which extend far beyond the journalistic practices of reporting and editorializing, are political organizing activities. As the book will show, political organizing is not a sideline or an occasional overstep but a long-standing tradition baked into many right-wing media outlets' practices at every level, especially during elections. To understand right-wing media, we must view them through the lens of political organizations.

Of course, right-wing media also provide day-to-day news reporting. Importantly, they can function as political organizations even—perhaps especially—in the midst of partisan journalistic reporting. When right-wing media follow Republican talking points—for instance, repeating claims that the 2020 election was stolen—they can become handmaidens of power, mobilizing audiences toward specific political goals. In doing so, they effectively replicate the core functions of a political organization.

This book adopts a functionalist approach, presenting evidence that right-wing media, whether through political organizing activities or partisan reporting, can function as political organizations. It is worth noting that the blending of journalistic practices with political organizing activities—what media scholar Andrew Chadwick called "hybrid organizational repertories"[14]—is a rather unique feature of right-wing media compared to other more traditional political organizations. The fusion of journalism and political organizing can create internal tensions within right-wing media, as employees must navigate the competing demands of upholding journalistic standards while advancing political objectives. However, as I will discuss in the conclusion chapter, this blending also makes right-wing media powerful as a political tool, as they enjoy broad legal protections afforded by their journalistic status.

Much like any political organizations, right-wing media outlets engage in resource mobilization, strategic selection of tactics, and the pursuit of political objectives. However, what makes them uniquely dangerous to American democracy is their willingness and ability to use information as a weapon to fight information warfare. By spreading disinformation in news format—either intentionally or inadvertently through partisan reporting—they have tapped into the credibility traditionally associated with journalism to mislead millions of American voters. Over the past decade, media and political elites on the right have increasingly weaponized journalistic practices to both spread ideologically convenient disinformation and to discredit truthful stories that threaten political harm. As Chapter 2 will show, this has resulted in systemic breakdowns in information quality—especially with regard to some of the most high-profile political stories that generated substantial audience engagement and, thus, potentially significant impact on American politics.

Part II: Three Models of Political Organizing in the Right-Wing Media Sphere

If right-wing media function as political organizations with distinct political and ideological goals, we can expect both contestation and cooperation among them. When their goals conflict, they may adopt contrasting stances on GOP candidates and issues. Conversely, when their goals align, they often coalesce around a shared narrative—particularly in response to significant political threats that endanger their collective interests. To examine how the political logic of right-wing media manifests in their interactions with one another and their relationship with the Republican Party, I propose a typology of three ideal types of political organizing, each designed to achieve strategic political objectives.

Ideologically contested political organizing: The right-wing media sphere is organized along internal ideological fault lines that divide the GOP and the conservative movement coalition.

Politician-led political organizing: Republican elites shape right-wing media coverage around a strategic narrative designed to advance political goals.

Media-led political organizing: A leading media organization rallies the right-wing media sphere around a strategic narrative designed to advance political goals.

The development of this typology stems from my observation of a series of political events that unfolded during the first Trump administration. In late July 2017, Trump's national security advisor, H.R. McMaster, fired several "anti-establishment" White House officials. After the firings, a group of right-wing media outlets published several damning stories about McMaster and called for his resignation. However, another group defended McMaster and criticized the anti-McMaster media outlets publicly. The feud among right-wing media outlets continued even after Donald Trump issued a public statement in support of McMaster.

Before long, a notable divergence of news coverage occurred again within the right-wing sphere. During the Republican primary in the U.S. Senate special election in Alabama in 2017, Rupert Murdoch instructed Fox News's CEO Suzanne Scott to support the incumbent GOP senator Luther Strange;[15] however, Breitbart's CEO Steve Bannon mobilized his employees to campaign for Strange's GOP challenger, Roy Moore, who was accused of sexual misconduct. In light of the accusations, Fox host Sean Hannity urged Moore to withdraw from the race,[16] whereas Breitbart's chief editor, Alex Marlow, sought to undermine the credibility of Moore's accusers.[17]

These two examples stand in stark contrast to previous theories of right-wing media. In the book *Echo Chamber*, political scientists Kathleen Jamieson and Joseph Cappella characterized right-wing media as "cousins with a shared commitment to Reagan conservatism, a common ideological ancestry, and a network of related kin."[18] Ten years later, the book *Network Propaganda* declared that the right-wing media sphere functions as network propaganda where outlets repeat each other's lies.[19] According to these two theories, right-wing media are governed by either a common commitment to Reagan conservatism (echo chamber) or a market force that incentivizes them to spread the same identity-affirming lies (network propaganda).[20] Both theories created the impression that right-wing media outlets are uniformly partisan and therefore homogenous.

While there is undoubtedly a significant amount of echoing among different right-wing media outlets, they've also pursued diverging political goals, resulting in disagreements over GOP candidates and government policies. The divergence between Fox and Breitbart in the coverage of Roy Moore's campaign is just one example of these disagreements. Unlike what previous theories suggest, right-wing media are not uniformly partisan. Neither are they homogenous. Rather, they are controlled by different individuals and families whose political goals and priorities do not necessarily align with each other or with those of the GOP. Their disagreements may not always be apparent in public, but when they emerge—for example, during GOP primaries, we may observe *ideologically contested political organizing* wherein different right-wing media outlets support different GOP candidates.

Having identified the first ideal type, I became interested in understanding when and how different right-wing media outlets could come together to promote a strategic narrative designed to address an emerging political problem. It is important to note that this question, which is based on the premise that right-wing media are different political actors pursuing distinct interests, differs from the central concerns of previous theories like those in *Echo Chamber* and *Network Propaganda*.

Both *Echo Chamber* and *Network Propaganda* emphasize that right-wing media tend to report much the same stories in much the same terms in many issue areas. The common thread in these issue areas is either a shared commitment to Reagan conservatism or a market incentive to appeal to the White Christian identity. This perspective makes sense for highly polarized issues such as abortion, where the sides and framing strategies have become largely well-enough established that different right-wing media outlets do not need to take cues from political elites or consult each other to know which sides to pick or what narratives to write.

However, when confronted with emerging political problems such as natural disasters, health crises, or political scandals, crafting a coherent narrative can become more complicated for different right-wing media outlets. In such situations, there might be no preexisting identity-based or ideology-based scripts that all right-wing media can intuitively follow. While a political crisis threatening the collective interests of the right typically triggers a rallying effect, the puzzle is how these diverse media outlets coalesce around a goal-oriented strategic narrative in response to the threat, especially without a centralized propaganda department dictating their messaging.

In September 2018, Christine Ford alleged that Trump's U.S. Supreme Court nominee Brett Kavanaugh had sexually assaulted her. Her allegation could derail Kavanaugh's confirmation, which, if successful, would shift the ideological balance of America's highest court. One would expect that some right-wing media may attack Ford. In fact, this did happen initially—mostly on far right, conspiratorial sites. However, attacking sexual assault victims only two months away from the 2018 midterm election carries a significant political cost for Republicans—namely that it may alienate a key voting bloc: women voters in suburban areas. As a result, Republican elites chose to support Kavanaugh while expressing sympathy toward Ford.[21] As most right-wing media outlets relied on Republican senators as their primary source, they also avoided personal attacks against Ford. This example demonstrates the influence of Republican elites over right-wing media when a common political threat emerges, which I characterize as *politician-led political organizing.*

A leading right-wing media organization can also rally the right-wing media sphere around a solution-based strategic narrative. In May 2017, the Justice Department was about to appoint Robert Mueller as special counsel to investigate Donald Trump's ties to Russia, which Trump characterized as an existential threat to his presidency.[22] Yet, Republicans were divided on how to respond to this threat.[23] To distract and potentially undermine Mueller's investigation, Fox News revived a debunked conspiracy theory with fabricated sources, falsely claiming that it was Seth Rich, a deceased Democratic National Committee (DNC) staffer, who handed the stolen DNC emails to WikiLeaks—not Russian hackers. This conspiracy theory suggests that Russian hackers did not interfere in the 2016 election and that therefore there was no collusion between Trump and Russia. Fox's disinformation story quickly spread to the rest of the right-wing media sphere. Within two days, most major right-wing media outlets repeated Fox's lie. This example shows the influence of a top right-wing media outlet over other right-wing media when a common political threat emerges, which I characterize as *media-led political organizing.*

Before previewing each chapter, I will provide a historical context for understanding right-wing media as political organizations. The postwar history of right-wing media is fundamentally a history of political organizing. The most influential right-wing radio broadcasters, TV hosts, and magazine editors from the early 1950s to the late 1980s were not just content creators; they were also political campaigners, founders of political organizations, town hall meeting organizers, and protest leaders. Their goal was not merely to win the intellectual debate but to defeat what they perceived as liberal hegemony in America.[24] In their pursuit of power, some right-wing media activists have decided to abandon journalistic integrity, using media instead as a weapon to wage information warfare against their perceived enemies.

From the Airwaves to the Frontlines

Between 1953 and 1956, about a million hydrogen balloons carrying biblical pamphlets floated over the Iron Curtain, which, according to historian Heather Hendershot, inspired the Hungarian Revolution of 1956.[25] The mastermind behind this balloon project was Billy Hargis, a right-wing broadcaster whose message once reached 500 radio and 250 TV stations across the United States.[26] As one might suspect, pulling off such a feat was no easy task. Hargis consulted with the U.S. State Department, hired meteorologists to test weather conditions, had the balloons specially manufactured to float in favorable winds, and organized a crew of refugees to assist the launch in a field in West Germany.[27] Hargis was not merely a broadcaster; he was also, as Hendershot called him, "a crafty political operator."[28] In the 1960s, he organized training seminars to coordinate actions among Christian leaders; he founded Christian Crusade, a nonprofit organization whose nonprofit status was revoked because of its overt political activities; he also pioneered direct mail and computerized mass mailings, a tactic that later became crucial in building the organizational infrastructure of the conservative movement.[29]

Like Hargis, prominent right-wing media figures engaged extensively in political organizing from the 1950s to the 1960s. Clarence Manion, the host of Manion Forum, led the Bricker Amendment campaign to weaken the president's power in 1953; in 1955, he also founded For America, a campaign organization for third-party candidate T. Coleman Andrews.[30] William Buckley Jr., the founding editor of *National Review* and former host of the PBS TV show *Firing Line*, helped found Young Americans for Freedom in 1960, an organization that mobilized conservative college students; In 1965, he even ran for New York City mayor.[31] William Rusher, the publisher of *National Review* and frequent PBS guest, cofounded the Draft Goldwater Committee, which helped Barry Goldwater secure the GOP nomination for the 1964 presidential election. For Manion, Buckley, and Rusher, disseminating conservative ideas through media was certainly central to their work. But they also took actions beyond merely speaking in front of a microphone, ensuring that their ideas did not just stay on the airwaves but led to tangible political change. As historian Nicole Hemmer put it, these conservative media figures were "the main source of activism and political organization,"[32] leading the charge at the forefront of the early conservative movement.

In the 1970s, the New Right emerged as a political movement centered around social issues such as abortion and homosexuality. Compared to the Old Right, the New Right took a more aggressive approach to organizing. Richard Viguerie, one of New Right's chief architects, declared that they "were more interested in winning the election than winning the debate."[33] He and Paul Weyrich secured the backing of rich donors to fund a sprawling network of think tanks, advocacy groups, and networking organizations, which have profoundly shaped America's political landscape.[34]

A key organization within this network is the Council for National Policy (CNP). Morton Blackwell, a cofounder of CNP, emphasized the importance of integrating media into the right-wing political machine, noting in a speech that "political technology can be roughly divided into communication technology and organization technology with no neat line of separation between communication and organization."[35] In the 1980s, CNP developed close ties with media activists of the Christian Right. Its members included the founders of three major Christian broadcasting companies—Salem Radio Network, Bott Radio Network, and American Family Radio—whose business models relied heavily on selling airtime and advertising to CNP-affiliated organizations.[36] It also counted among its members prominent televangelists—Christian evangelical leaders who primarily use TV broadcasting as a medium to preach.

Like the early conservative media activists, televangelists established brick-and-mortar political organizations to advocate for their causes. Jerry Falwell Sr., the host of *The Old Time Gospel Hour*, cofounded the Moral Majority, a powerful organization with a lobbying arm aimed at influencing legislations and a political action committee (PAC) designed to support political campaigns.[37] Pat Robertson, host of *The 700 Club*, founded the Christian Coalition, which used a variety of tactics—including sending videotapes of a homosexual film to each member of the House of Representatives—to influence public policy.[38] James Dobson, the host of *Focus on the Family*, cofounded the Family Research Council, which supported conservative candidates through its affiliated political action committee and lobbied for the 1996 Defense of Marriage Act, a law that denied federal recognition of same-sex marriage.

Televangelism was only one facet of the New Right's media activism. While figures like Falwell, Robertson, and Dobson were mobilizing their followers through religious broadcasting, a parallel effort was underway to build a robust network of secular conservative media, including neoconservative and libertarian publications. This network was heavily supported by wealthy individuals who recognized the power of media to shape public opinion. For instance, Television News Inc. (TVN), an outlet that provided syndicated news services, received millions of dollars in seed money from the Coors family in the 1970s. The *American Spectator* magazine received $1.5 million from the Olin, Coors, Bradley, Scaife, and Starr foundations in the 1980s.[39] The *Washington Times*, founded in 1982, received over $900 million in financial support from Sun Myung Moon during its first decade. The neoconservative magazines *National Interest* and *Public Interest*, and the libertarian magazine *Reason*, similarly benefited from substantial financial backing by conservative foundations.[40] By the early 1990s, the three biggest conservative donors were contributing a significantly larger proportion of their wealth to fund ideological media compared to their liberal counterparts.[41]

It wasn't until the 1980s that the talk show host Rush Limbaugh transformed right-wing media into a sustainably profitable business. As Limbaugh's radio audience grew, he became a GOP kingmaker, performing crucial party functions, such as assessing candidates' fitness for office.[42] Limbaugh's political influence was widely recognized by Republican leaders. Ronald Reagan praised Limbaugh as his spiritual heir in 1992; George H. W. Bush invited him for a sleepover at the White House in 1994, personally carrying his bag to the Lincoln bedroom.[43] In 2020, Donald Trump awarded Limbaugh the Presidential Medal of Freedom, cementing his legacy within the conservative movement.

From Hargis to Limbaugh, prominent right-wing media personalities actively participated in politics, using media as a tool to pursue political objectives. The lack of separation between media and political organizing reflects a long-standing tradition in American history. In the 18th century, American revolutionaries did not just print pamphlets—they also organized local militia groups to resist British rule. In the 19th century, partisan newspaper editors did more than just edit newspapers—they set up county meetings, organized conventions, and served on committees to advance the interest of their party.[44] Throughout most of American history, media was almost always intertwined with politics.

However, when we discuss political organizations in the contemporary United States, we tend to focus on party organizations, issue advocacy groups, and think tanks.[45] With a few exceptions,[46] right-wing media are often excluded from this discussion, as we commonly perceive them as belonging to a separate realm—journalism.

In the United States, journalism gained a significant degree of independence from politics during the high-modern period of the mid-20th century. During this time, the field developed powerful professional norms that profoundly shaped public expectations of journalism in America.[47] Journalistic ideals such as seeking truth, maintaining editorial independence, and striving for accuracy have gained such social and cultural authority that they became nearly universal in media outlets' branding.

Unsurprisingly, almost every major right-wing media outlet today presents itself as a news media enterprise rather than a political organization. Keenly aware of the symbolic power and legal protections associated with journalism, they often emphasize their commitment to basic journalistic standards in their self-narratives. For example, Fox branded itself as "fair and balanced"; Breitbart declared its commitment to truthful reporting on its website; even the Gateway Pundit, which filed for bankruptcy in 2024 following defamation lawsuits over its promotion of the Big Lie, claimed that its mission was to seek the truth.

For any media enterprise that claims journalistic status while operating as a political organization, tensions between political expediency and truthfulness are bound to arise. When such tensions arise, a choice must be made: One can uphold truthfulness, even at the risk of political costs, or sacrifice truthfulness in favor of advancing a political agenda. To understand why so many right-wing media outlets have chosen the latter, we must revisit history and examine a defining narrative that has animated the right-wing media sector for decades. This narrative holds that right-wing media must engage in information warfare to counter what they perceive as liberal dominance in the American media landscape. The imperative to win ultimately led some right-wing media activists to compromise journalistic integrity in favor of political expediency.

Conservative Media Activism as Information Warfare

In 1968, ABC News invited Gore Vidal, a liberal public intellectual, and William Buckley Jr. to discuss the Republican and Democratic national conventions. By that time, Buckley was widely recognized as a leading figure of the modern conservative movement. As the chief editor of the *National Review*, he had worked to distance the movement from its extremist elements, such as the John Birch Society, shaping a brand of conservativism that reflected his own image: reasonable, respectable, and responsible. However, during the ABC broadcast, Buckley lost his temper. When Vidal called him a "crypto-Nazi," he threatened physical violence on national television.

"Now listen, you queer," said Buckley, "stop calling me a crypto-Nazi or I'll sock you in the goddamn face, and you'll stay plastered."

Buckley's outburst revealed the conflicted psyche of postwar conservative media activists. On the one hand, many held journalistic aspirations, believing that conservatism would ultimately prevail through the intellectual merit of its ideas. At their best, they saw no need to compromise accuracy because they believed that their conservative worldview was inherently correct—and therefore accurate. When Buckley founded the *National Review* in 1955, he proudly declared, "We shall recommend policies for the simple reason that we consider them right . . . and we consider them right because they are based on principles we deem right."[48]

Moreover, early conservative media outlets also believed that they could achieve objectivity by covering conservative stories overlooked by the mainstream press, which they perceived as having a liberal bias. Although there would inevitably be a conservative slant in how they selected stories, they maintained that the stories would be rooted in facts. For example, by the early 1960s, the magazine *Human Events* defined its mission as being objective in reporting the news and representing the facts accurately; while it admitted that its stories might be biased in favor of limited government, private enterprise, and individual freedom, it pledged to dedicate "the reporting to the facts that other newspapers overlook" and "never be classified as vindictive, misleading, or deliberately propagandistic."[49]

On the other hand, many early conservative media activists harbored a deep animus toward the mainstream media, which they believed were shutting out conservative points of view and working in concert with one another to portray them—because of their ideological beliefs—as outside the bounds of respectable politics.[50] It wasn't just Vidal who referred to conservatives like Buckley as crypto-Nazis. Richard Hofstadter, the author of *The Paranoid Style in American Politics*, accused conservatives in the 1960s of being "protofascists" hiding behind the veneer of traditional conservative rhetoric.[51] During that time, the mainstream media often lumped different elements of the conservative movement together under pejorative labels such as "ultras," "radicals," or "extremists."[52] The efforts to marginalize conservatives in the 1950s and 1960s intensified their resolve to fight back through their own media enterprises.

In its early years, *National Review* embraced the idea that it must fight a war against the enemy of liberalism. It believed that media outlets ranging from the mainstream press such as the *New York Times* to liberal opinion magazines such as the *New Republic* all worked together to enforce conformity with their liberal agenda.[53] To counter liberalism, William Rusher, the magazine's publisher, defined its mission as "militantly *engagé*, dedicated to waging political war against the liberals, rather than merely restating conservative principles in some safely abstract form."[54] In a similar vein, the publisher of *Human Events*, Henry Regnery, believed that liberals manipulated public opinion and that conservatives should therefore replicate the tactics of the liberals by eroding public faith in the mainstream press.[55]

The narrative of waging warfare against perceived enemies is fundamentally incompatible with journalistic ideals. Contemporary journalism in the United States prioritizes enlightenment through accurate representation of facts and reasoned argument. Political warfare, however, involves employing all available means, short of war, to achieve its objectives.[56] Similarly, information warfare relies on using information as nonlethal weapons to subdue adversaries rather than engaging them in reasoned debate.[57] The warfare mindset effectively creates a permission structure for conservatives to abandon journalistic integrity. If the goal of media is to win an information war, then why should anyone be constrained by the journalistic norms of fairness, independence, or accuracy? Indeed, 77 years after its founding, the once-revered *Human Events* magazine hired Jack Posobiec as senior editor—a notorious conspiracy theorist who had promoted the baseless Pizzagate conspiracy theory, falsely claiming during the 2016 election that Hillary Clinton ran a sex trafficking ring out of a pizza parlor.

Few right-wing media personalities could better encapsulate the rationale for readily giving up journalistic ideals than Matthew Boyle, Breitbart's Washington bureau chief. In a 2017 speech at the conservative think tank the Heritage Foundation, Boyle summarized Breitbart's goal:

> Journalistic integrity is dead. There is no such thing anymore. So, everything is about weaponization of information. Both sides are fighting on the battlefield of ideas and you know CNN, the New York Times, the Washington Post, Politico, Associated Press, MSNBC, NBC, CBS, the whole alphabet soup they've all thrown in together with the institutional left. . . . The goal eventually is the full destruction and elimination of the entire mainstream media.[58]

Boyle's boss, the former Breitbart CEO Steve Bannon, who ran a podcast called the "War Room," laid out a strategy to destroy the media. "Democrats don't matter," Bannon said in an interview with Bloomberg, "The real opposition is the media. And the way to deal with them is to flood the zone with shit."[59] In other words, Bannon's plan to destroy the media is to pollute the information environment with disinformation, which creates widespread doubts about the press.

Boyle's and Bannon's words about fighting information warfare were echoed by many right-wing personalities. For example, conspiracy theorist Alex Jones built his entire brand on the idea of information warfare against the press. During a 2021 interview, talk radio show host Dan Bongino told the *New Yorker*'s journalist Evan Osnos that talking to journalists like Osnos is itself an act of asymmetric warfare.[60] Similarly, Fox News host Pete Hegseth, who was recently chosen be secretary of defense by Trump, said that "I carried a rifle in the military, and now I get to serve in information warfare."[61]

To be sure, not all right-wing media outlets share Steve Bannon's mission. However, even good-faith conservative journalists can easily become the handmaidens of Republican officials to spread lies.

Political communication scholars have long warned that politicians can manipulate journalistic practices to spread false information. The Bush administration, for example, manipulated the press by managing competing news sources during the war in Iraq.[62] They discouraged dissenting voices in the government from participating as news sources so that the press, which framed stories based on perceived power balances within political institutions,[63] had less opportunity to cover legitimate criticisms of government policies. In addition, political elites can escort factually dubious information through news gates via the journalistic norm of balance.[64] For example, Republicans in Congress pushed a significant amount of misleading, contrarian climate change discourse into the news by exploiting the press's adherence to balanced reporting.[65] Therefore, to provide high-quality journalism, even professional news organizations had to rely on the assumption that public officials operate in good faith with public interest in mind. As communication scholars Lance Bennett, Regina Lawrence, and Steven Livingston argued, the press tends to do a poor job fulfilling its watchdog role of journalism when government officials bend facts in service of poorly examined policies.[66]

Partisan journalism is even more reliant on the assumption that their sources behave responsibly. Unlike professional journalists who seek input from a variety of government officials, partisan journalists tend to rely on ideologically congruent sources. When their sources bend facts to serve ideological goals, partisan journalists may find it relatively easy to go along with it. Thus, for right-wing media to fulfill its essential journalistic role, Republican officials as news sources must operate in good faith, keeping public interest above partisan goals. But do they?

According to PolitiFact's 2013 report, Republicans were three times more likely than Democrats to lie.[67] Bill Adair, founder of PolitiFact and journalism professor at Stanford, found this discrepancy persisted from 2016 to 2021. In his book *Beyond the Big Lie*, Adair reported that Republicans distorted facts in 55% of the cases PolitiFact reviewed, compared to just 31% for Democrats.[68] Trump alone made 30,573 false or misleading claims during his first term in office, with minimal electoral repercussions, despite frequent debunking by the press.[69] Given the sheer volume of falsehoods from Republicans, many right-wing media outlets have become de facto conduits for disinformation, often failing to fact-check Trump and his fellow Republicans amid partisan reporting.

Consider, for example, the Trump administration's spread of disinformation around hydroxychloroquine (HCQ) during the height of the Covid-19 crisis in 2020. Facing an economic shutdown that threatened his re-election, Trump promoted HCQ as a miracle cure for

Covid-19.[70] Despite public health experts' warnings about the drug's risks, over 90% of right-wing media coverage of HCQ in my sample echoed the Trump administration's false narrative without including expert warnings or fact-checking the president. As I'll show in Chapter 2, right-wing journalism can take the form of information warfare, not only because outlets like Breitbart aimed to "flood the zone" but also because so many outlets consistently failed to fact-check the deluge of misleading claims from Republican officials.

A handful of small, principled center-right outlets remain dedicated to the journalistic role of truth-seeking, even as the pressure to conform to the Make America Great Again (MAGA) Republican agenda has intensified. For example, The Dispatch, an online magazine launched in January 2020, repeatedly debunked MAGA Republicans' false claims of election fraud. Likewise, The Bulwark, founded by former conservative commentators disillusioned with Trumpism, has consistently provided fact-based analysis and confronted conspiracy theories. Though small in audience size, those outlets serve as reminders that conservative media can be a bastion for truth and a safeguard of American democracy.

Structure of the Book

Chapter 1, "All the Billionaires' Men," offers an in-depth look at the political organizing activities of right-wing media. Drawing on Federal Election Commission filings, internal emails, and other qualitative data, it reveals that outlets like Breitbart received hundreds of thousands of dollars from GOP PACs and super PACs for their campaign activities between 2015 and 2022. The chapter traces these political activities back to the "privatized political patronage" of billionaires who support right-wing media as part of a political infrastructure to advance their personal ideological agendas. Using Fox and Breitbart as examples, it shows that these billionaires can shape editorial processes through a combination of direct influence and anticipated compliance. Chapter 1 argues that right-wing media can effectively parallel traditional political organizations in mobilizing resources, selecting tactics, and achieving political goals.

Chapter 2, "Flood the Zone with Shit," provides a systemic analysis of right-wing media's online content. Through a computational analysis of 4 million online stories published by 30 right-wing media outlets from 2017 to 2020, it shows that disinformation was consistently a defining feature of the most highly engaging content. Drawing on an in-depth analysis of the coverage of four high-profile disinformation campaigns, the chapter shows four important ways political and media elites on the right weaponize journalistic practices to spread falsehoods. Chapter 2 shows that when right-wing media, as political organizations, spread disinformation as news, they pose a distinctive threat to American democracy.

Through Chapter 3, 4, and 5, I shift the analysis to the network level, focusing on three key organizing mechanisms within the right-wing media sphere. In Chapter 3, "Divided We Fall," I use the controversy surrounding H. R. McMaster as a case to illustrate ideologically contested political organizing, which foregrounds ideological contests as a key driving force of political organizing within the right-wing media sphere.

The second and third mechanisms explain how different right-wing media outlets can unite behind a strategic narrative designed to solve an emerging political problem. In Chapter 4, "In GOP We Trust," I use the controversy surrounding Justice Brett Kavanaugh as a case to illustrate politician-led political organizing. Chapter 4 demonstrates that when right-wing media outlets lack a preexisting script to write a coherent narrative in response to an emerging threat, prominent Republican elites with the power to generate news can significantly shape coverage toward a strategic political objective.

In Chapter 5, "The Fox News Effect," I examine the Seth Rich conspiracy theory as an example of media-led political organizing. Between 2016 and 2017, various media outlets attempted to promote this conspiracy for different political purposes. However, it wasn't until the theory became useful in defending Donald Trump against the Mueller investigation—and Fox News championed it—that it gained widespread traction across the right-wing media sphere. This chapter illustrates how media-led political organizing can unify right-wing media around a strategic narrative, particularly when a dominant outlet like Fox News takes the lead.

In Chapter 6, "Conclusion," I conclude this book by addressing three questions that likely arise from its finding. First, what about the mainstream and left-wing media? Have they, too, engaged in paid campaign activities during elections? Second, do today's right-wing media mirror the 19th-century partisan press, which operated as political organizations? And third, what, if anything, can be done to hold right-wing media accountable?

Why It Matters

The book's thesis—that right-wing media function as political organizations—has both theoretical and practical implications. Theoretically, it provides a more accurate understanding of right-wing media behavior, challenging prior scholarship that often depicts these outlets simply as content producers (whether journalistic or propagandistic) uniformly aligned with the GOP. As this book will demonstrate, right-wing media outlets do far more than produce media content; they engage in a wide range of political organizing activities; they are not uniformly biased toward the GOP either, as they have repeatedly challenged high-ranking GOP officials and engaged in ideological infighting. Moreover, the book's thesis also pushes the field of political communication to shift its analytical focus. Instead of continuing to refine measures of partisan bias in right-wing media's content, it suggests prioritizing investigations into their editorial processes, flows of money within these outlets, their coordination with other political entities, and their role as a partisan governing tool for the Trump administration.

In terms of its practical implications, the book's thesis highlights a significant risk to American democracy. Today's right-wing media operate under the control of wealthy owners who have amassed tremendous fortunes and remain outside any form of democratic accountability. This lack of accountability raises serious concerns about the disproportionate influence of a small elite minority in shaping public opinion, especially when these elites have cultivated large audiences that closely align with the Republican voting base. The sizable publics they have mobilized provide political cover and electoral support for GOP politicians, enabling billionaires to capture the Republican Party and push it toward adopting extremist positions on issues like abortion—stances that do not align with the will of most Americans.

In 2024, Donald Trump again won the presidential election, aided by Elon Musk, the richest man in the world, who owns the social media platform X (formerly known as Twitter) and has openly floated the idea of purchasing MSNBC. The alliance between right-wing media oligarchs and authoritarian political figures is a deeply troubling trend. It portends a future in which media enterprises are increasingly captured by wealthy ideologues, pushing America toward illiberalism—much like Hungary, where Prime Minister Viktor Orbán's close allies purchased private television and radio outlets to turn them into pro-government platforms.

Understanding right-wing media as political organizations, along with the system of privatized political patronage that sustains them, is essential for addressing this pressing challenge. Without structural reforms to ensure media accountability and limit the concentration of ownership, the United States risks sliding further into a system where democracy exists in name only, dominated by a few select elites who control both the political narrative and the levers of power.

I

All the Billionaires' Men

SHORTLY AFTER ENDING HIS TENURE as the chief strategist at the White House in 2017, Steve Bannon returned to Breitbart as its executive chairman. "Now I'm free," Bannon told the *Weekly Standard* in an interview, continuing, "I've got my hands back on my weapons.... I've built a fucking machine at Breitbart. And now I'm about to go back, knowing what I know, and we're about to rev that machine up."[1]

Bannon got one thing wrong: The weapon of Breitbart did not belong to him. He was only a hired hand. When Bannon had a falling-out with Donald Trump in early 2018, he was pushed out of Breitbart by its owners—the Mercer family. The real influence over Breitbart came from the veteran GOP donor Robert Mercer,[2] who poured $10 million into Breitbart in 2011.[3]

Like Breitbart, many major right-wing media outlets are kept afloat by rich conservative donors. For instance, the Daily Caller, Real Clear Politics, the Washington Free Beacon, the Daily Wire, and the Federalist have all received lavish funding from billionaires. These funds have provided crucial seed money for right-wing media and, in some cases, have continued to cover the operating costs of content production for years.

We are accustomed to thinking of today's right-wing media outlets as profit-making businesses. Exemplified by Fox and the late Rush

Weapons of Mass Deception. Yunkang Yang, Oxford University Press. © Yunkang Yang (2025).
DOI: 10.1093/9780197820339.003.0002

Limbaugh, they are dubbed "the second generation" of right-wing media, adept at building successful corporate brands based on populist and tabloid appeals.[4] The commercial success of Fox and Limbaugh has led us to believe that the right-wing media sector must be primarily driven by a profit motive.

This chapter reveals a much less frequently told story about the right-wing media outlets in addition to Fox. In a much-saturated right-wing media market that is dominated by Fox and flooded with small-budget online blogs such as Zero Hedge, many major media companies such as the Daily Caller and Breitbart have relied on billionaires' donations to stay competitive. The billionaires who have long supported right-wing media include Charles and David (deceased) Koch, Rupert Murdoch, the Mercer family, the Wilks brothers, the Scaife family, and the Uihlein family—all have given away millions of dollars to advance their personal ideological agendas. This form of privatized political patronage is of critical importance in understanding the behavior of right-wing media.

In Chapter 1, I first delve into greater detail on why we should move beyond the traditional "partisan media" paradigm, focusing on two fundamental journalistic norms that prominent right-wing media outlets have frequently violated for political gain. I then present a systemic analysis of payments from GOP political action committees (PACs) and super PACs to right-wing media, illustrating how this financial arrangement serves as foundational evidence for the book's thesis that right-wing media have functioned as political organizations.

The next part of this chapter focuses on "privatized political patronage," a funding model that explains why many right-wing media outlets have prioritized political objectives, even at the expense of financial losses. The analysis delves into the financial structures of right-wing media and the personal background of their financial backers, highlighting how patrons such as the Murdoch family and the Mercer family can shape editorial decisions, using right-wing media as a tool to pursue their personal ideological agendas.

In the final part, I draw on additional sources, including investigative journalism, to outline the key resources leveraged by right-wing media, the tactics they have employed, and the political objectives they have pursued. This analysis aims to systematically demonstrate that right-wing media can fulfill the functions of political organizations, particularly in resource mobilization, tactics selection, and the pursuit of political goals.

Beyond Partisan Media

Political communication scholars have long analyzed right-wing media within the paradigm of partisan media, media that is "framed, spun and slanted so that particular agendas are advanced."[5] Partisan media stoke outrage through slanted story selection and framing but are still expected to generally operate according to the basic journalistic norms of facticity and editorial independence. Hence, scholars argued that right-wing media outlets have played an important journalistic role in democratic politics: They inform public debate by providing access to alternative ideas unconstrained by the "fair and balanced" norm of objective journalism.[6]

Following the partisan media paradigm, many scholars focused on identifying partisan bias in right-wing media and measuring its effects. They found that Fox News often covers stories and polls that favor Republicans and reframes mainstream news stories with conservative perspectives.[7] These scholars have shown that the right-wing media's biased news coverage can significantly shape their audiences' beliefs, behaviors, knowledge, and attitudes.[8]

However, empirical evidence about right-wing media's conduct has challenged two key assumptions of the partisan media paradigm.

The first is about facticity. The principle of presenting facts or some documentary support of claims, even with a partisan spin, is considered an essential characteristic of a news organization. As media historian Michael Schudson argued, news organizations must at least make a sincere effort to be factual and truthful.[9] While the assumption about facticity—or at least an effort to be factual—is still valid for principled conservative news outlets such as the Bulwark, it does not hold water for some of the most prominent right-wing media outlets like Fox.

During the Obama administration, there were signs that Fox deliberately bent facts in the service of politics. For instance, Fox News then

Washington deputy managing editor Bill Sammon, who on multiple occasions claimed that Barack Obama was drawn to Marxism, privately admitted in 2009 that he spread what he had believed to be far-fetched speculation.[10] Similarly, Fox News host Sean Hannity amplified the Birther conspiracy theory, which falsely claimed that Obama was not born in the United States and therefore not a legitimate president, even though he admitted that he did not personally believe it.[11]

In 2023, Fox paid a hefty price for deliberately endorsing and amplifying false claims about voter fraud in the 2020 election. Text messages and testimonies that emerged from the Dominion Voting Systems defamation lawsuit showed that Sean Hannity did not believe the voter fraud claims. However, he went on air and told his audiences that he can "factually" say it would be impossible to ever know the true, fair, accurate election results.[12] Court documents also showed that then Fox host Tucker Carlson privately called voter fraud claims "ludicrous" and "totally off the rails."[13] Nevertheless, Carlson continued to sow doubts about the 2020 election well into March 2023, calling it the biggest scam in his life.[14] Deliberate deception, as such, is not journalism. It is a form of distorted and dysfunctional communication that undermines democratic self-governance.[15]

The second assumption is about editorial independence. The question about how independent the press coverage of political news truly is from government's spin is a subject of much scholarly debate.[16] However, most journalism scholars agree that even though specific press coverage may vary along the spectrum of independence and dependence on different issues and events, news organizations operating in good faith should act independently—for instance, refusing to accept money or gifts from special interests.[17] Violating editorial independence—for example, acting on behalf of politicians to shape news coverage in favor of certain candidates in elections—raises serious questions about whether the media organization is truly functioning as a journalistic enterprise.

During the 2016 election, Breitbart published several hit pieces—under Breitbart's own byline—on Trump's political opponents at the direct order of Stephen Miller, a political operative who joined the Trump campaign in January 2016. In July 2015, Miller directed Breitbart to attack Trump's then GOP rival Senator Marco Rubio.[18] According to leaked emails, Miller instructed the Breitbart editor

Katie McHugh to cite a study by the think tank Center for Immigration Studies and hit Rubio on immigration. Once McHugh's anti-Rubio article—which was written under Breitbart's own byline—was out, Trump tweeted her story. Miller then told McHugh to continue to attack Rubio every day.

Similarly, Rupert Murdoch directed Fox to influence the U.S. Senate race in West Virginia at the behest of Donald Trump and Mitch McConnell during the 2018 midterm election. Both Trump and McConnell sought to prevent the nomination of Don Blankenship, a former mine owner with a record of violating mine safety laws. In a note to Fox executives, Murdoch wrote, "Both Trump and McConnell are appealing for help to beat unelectable former mine owner who served time." He directed his employees to air anything during the day that would be helpful. He also encouraged hosts Sean Hannity and Laura Ingraham to attack Blankenship, stating that "dumping on him hard might save the day."[19]

These examples show that Fox and Breitbart have stepped out of the bounds of journalism, although they may still provide day-to-day journalistic reporting. To understand right-wing media outlets and their role in American democracy, we must move beyond the partisan media paradigm and view them as political organizations.

Right-Wing Media as Political Organizations

A political organization first and foremost seeks to advance political goals, which may vary across different types of political organizations. For instance, the goal of a political party is to form a government, while a social movement organization aims to raise social awareness. Political organizations pursue these objectives by engaging in political organizing activities, or "repertoires," which are routines learned, shared, and executed through a relatively deliberate decision-making process.[20] For example, a political party engages in election campaigns, whereas a social movement organization participates in protests. A key factor in the success of a political organization is its ability to mobilize resources, both material (e.g., labor and money) and symbolic (e.g., attention and information), which enable the recurrence of these political organizing activities.[21]

A right-wing media organization can function as a political organization if it mobilizes resources that enable it to participate in organizing activities in pursuit of political objectives. Consider the example of right-wing media leasing their mailing lists to PACs and super PACs. According to Federal Election Commission (FEC) filings, the Daily Caller and the Daily Wire leased their mailing lists to the National Republican Congressional Committee (NRCC) for a payment of $126,768 and $442,663, respectively, in the 2020 election cycle, which went toward funding no fewer than 36 Republican candidates who voted to overthrow the 2020 election. Likewise, Breitbart, Western Journal, Townhall, the *Washington Times*, and Newsmax all leased mailing lists to Republican PACs and super PACs (see Table A.1.1 in the appendix). By sharing their readers' contact information, right-wing media outlets mobilized a highly valued political resource to help elect Republican candidates.

Leasing mailing lists is just one of many ways major right-wing media participated in campaigns. Other types of campaign activities include fundraising, voter contact services, voter data acquisition, website development, research, and political marketing on social media, according to the itemized payment receipts from FEC filings. Table 1.1 shows the major categories of activities as indicated on the receipts for a few major right-wing media outlets, excluding subscription and advertising. Figure 1.1 shows a network of payment flows from right-wing campaign organizations (small text labels) to right-wing media (large text labels). Arrows point to the direction of the payment. Edge width is proportional to the amount of payment. The network graph was created via the visualization tool Gephi.

As Figure 1.1 and Table 1.1 show, Breitbart, the Daily Wire, the *New York Post*, Conservative Review, WorldNetDaily (WND), the *Washington Times*, Western Journal (Liftable Media), Townhall, Newsmax, and the Daily Caller received payments from PACs or super PACs to conduct a variety of campaign work during elections. Daily Wire received the largest amount of money, totaling $1,112,865, for list rental exclusively. Newsmax received money from most PACs and super PACs.

In fact, many of the super PACs that paid right-wing media to do campaign work were funded by the same group of donors that have

Table 1.1 Paid Campaign Activities of Right-Wing Media (2015–2022)

Media	Type	Amount
Breitbart	List rentals	$176,341
	Online fundraising	$3,000
Conservative Review	Campaign events	$6,500
Daily Caller	List rentals and acquisitions	$227,197
Daily Wire	List rentals	$1,112,865
Liftable Media	Digital management and website services	$31,622
	Fundraising services	$1,605
	Voter data acquisition	$7,500
	Party email acquisition	$5,000
	Social marketing	$23,500
Newsmax	Fundraising	$39,431
	Email blast services	$3,400
	Finance consulting	$6,089
	List rentals	$247,860
	Online voter contact	$6,300
	PAC media editing	$1,260
New York Post	Research materials	$897
The Blaze	Digital advertising and list rentals	$5,000
Townhall	List rental	$7,500
	Telephone service	$19,000
	Web service	$254
Washington Times	List rental	$7,087
WND	List rental	$13,000
	Web service	$5,000
	Fundraising	$6,483

long supported right-wing media. For example, during the 2015–2016 election cycle, the right-wing super PAC Make America Number 1 received $15 million from Breitbart's owner, the Mercer family;[22] likewise, the super PAC Keep the Promise III received $15 million from the Wilks family, who funded the Daily Wire.[23] It turned out that

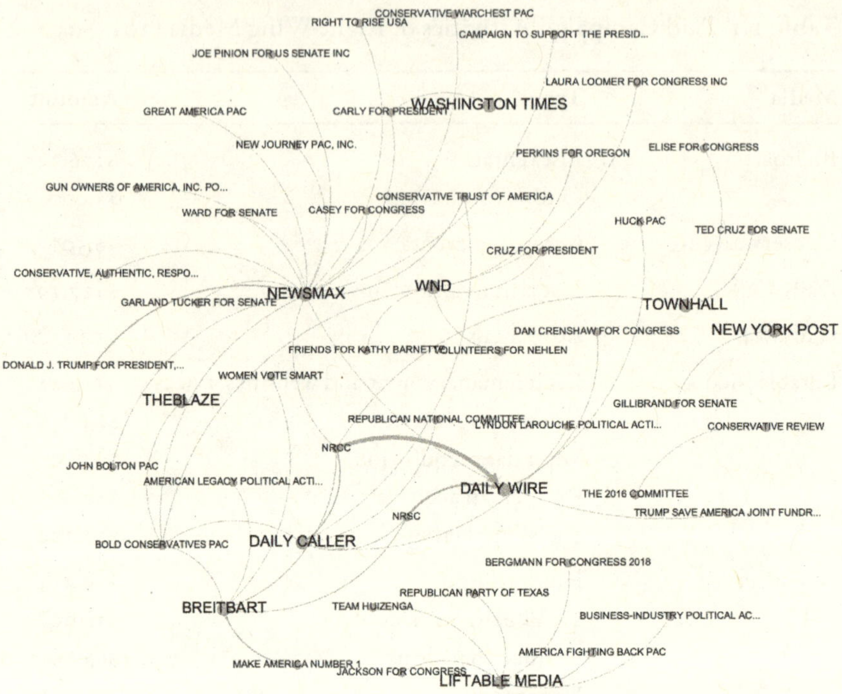

FIGURE 1.1 Payment network of right-wing media and right-wing campaign organizations between 2015 and 2022.
Source: FEC

both these right-wing media and campaign organizations were part of a sprawling political infrastructure created by rich individuals and families to promote their personal, ideological agendas.

A Donor-Supported Business

On a summer night in London in 2018, Breitbart's then CEO Steve Bannon was dining with European far-right politicians. When asked about the financial situation of Breitbart, he made a stunning confession:

> When I left to take over the campaign, we were going to make, like, 8 million dollars of free cash flow that year. After we won, this group called Sleeping Giants, a group of tech executives, they literally

> stripped down. . . . They went to 35 exchanges that sell the ads. 31 went away. So the ad revenues dropped, like, 90%.[24]

Bannon was referring to a boycott campaign led by the activist group Sleeping Giants in late 2016. By mid-2017, the campaign forced nearly 2,600 advertisers to drop Breitbart, including household names such as AT&T, BMW, and Visa.[25] Meanwhile, Breitbart's online traffic started to fall; by May 2020, it had declined by nearly 75% since the beginning of 2017.

"All the right-wing media—the top ten companies by the end of the year, except for Fox, will be donor-base," Bannon lamented in 2018, asserting that "there is no economic model. You will have a donor come in and write a check."[26]

While Bannon may have overstated his financial predicament, his remarks suggest that today's right-wing online media landscape differs significantly from the heyday of Fox or Limbaugh. It is now more saturated and competitive, largely due to the low barriers to entry in the digital space.

Fox and Limbaugh owed their extraordinary commercial success to a number of fortuitous factors in the 1980s and 1990s: the emergence of a conservative media market segment looking for alternative news sources beyond the mainstream media, technological advancement in radio and cable TV that lowered the cost for media entrepreneurs to capitalize on the market demand, and regulatory changes such as the repeal of the Fairness Doctrine that paved the way for the use of highly polarizing language in programming.[27] But most important, there were simply not as many national right-wing media outlets as there are today.

By 2016, the number of right-wing media had skyrocketed. Figure 1.2 shows the number of newly registered right-wing media website domains each year from 1994 to 2016. For much of the 1990s and 2000s, the annual number remained below 20. In 2016, it went up to 150.

The rise of social media platforms that connect news consumers to publishers wore down, if not completely obliterated, entry barriers. Their algorithms prioritize audience engagement metrics over firm reputation in content distribution.[28] As a consequence, small-budget clickbait sites quickly developed a competitive edge. In the 2010s, a

FIGURE 1.2 Right-wing media website domain registrations between 1994 and 2016.

Source: BuzzFeed (Silverman et al., 2017)

flood of clickbait fake news sites such as Endingthefed, YourNews Wire, and Truthfeed sprung up on the political right. Despite having no firm reputation and no original reporting, they were able to compete with more established brands such as Breitbart by spreading made-up or plagiarized fake news stories on Facebook. For outlets like Breitbart, investing in original reporting makes commercial sense only if consumers care about their brand, but as it turned out, many social media users simply do not care much about firm reputation.[29]

Facing competition from both the industry giant of Fox, which had cultivated a loyal brand community, and clickbait sites such as Truthfeed, which had no organizational overhead, top right-wing media outlets such as Breitbart and the Daily Caller needed sustained financial support to stay competitive. They fell back on privatized political patronage, a long-standing funding model that has kept modern conservative media alive for decades.

Among the 10 right-wing media companies that received largest online traffic,[30] nine were supported by donors on the political right. Table 1.2 shows a non-exhaustive list of top right-wing media outlets' funding sources. The media outlets were ranked by the number of combined monthly total unique visitors from September 2018 to May 2021.

As Table 1.2 shows, Fox is one of a kind: Its online traffic is larger than the combined total of the next nine highest ranking right-wing media.

Table 1.2 Top Right-Wing Media Outlets and Their Donors

Media	Online Traffic (09/2018–05/2021)[31]	Funding	Donors/ Funders	Year
1 Fox News	2,756,603,000	N/A	N/A	N/A
2 *Washington Examiner*	332,114,000	Undisclosed	Phil Anschutz	2004
3 The Blaze[32]	244,476,000	$41,906	Charles Koch Foundation	2017
		$7,500	Charles Koch Foundation	2017
		$1,585,159	FreedomWorks	2011–2012
		$40 million	Undisclosed donors	2013
4 *Washington Times*	243,923,000	$1.7 billion	Sun Myung Moon	By 2002
5 *National Review*	181,351,000	$10,000	Charles Koch Foundation	2010
		$11,626	Charles Koch Foundation	2015
		$200,000	Bradley Foundation	2014–2015
		$10,500	Donor Trust	2010–2011
6 Breitbart	179,776,000	$10 million	The Mercer Family	2011
7 Western Journal	169,502,000	$150,000	William Donner Foundation	1997–2002
		$25,000	Armstrong Foundation	1997–2002
		$98,500	Castle Rock Foundation	1997–2002
		$3,000	Roe Foundation	1997–2002
8 Daily Wire	153,248,000	Undisclosed	The Wilks Family	2015
9 Daily Caller[33]	141,705,000	$3 million	Foster Friess	2010

Continued

Table 1.2 *Continued*

Media	Online Traffic (09/2018–05/2021)[31]	Funding	Donors/ Funders	Year
		$3,376,250	Charles Koch Foundation	2015–2018
		$800,000	Fidelity Charitable Gift	2015
		$100,000	National Christian Foundation	2017
		$130,000	Donor Trust[34]	2014–2015
		$100,000	Bradley Foundation	2014
		$260,000	Searl Freedom Foundation	2014–2015
10 Newsmax	130,301,000	$25,000	Richard Mellon Scaife	1998
		$15 million	Chris Rudy and Richard Scaife[35]	2000

Source: Politico, Center for Public Integrity, Center for Media and Democracy, Folio, Source Watch, and Sludge

All the remaining top right-wing media have received funding from rich conservative donors. Besides those listed in Table 1.2, other well-known privately funded right-wing media outlets included the *Weekly Standard* first owned by Rupert Murdoch who later sold it to Phil Anschutz, PragerU, funded by the Wilks brothers and the Bradley Foundation, the *New York Post*, funded by Rupert Murdoch, Real Clear Politics and the Federalist, both funded by Richard Uihlein, and the Washington Free Beacon funded by Paul Singer.[36]

In some cases, private funding provided crucial seed money for right-wing media to develop a successful business model and attract new investors. For instance, Newsmax's CEO Chris Ruddy obtained his seed money of $25,000 from the veteran GOP donor Richard Scaife in 1998.[37] Ruddy and Scaife raised another $15 million from 200 investors in the subsequent year, only to lose roughly $8.4 million in 2000 and 2001.[38] In 2017, it sought funding from Qatar's sovereign wealth fund and secured $50 million from a member of the Qatari royal family.[39] The Daily Wire is another example of a few commercially successful right-wing media outlets. With the initial investment from the Wilks brothers, it built a successful business model centered on subscription.[40] By 2023, it had significantly grown its revenue as it ventured into films, book publishing, podcasts, and social media.[41]

However, many major right-wing media outlets continued to operate at a loss. The now shuttered *Weekly Standard* magazine lost more than $30 million in total under Murdoch's ownership.[42] Under its second owner, Phil Anschutz, it lost $3 million per year during the last five years of its existence.[43] Similarly, the *New York Post* has rarely made a profit for Rupert Murdoch. Between 1976 and 1988, the newspaper lost $100 million; in 2012 alone, it lost $15–20 million. According to Robert Thomson, the CEO of News Corp, which owns the *New York Post*, the *New York Post* had not been profitable in modern times until 2021 when it reported its first profit.[44] Like Murdoch, the owner of the *Washington Times*, Sun Myung Moon, poured nearly $2 billion into subsidizing the newspaper.[45]

Unable to develop a successful business model, some right-wing media outlets chose to rely on their nonprofit affiliates to cover operating costs or simply to become nonprofits. For example, the Daily Caller has relied on donor support since it was founded in 2010. Its content mainly comes from its donor-based nongovernmental organization (NGO) affiliate the Daily Caller News Foundation (DCNF); 40% of DCNF's revenue came from the Koch family alone, which went to fund approximately 50 reporters in 2017.[46] Others, such as the Western Center for Journalism, the Franklin Center for Government and Public Integrity, the *American Spectator*, *Commentary* magazine, and the Media Research Center have operated as nonprofits, with significant and regular funding from billionaires and political foundations such as the Charles Koch Foundation and Scaife Foundation.[47]

Using donors' money to support media that operate at a loss has been a tradition in the right-wing media sector. *Human Events*, the oldest postwar conservative publication, which led the modern conservative movement, was borne out of funds and subscriptions from a handful of donors in Chicago in 1944. At its inception, it was losing approximately $10,000 per year, and by 1974, its annual loss ballooned to hundreds of thousands of dollars.[48] Donors' support remained crucial for the survival of *National Review* too. The magazine, which was propped up by William Buckley Jr.'s father's $100,000 and another $300,000 Buckley raised from a group of wealthy conservatives in 1955,[49] was operating at a deficit in the 1970s.[50] The only year it reported a profit was 1994.[51] It eventually merged with the nonprofit National Review Institute in 2015, which allowed it to tap into the nonprofit's pool of donations from the Bradley Foundation and the Charles Koch Foundation.[52]

When right-wing billionaires decided to support right-wing media, they likely knew that the odds of commercial success were against them. When Rupert Murdoch helped launch the *Weekly Standard* magazine in 1995, he reportedly said, "Let's make sure we don't lose too much money."[53] Why did billionaires on the right fund these right-wing media outlets, knowing full well that doing so would more likely than not lose money?

The Billionaires and Their Political Machine

A year after the Daily Caller was founded in 2010, it still had not turned a profit. However, its largest shareholder and funder, Foster Friess, a veteran GOP donor who also funded many GOP candidates and right-wing political causes, told journalist Lee Fang that he was not worried. "They are breaking great stories and changing the discussion," Friess said.[54]

Individuals like Friess had an enormous fortune to spend on right-wing media. According to Bloomberg, in 2020 the financier of Real Clear Politics, the Uihlein family, had a net worth of $4 billion; Paul Singer, who funded the Washington Free Beacon, had $4 billion; Charles Koch, who funded the Daily Caller had $46.1 billion; Phil Anschutz, who owns the *Washington Examiner*, had $10.4 billion; Robert Mercer, the owner of Breitbart, obtained his $1 billion of wealth in the finance industry; and Dan and Farris Wilks, who funded the Daily Wire and PragerU, had $3.5 billion. Rupert Murdoch had approximately $21 billion in 2022.

There is little doubt that these billionaires had different views on several issues. Compared to the Kochs, Rebekah Mercer was less supportive of immigration.[55] In the 2016 election, she backed Donald Trump, who launched the "Muslim ban," a series of executive orders that prohibited travel from predominantly Muslim countries. The Kochs, by contrast, were supportive of immigration. In 2017, they criticized Trump's Muslim ban, arguing that it was antithetical to their approach to building a free and open society.[56] On the issue of LGBTQ rights, Paul Singer has been an active advocate—he founded the American Unity PAC and the American Unity Fund, both of which mobilized Republicans to support LGBTQ rights,[57] and he spent more than $10 million pushing states to legalize same-sex marriage and recruiting Republicans to join the cause between 2010 and 2014.[58] Farris Wilks, by contrast, said that same-sex marriage would lead to the acceptance and promotion of bestiality, claiming that his goal was to bring the Bible back and counter the gay agenda in schools.[59]

However, all these billionaires have a keen interest in promoting free-market policies and government deregulation, which disproportionately benefit the wealthy. For example, Charles and David Koch advocated for the elimination of social welfare programs, the dismantling of the FEC and campaign finance laws, and the abolition of all income and corporate taxes.[60] Robert Mercer sought to shrink the U.S. government to a mere fraction of its size.[61] And Paul Singer, Foster Friess, and the Wilks brothers donated millions of dollars to free-market organizations like the Heritage Foundation, the Cato Institute, the State Policy Network, and the American Enterprise Institute. Rupert Murdoch, too, contributed $1.25 million to the Republican Governors' Association during the 2020 election, aiming to bolster "the power of free markets."[62]

Few can articulate the billionaires' strategy to reshape American politics better than Richard Fink, who helped the Koch brothers build their political machine in the 1970s.[63] Fink outlined a three-step plan to enact long-term social and political change. First, they should invest in intellectuals who produce ideas; second, they must fund think tanks to turn these ideas into policies; and third, they should create "citizens' groups"—also called "astroturf organizations" as opposed to genuine grassroots movements—to manufacture popular support for these policies.[64]

Over the past five decades, a great many think tanks and "astroturf organizations" have mushroomed on the right, coordinating with right-wing media to pursue billionaires' political agendas. Among the most high-profile right-wing think tanks are the Heartland Institute, which is known for rejecting the scientific consensus on climate change, the Cato Institute, which advocated the privatization of social security and a host of other policies that benefit the rich, the Heritage Foundation, which sponsored project 2025,[65] a blueprint of radical agendas for Trump's second term, and the Government Accountability Institute, which produced opposition research about Hillary Clinton and Joe Biden that widely circulated within the right-wing media sphere.

The earliest, most well-known "astroturf organization" is Citizens for a Sound Economy, which was cofounded by Charles Koch in 1984. It was later split into two organizations in 2004: FreedomWorks, funded by the Mercer and Scaife families, and Americans for Prosperity (AFP), funded by the Kochs.[66] The Wilks brothers funded American Majority.[67] All these three astroturf groups were actively involved in the Tea Party movement in 2009 and 2010, trying to direct Tea Party activists' energy toward their policy goals. For instance, FreedomWorks helped orchestrate town hall protests and sponsored Tea Party rallies, American Majority hosted 400 workshops to train Tea Party participants, and the AFP placed its own speakers in local Tea Party meetings to promote arguments against environmental regulations.[68] As I will later show, many of these astroturf organizations coordinated with right-wing media to fundraise and drive membership.

Mechanisms of Control

Command and Control

Kurt Bardella, a spokesperson for Breitbart between 2014 and 2016, characterized the editorial process within Breitbart as no less than military-style command and control:

> As Steve Bannon became a central figure and asserted himself as the leader of Breitbart and began to remake the image of Breitbart

> around his agenda, it morphed from an entity that wanted to tell another side of the story to an entity that wanted to be politically active; that was an active organization; that was command and control; that sought to not just chronicle what was happening but to shape the events around what was going on.[69]

In a subsequent interview with CNN, Bardella added that all the stories on Breitbart's home page were personally directed by Steve Bannon.[70] Bardella's description of Breitbart's top-down editorial control is very much in line with investigative journalist Jane Mayer's work. According to Mayer, Breitbart's financier, Rebekah Mercer, was highly involved in its content production: She suggested areas of coverage, read every story, and even called editors to correct grammatical errors and typos.[71]

This top-down management style at Breitbart ensured that Breitbart's stories served the Mercers' foremost political agenda: replacing establishment Republicans with hardliners on immigration. During the 2016 election, Steve Bannon personally oversaw all Breitbart stories about Donald Trump.[72] During the U.S. Senate special election in Alabama in 2017, Breitbart's editor Matthew Boyle directed all Breitbart employees take an all-hands-on-deck approach to make sure that the anti-establishment GOP candidate Roy Moore wins the election. In an internal Slack channel, Boyle told his staff, "As of now, everyone is working on the Alabama race," saying that it would decide "the future of the economic nationalist movement and whether Trump is going to win."[73]

Likewise, employees of Fox also followed direct orders from its owner Rupert and Lachlan Murdoch during the 2020 election. According to testimonies and depositions, Rupert and Lachlan Murdoch routinely intervened in the editorial process to shape decisions on which stories to cover, how to cover them, which guests to invite, what questions to ask them, and even the length of the ticker at the bottom of Fox's screen. Rupert Murdoch, for example, conveyed his directives primarily through Fox's CEO, Suzanne Scott, who then passed them on to top and mid-tier executives, show-level producers, and hosts. During the 2020 election, he spoke with Scott multiple times a week, instructing her to put the commentator Victor Davis Hanson on air, sign Miranda Devine and Michael Flynn as contributors, ask Shepard Smith to tone down his criticism of Trump, prevent Steve Bannon from appearing on Fox, urge Hannity to say something positive about Lindsey Graham, and fire Lou Dobbs and Bill Sammon, to name but a few.

Like Rupert Murdoch, Lachlan Murdoch regularly communicated with Scott. He spoke to Scott every day and attended Fox's two daily editorial calls whenever he was available. His directives to Scott included adopting a celebrative tone in the coverage of Trump's rallies, suggesting lead stories for Fox's website, proposing stories for Fox's streaming platform Fox Nation, and shortening the ticker at the bottom of Fox's screen. Lachlan stated that he could not recall a single instance when Fox News did not follow his suggestions.[74]

Rupert and Lachlan Murdoch's close involvement in Fox's editorial process during the 2020 election is consistent with the way they've managed other media outlets they own. In a profile for the *New Yorker* magazine, reporter Ken Auletta spent 10 days shadowing Rupert Murdoch in his office. He observed that Murdoch suggested story ideas to editors several times a day on the phone. When asked about what gave him the most pleasure in the news business, Murdoch responded without hesitation: "being involved with the editor of a paper in a day-to-day campaign and trying to influence people."[75]

Anticipated Compliance

The owners of right-wing media can also exert their influence through anticipated compliance from their employees without explicitly giving them instructions. This is especially true for Rupert Murdoch, who managed multiple media outlets in the United States, the United Kingdom, and Australia. According to media scholar David McKnight, Rupert Murdoch hired editors who were "on the same wavelength as him" about politics.[76] These editors, as News Corporation former executive Bruce Dover characterized, often tried to please Rupert Murdoch.[77] David Yelland, an editor of the *Sun*, told McKnight that most editors do not need to receive specific instructions on how to cover every story: They habitually think about Rupert Murdoch's personal preferences when they react to news events.

The *Weekly Standard* is one example of how a Murdoch-owned media outlet can independently promote specific ideological agendas that align with those of Rupert Murdoch. In the early 1990s, Rupert Murdoch began to associate himself with neoconservatives, a group of conservative intellectuals known for their hawkish views of U.S. foreign policy. When the group approached Murdoch for money to fund a nonprofit organization, Murdoch decided to invest $3 million into a new magazine—the *Weekly Standard*—within the News Corporation. He hired Bill Kristol, a well-known neoconservative, as its chief editor. Since its founding, editors at the *Weekly Standard* have been given significant editorial freedom.[78] Led by Kristol, the magazine quickly became one of the most influential publications in Washington, D.C., earning the name of inflight magazine on Air Force 1 during the George W. Bush administration. Read regularly by influential politicians such as then Vice President Dick Cheney, the magazine became the incubator and champion of America's war in Iraq, a cause that Rupert Murdoch himself cared deeply about.[79]

However, the owner can also shut down the media outlet if he or she can no longer anticipate compliance. When the conservative billionaire Philp Anschutz first bought the *Weekly Standard* from Rupert Murdoch, the magazine was losing at least $1 million a year. But that did not bother Anschutz: Anschutz liked the influence of the *Weekly Standard* among the Bush administration and wanted the magazine to keep its ideological focus.[80] Owning the magazine allowed Anschutz to connect with Republican elites inside Washington.

Since Trump began his 2016 campaign, Kristol made the magazine the epicenter of the never-Trump movement on the political right. When Kristol's attempt to find a challenger to Trump in the 2016 election became public, Anschutz was upset. Anschutz's executive Ryan McKibben told Kristol that "this wasn't what Phil Anschutz wanted from the magazine."[81] Anschutz did not intend to lose millions of dollars every year only to support the beachhead of the anti-Trump movement when the political tide on the right clearly turned in Trump's favor. Although its readership did not experience a significant decline,[82] the *Weekly Standard* lost its political usefulness for Anschutz. In December 2018, Anschutz shut down the magazine.

The degree to which donors influenced or controlled the editorial process inevitably varies across different right-wing media organizations. Charles Koch and the Wilks brothers may not have managed the Daily Caller and the Daily Wire in the exact same way as the Mercers did with Breitbart. However, their financial support of right-wing media reveals an undeniable truth: Media organizations have become increasingly important for political organizing on the right, with the donors and owners of media gaining audiences, the most important resource in an attention economy.

How Right-Wing Media Function as Political Organizations

Mobilizing Resources

> *FreedomWorks is the only organization we have seen that really truly has the organizational power. . . . I want you to go to FreedomWorks.org because freedom works.*[83]

This lavish praise of FreedomWorks came from Glenn Beck, a talk radio host and the owner of TheBlaze. In 2010, Beck touted the organization multiple times on his radio show, encouraging his listeners to join it. As one may suspect, Beck received $250,000 for promoting FreedomWorks on air, which witnessed a significant spike in both online traffic and new email sign-ups three months after its first deal with Beck in 2010.[84] Like Beck, Sean Hannity, Rush Limbaugh, and Laura Ingraham sold millions of dollars of endorsements to the right-wing think tank Heritage Foundation. These talk radio hosts' paychecks from these political organizations show the value of a highly coveted resource of right-wing media: audiences.[85]

Today, leading right-wing TV programs, radio shows, and websites reach millions of Americans. In August 2024, Jesse Watters *Primetime* and *The Five* each drew 3.3 million viewers. During the same period, the Fox News website attracted 85 million unique visitors, with Newsmax reaching 5.5 million, and both the *Washington Times* and the Daily Wire drawing 3.1 million each.[86] In talk radio, Sean Hannity, Glenn Beck, Dan Bongino, and Mark Levin commanded audiences of 16.25 million, 8.75 million, 8.5 million, and 8.25 million listeners, respectively.[87] As of November 2024, Fox News, the Daily Wire, and Breitbart had amassed 24 million, 3.7 million, and 5.2 million followers on Facebook, along with 25 million, 2.3 million, and 2.2 million on X.

Nevertheless, not all audiences are created equal. While more profit-driven outlets such as Fox News and Daily Wire focused on creating a popular brand that appeals to large audiences, smaller publications such as *Human Events* and the *Weekly Standard* aimed at cultivating a small circle of elite audiences. Both mass readership and elite audiences have their own political value. While mass readership can translate into votes, donations, phone calls, and email sign-ups, elite audiences can give the billionaires access to influential politicians inside Washington, allowing them to directly influence political and judicial appointments, legislation, and policy initiatives.

The *Weekly Standard*, for example, boasts of its access to influential elites in Washington. Its website used to read, "Lots of Washington publications say they have influence. The Weekly Standard delivers it. . . . Each issue is hand-delivered—by request—every Sunday morning to an exclusive list: the most powerful men and women in government, politics, and the media."[88] According to historian Nicole Hemmer, the editors of *Human Events* once worried about gaining too many readers, lest the magazine be degraded by popular demand.[89]

Mobilizing mass audiences, as Glenn Beck did in his show, often takes the most direct form of calling on the listeners, viewers, and readers to take specific actions. During election cycles, conservative talk radio hosts regularly encourage their listeners to vote for GOP candidates. In the Tea Party era, multiple Fox News hosts called on viewers to join the protests, and right-wing media sites routinely sent mass emails imploring subscribers to donate to GOP campaigns. Below are two examples from the 2020 election cycle. The first one is an excerpt from an email that Breitbart sent to its subscribers in October 2020 on behalf of Jim Jordan's campaign; the second one is an excerpt from a June 2020 email the Daily Caller sent on behalf of Senator Lindsey Graham's campaign:

> BREITBART: SPECIAL MESSAGE
>
> JIM JORDAN FOR CONGRESS
>
> Fellow Conservatives,
>
> In 2006, I was elected to defend the Constitution of the United States of America. I've never let anything distract me from that mission—and it's exactly what I'll continue doing if re-elected to on November 3rd.
>
> Please take a moment to watch our final campaign ad of 2020, and if you are inclined to chip-in a couple bucks to help me keep this ad running through Election Day, please know how grateful we are for your continued support.

> DAILY CALLER: A message from our sponsor
>
> Friend,
>
> Thought we left Hillary Clinton in 2016? Think again!
>
> Hillary Clinton: Incredible news: @HarrisonJaime has outraised Lindsey Graham in his race to replace Graham in the Senate—the first time Graham has been outraised in his entire career. Let's keep it going and flip the Senate.
>
> Out of nowhere, Hillary took to Twitter to celebrate the fact that my Democrat opponent outraised me in the first three months of this year by nearly $2 million!
>
> Friend, the Left is SWARMING following the news that I was outraised. Hillary's tweet comes just days after we learned my opponent is spending $2.2 million over three weeks to flood South Carolina television and radio airwaves with ads.
>
> 91% of my opponent's money is donated from out of state, and it is flooding into South Carolina like never before.
>
> We cannot take this lying down! Please make a rush contribution today and tell Hillary Clinton that South Carolinians will not be swayed by her or any other New York liberal.
>
> STAND UP TO HILLARY WITH A DONATION TODAY
>
> With Hillary jumping into my race, more liberals will donate to my Democrat opponent with the hope of defeating this "deplorable!"

Mobilizing elite audiences takes a more subtle form than a direct call to action. If the goal is to influence policymakers in elite circles, then telling them how to articulate the rationale for a position on an issue matters a great deal. To cultivate experts who can articulate intellectual justifications for preferred polices, right-wing media outlets have developed connections to right-wing think tanks. For example, Rupert Murdoch was on the board of three conservative think tanks: the Hoover Institution, the Cato Institute, and Institute for Public Affairs.[90] Fox's former host Tucker Carlson was a senior fellow at the libertarian think tank the Cato Institute, funded by the Koch brothers; Breitbart's former CEO Steven Bannon and senior editor Peter Schweizer cofounded the Mercer-funded Government Accountability Institute; Fox's Laura Ingraham, Mark Levin, and Daily Wire's Ben Shapiro were all fellows at the Claremont Institute, a think tank funded by the Dick and Betsy DeVos Foundation, the Bradley Foundation, and the Scaife Foundation. These formal ties between right-wing media figures and think tanks provide opportunities for right-wing media to circulate experts' opinions and influence elites' decision-making.

In addition, social events were regularly organized to introduce right-wing media personalities to political elites. As journalist Lee Fang revealed, one of these events, organized by the Heritage Foundation around 2009, was called "President's Club" conferences. During the conferences, talk radio hosts such as Rush Limbaugh socialized with Republican donors and politicians who gave speeches on how the GOP could thwart President Obama's agendas.[91] Another regular event is the Norquist's Wednesday Meetings. They are invite-only, off-the-record events across many states that provide networking opportunities for right-wing media personalities, GOP staffers, political operatives, and representatives from various right-wing groups.[92] The meetings eventually became one of the most significant institutions in American conservative political organizing.

Selecting Tactics

In March 2023, the Manhattan District Attorney Alvin Bragg indicted Donald Trump on 34 felony counts of falsifying business records related to a hush-money payment to adult film actress Stormy Daniels during his 2016 presidential campaign. The evidence about the hush money payment first emerged from Fox News reporter Diana Falzone's investigation during the 2016 election, but this story remained unknown to the public until the *Wall Street Journal* published it in 2018.[93] It turned out that Fox News had buried the story to protect then candidate Donald Trump in 2016. The head of Foxnews.com, Ken LaCorte, reportedly told Falzone, "Good reporting, kiddo. But Rupert wants Donald Trump to win. So just let it go."[94] Falzone later signed a nondisclosure agreement with Fox, which prevented her from talking about her work at Fox.

The tactic to prevent reporters from revealing damaging information about a third party is known as "catch and kill," which gained notoriety following the revelation that the *National Enquirer* bought and buried damning stories about Donald Trump's extramarital affairs in order to help elect Trump in 2016.

"Catch and kill" is one of many tactics that right-wing media have employed to pursue political objectives. The flip side of killing damaging information is spreading disinformation. Chapter 2 will focus on right-wing media's disinformation tactics, but it is worth noting here that some of the most high-profile disinformation stories on the political right in the past few years—for instance, the Clinton Foundation story[95] and the Biden-Ukraine conspiracy theory[96]—were borne of concerted, elites-driven efforts between right-wing media and other donor-supported political organizations.

Apart from spreading and suppressing strategic information, many right-wing media outlets also engaged in extensive campaign work. As the payment receipts from FEC filings indicated, their campaign work includes contacting voters, managing digital assets, organizing events, fundraising, and many other activities. It is difficult to evaluate the specific ways right-wing media conducted these campaign activities, as the receipts themselves only described general categories of activities. However, there is ample evidence, at least in fundraising, that some right-wing media personalities personally attended fundraisers,[97] sent fundraising emails to their readers, published donation links on their websites, and called on their listeners and viewers to make donations.

More overt forms of campaign work involved right-wing media personalities personally stumping for GOP candidates. For example, Steven Bannon, then CEO of Breitbart, personally appeared onstage at a rally for Roy Moore, the GOP candidate for the 2017 U.S. Senate special election in Alabama. Fox personalities—including Sean Hannity, Jeanine Pirro, Laura Ingraham, Dan Bongino, and Mark Levin—also attended campaign events, which was sometimes criticized but largely condoned by their employer.[98] According to *Washington Post* reporting, Fox News, which occasionally paid lip service to journalistic independence, did occasionally ask several hosts, including Jeanine Pirro, Brian Kilmeade, and Pete Hegseth, to cancel GOP fundraising events.[99] But its biggest stars, such as Sean Hannity, have continued to stump for candidates, such as Donald Trump, without any disciplinary actions from Fox.

Achieving Political Objectives

The evidence of right-wing media's political organizing activities points to a set of well-defined, predetermined political goals, which involve helping GOP candidates win elections and driving online traffic or membership to political organizations. Recent work by other scholars and observers revealed additional goals: Many right-wing media outlets sought to influence public policies, stop legislation, and intervene in U.S. Supreme Court nominations.[100] This book will delve into additional examples in later chapters, such as influencing staffing changes (Chapter 3) and shielding political allies from investigations (Chapter 5).

As this chapter showed, privatized political patronage explains how some right-wing media outlets came to develop these political objectives. At Breitbart, the push to elect Donald Trump in 2016 and Roy Moore in 2017 stemmed directly from Steve Bannon, supported by the Mercer family, who advanced an anti-immigrant, nativist agenda. At Fox, the effort to defeat Blankenship in the GOP primary in West Virginia in 2018 came directly from Rupert Murdoch. In these cases, patrons of right-wing media provided clearly defined political goals.[101]

In other instances, right-wing media can achieve numerous political objectives even without direct influence from their owners or managers. When conservative journalists report the news without fact-checking or providing context, they may inadvertently become handmaidens of power, enabling GOP elites to exploit journalistic practices to further their agendas. The next chapter explores how right-wing media can function as de facto political organizations through reporting.

2

Flood the Zone with Shit

IN 2018, PETER SCHWEIZER, A senior editor-at-large at Breitbart, wrote a book titled *Secret Empires*, which implied—with no credible evidence—that then Vice President Joe Biden abused his power to protect Burisma, a Ukrainian gas company where Biden's son Hunter served as a board member. After Fox News began to cover Schweizer's book in March 2018, more right-wing media outlets started to pile onto the narrative. For example, Zero Hedge, an outlet followed by Steve Bannon, who described himself as a "huge fan,"[1] concocted the false claim that the head of Burisma had been indicted over money laundering for Biden.

As the Ukraine–Biden conspiracy theory gained traction in the right-wing media sphere, Lindsey Graham, then Senate Judiciary Committee chairman, launched an official investigation into Joe Biden in 2019. As Graham leaned into the allegations, the disinformation narrative became a news story, one that right-wing media found too enticing to overlook. In contrast to professional news coverage that provided the context of Graham's probe[2]—for example, highlighting that it was based on unsubstantiated allegations—many right-wing media outlets omitted that important context in their biased reporting. This omission created the false impression that Biden abused his power as vice president, potentially damaging his candidacy in the 2020 election.

Weapons of Mass Deception. Yunkang Yang, Oxford University Press.
DOI: 10.1093/9780197820339.003.0003

The Biden–Ukraine conspiracy theory shows that right-wing media can function as political organizations by spreading disinformation under the guise of news. It first took an editor at Breitbart to manufacture a misleading narrative presented in a documentary format. Then, Fox News legitimated and amplified the narrative, presenting it as a form of investigative journalism. Subsequently, Republican elites provided the narrative with an official news angle, which prompted more right-wing media to cover the story.

Chapter 2 begins with a comprehensive overview of the online right-wing media sphere in the United States, extending the analysis beyond the top 10 outlets explored in Chapter 1. Next, it presents the results from an analysis of approximately 4 million online articles published by right-wing media outlets between 2017 and 2020, showing that disinformation stories consistently featured prominently among the most engaged-with online content. The chapter goes on to analyze four prominent disinformation stories, identifying four common tactics used by media and political elites on the right to weaponize journalistic practices for spreading disinformation.[3] These tactics were employed not only by established outlets like Fox News but also by platforms such as Breitbart, a midsized digital-native site known for its pro-Trump stance and anti-immigration agenda, and Zero Hedge, a small operation of three individuals.[4]

The Online Right-Wing Media Sphere

To understand the fast-changing right-wing media sphere in the digital age, it is important to start with some basic questions. For example, how many people do right-wing media organizations hire? What journalistic standards do they claim to follow? How many articles do they produce every year? How well do they perform on social media?

Some right-wing media organizations are notoriously secretive.[5] Fox, for instance, is known for demanding its employees sign nondisclosure agreements. Basic questions such as how Fox enforces journalistic standards still largely remains an enduring mystery.[6] Our understanding of the inner workings of right-wing media has largely relied on the work outside academia—for instance, the work by journalists[7] and liberal media watchdog groups,[8] which tend to focus on one media outlet at a time. Due to the lack of systemic analyses, we know relatively little about the right-wing media sphere, especially how different media outlets compare to one another.

Two studies explored some of these questions beyond a single right-wing media outlet. In one study, researchers interviewed 22 employees working at 14 online conservative media outlets.[9] They found that many right-wing media employees saw their work as journalism rather than propaganda. In the other study, researchers provided estimates of the content supply of 36 alternative U.S. right-wing online news sites between June and July 2018.[10] They found that some right-wing media outlets such as Breitbart, Townhall, and the Daily Caller were more productive than others such as Gotnews.com, the Federalist, and Disobedient Media.

Both studies excluded some major U.S. right-wing media outlets, such as Fox News and the *New York Post*. Additionally, some metrics used by prior studies were likely inaccurate.[11] Consequently, there remains a lack of precise understanding of fundamental aspects of the right-wing media sphere, despite its growing influence on American politics.

To describe the online right-wing media sphere in the United States,[12] I included 46 digital native sites, as well as TV and print media that operate a separate online version.[13] These media outlets offer U.S. audiences current, nonfictional, periodic, and right-leaning online political content. The "Chapter 2" section in the appendix explains how I constructed the right-wing media list and includes Table A.2.1, which lists the 46 media outlets.

Of the 46 right-wing media sites, I was able to collect data on staff size for 28 national media outlets that consistently produced content between 2017 and 2020.[14] Fox News stood out as the only outlet with more than 1,000 employees. In 2021, The *Washington Examiner*, the Daily Caller, the *Washington Times*, Newsmax, the Daily Wire, and the *New York Post* fell within the 100 to 1,000 employee range. Thirteen outlets—Political Insider, Western Journal, The Blaze, Real Clear Politics, Breitbart, PJ Media, Front Page Magazine, Infowars, the Federalist, *Spectator*, Washington Free Beacon, WorldNetDaily (WND), and the *National Review*—employed between 10 and 100 staff members.

The remaining eight outlets—Gateway Pundit, Geller Report, Twitchy, Hot Air, American Thinker, Conservative Review, Zero Hedge, and YourNewsWire—operated with fewer than 10 employees.

Right-wing media outlets also vary in their claims regarding journalistic standards. Eleven outlets asserted commitments to seeking truth (e.g., Gateway Pundit), providing accurate reporting (e.g., PJ Media), offering well-sourced information (e.g., Political Insider), or producing original reporting (e.g., Real Clear Politics). Five claimed to separate facts from opinions, while another five stated that they maintain editorial independence (e.g., Daily Caller), avoid or disclose conflicts of interest (e.g., TheBlaze and Western Journal), or enforce conflict-of-interest policies prohibiting employees from working for political parties or accepting external payments (e.g., Washington Examiner).

None of the media outlets with fewer than 10 employees or more than 500 employees have any ethics policies on their websites. It is the midsized right-wing media organizations such as Breitbart that are most vocal about their purported standards. It stands to reason that these outlets are perhaps most incentivized to perform journalistic legitimacy, as they need to compete with other similar-sized outlets.

Figure 2.1 shows the volume of right-wing media's content supply as well as user engagement on Facebook (i.e., the sum of likes, comments, shares, and reactions). To provide context, I also include 21 mainstream media organizations.[15] Table A.2.9 in the appendix lists the number of articles and Facebook engagement for each mainstream media outlet. The x-axis in Figure 2.1 indicates the total number of articles, and the y-axis shows user engagement. Triangles represent right-wing media, and circles represent the mainstream media. Their size is based on the average Facebook engagement per article.

As Figure 2.1 shows, many right-wing media outlets were quite popular on Facebook. For example, between 2018 and 2020, Fox News consistently outperformed most mainstream media outlets. Medium-sized right-wing outlets claiming to be factual or independent also performed remarkably well, often matching or even surpassing the engagement levels of much larger organizations like ABC, MSNBC, and CBS. The Daily Wire, while publishing a significantly smaller number of articles than most media outlets, has been particularly adept at maximizing Facebook engagement since 2018.

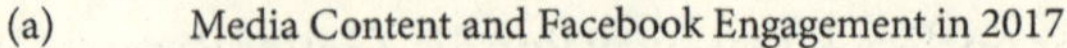

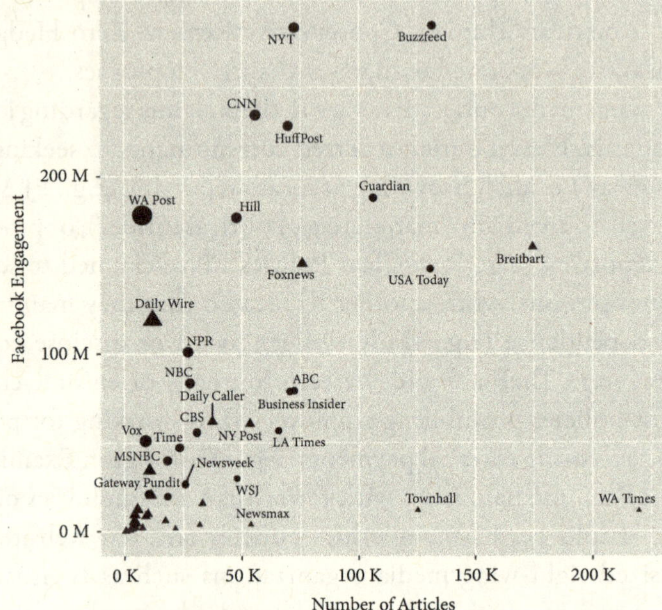

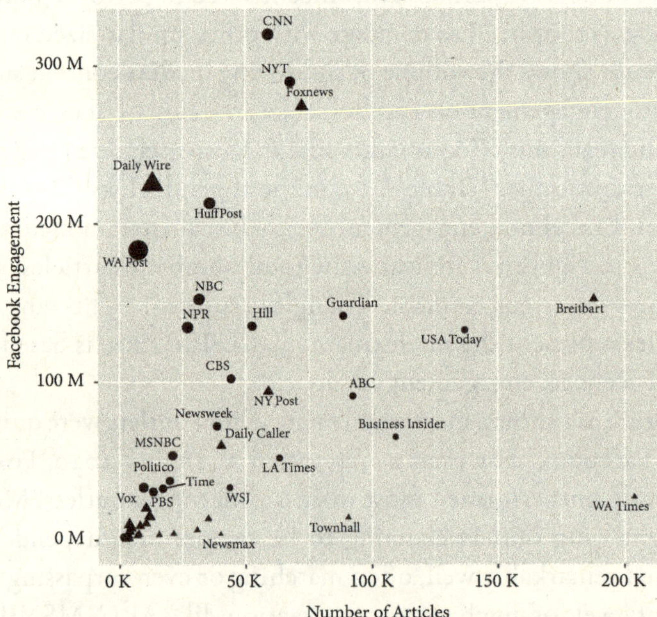

FIGURE 2.1 Media content and Facebook engagement for right-wing media and the mainstream media outlets between 2017 and 2020.

Note: a, b, c, and d are on difference scales, and for visualization purposes, certain data points were unlabeled due to overlaps.

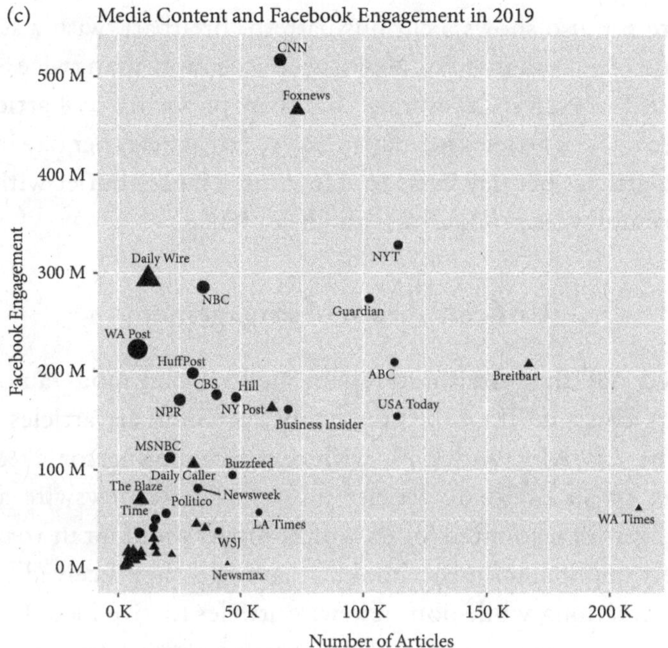
(c)
Media Content and Facebook Engagement in 2019
Facebook Engagement
Number of Articles
500 M
400 M
300 M
200 M
100 M
0 M
0 K
50 K
100 K
150 K
200 K
CNN
Foxnews
NYT
Daily Wire
NBC
Guardian
WA Post
HuffPost
ABC
Breitbart
CBS
Hill
NPR
NY Post
USA Today
Business Insider
MSNBC
Buzzfeed
Daily Caller
The Blaze
Newsweek
Politico
Time
LA Times
WA Times
WSJ
Newsmax

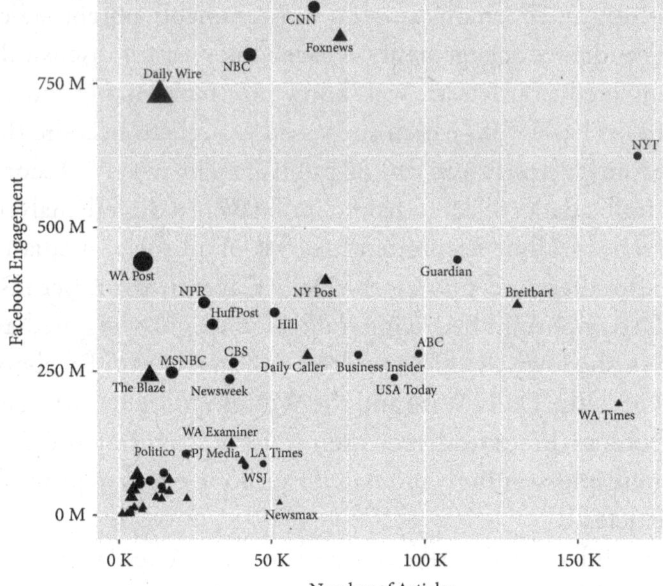
(d)
Media Content and Facebook Engagement in 2020
Facebook Engagement
Number of Articles
750 M
500 M
250 M
0 M
0 K
50 K
100 K
150 K
CNN
Foxnews
NBC
Daily Wire
NYT
WA Post
Guardian
NPR
NY Post
Breitbart
HuffPost
Hill
ABC
CBS
MSNBC
Daily Caller
Business Insider
The Blaze
Newsweek
USA Today
WA Times
WA Examiner
Politico
PJ Media
LA Times
WSJ
Newsmax

Figure 2.1 also shows a curious pattern. Breitbart, with a staff size less than 1/100th that of Fox News, produced more than twice as many articles as Fox News. On average, Breitbart published 478 articles per day in 2017, 514 articles per day in 2018, 457 articles per day in 2019, and 356 articles per day in 2020. How can a media outlet with fewer than 50 employees produce this much content?

Concentration of Engagement

It turned out that Breitbart republished an enormous amount of newswire content. The top three bylines of Breitbart articles turned out to be AP, AFP, and UPI, with each accounting for 31%, 23%, and 11% of all Breitbart articles in 2020. These newswire articles, which together accounted for 65% of Breitbart's content in 2020, were extremely unpopular on Facebook. On average, they received 24 Facebook interactions, while non-newswire articles received 8,008 interactions in 2020; moreover, 99% of Breitbart's newswire articles received zero Facebook engagement.

Publishing an enormous amount of presumably purchased content with zero audience engagement on Facebook seems nonsensical. Many right-wing media outlets are well-known for maximizing audience engagement on Facebook, which surpassed Google to become the main traffic driver for nearly 400 online publishers in 2015.[16] According to my web traffic data collected from SimilarWeb, a digital analytic company, Facebook alone accounted for 67% of all social media referred traffic to Breitbart and 55% for the Daily Caller in 2017. Because Facebook was so important in driving traffic, some right-wing media outlets engaged in shadowy practices to drive engagement on Facebook. Not only did both the Daily Wire and the Western Journal use targeted ads on Facebook to direct readers to their websites, but they also created or funded multiple seemingly unrelated Facebook pages to promote their online articles.[17]

So why did Breitbart republish so many unpopular newswire articles from AP, UPI, and AFP? It is likely that Breitbart aimed to bolster its claim of engaging in regular, legitimate news coverage to ensure protection under the press exemption of the Bipartisan Campaign

Reform Act (BCRA). The BCRA prevents media organizations from being classified as campaign contributors when conducting regular journalistic activities, such as reporting on or editorializing about candidates or political campaigns. By republishing newswire articles, Breitbart reinforced its appearance as a journalistic entity, strengthening its claim to press exemption and shielding itself from regulatory scrutiny. I will revisit this point in the conclusion chapter, illustrating how a media organization's overt political activities could constitute campaign contributions, thereby violating the Federal Election Commission's ruling on corporate contributions.

In fact, most online articles published by right-wing media outlets had modest user engagement. This is due to the tendency of concentration in the digital economy, where the most attention-grabbing articles tend to get most attention while most articles tend to attract little attention.[18] Because Facebook engagement is closely tied to content visibility,[19] articles with higher engagement become more visible.[20]

The pattern of concentration of engagement holds across different right-wing media outlets. Figure 2.2 shows Facebook user engagement for all the online articles published by Fox (n=293,665), Breitbart (n=659,217), and Zero Hedge (n=84,280) between 2017 and 2020. In each graph, a dot represents an article ranked by engagement. The x-axis shows the log rank of the article, and the y-axis shows the log engagement of the article. A log-log plot is often used to demonstrate power-law distributions, which are particularly valuable in identifying systems or processes where "concentration" or "dominance" exists. On a log-log scale, the power-law relationship will appear as a straight line.

As Figure 2.2 shows, user engagement with the top 10,000 articles for all three media outlets exhibits a strong tendency of concentration, as indicated by the near linear relationship between log rank and log engagement between the first article and the 10,000th article. Beyond the 10,000th article, the distribution of engagement starts to drop below the linear line, indicating that many lower-ranked articles receive little to no engagement. For Fox News, the top 5.7% of the most engaging

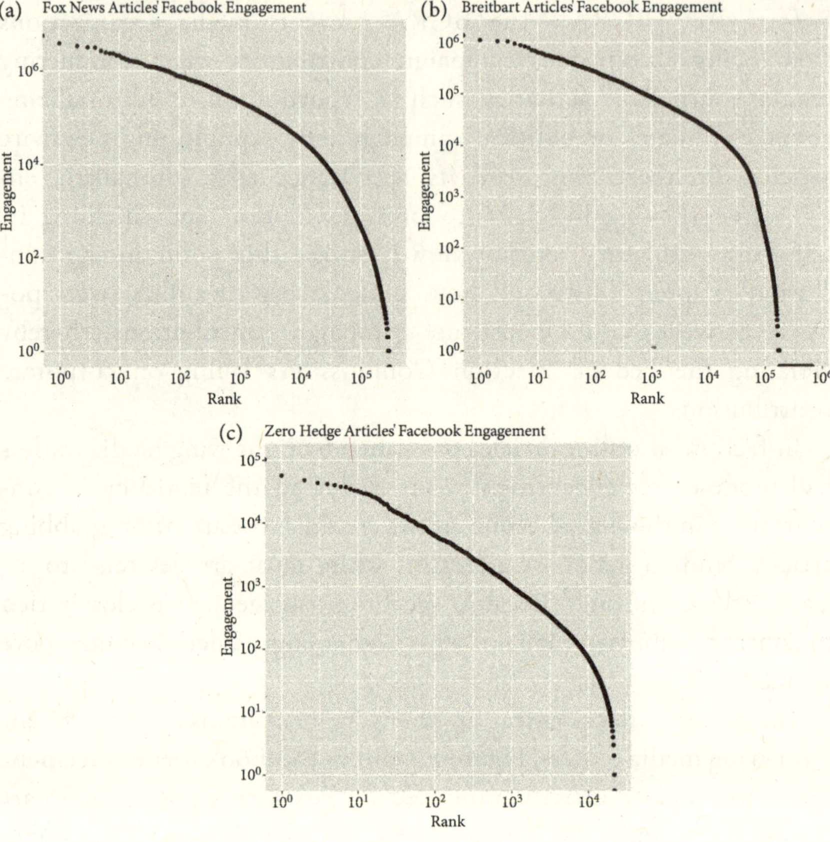

FIGURE 2.2 Log-log plots of rank and Facebook engagement for online articles from Fox News (a), Breitbart (b), and Zero Hedge (c).

Source: NewsWhip

articles produced 80% of all engagement with articles between 2017 and 2020; for Breitbart, it is the top 4%; and for Zero Hedge, it is the top 13.6%.

As a communication scholar, I am mainly interested in communication phenomena, which necessitate an audience. An article that no one reads or engages with is not the same as an article that is read by tens of thousands of people. To understand the topic patterns in stories that generated significant social impact through mass readership, it is important to focus on high-engagement content.[21] In the next section, I turn to the highest-engagement articles, which together generated more than 80% of total user engagement for each media outlet.

High-Engagement Content

To ensure balanced representation across media outlets and time periods, I collected the highest-engagement articles on a per-media, per-week basis. For each of the 30 national right-wing media outlets that regularly produced content between 2017 and 2020, I gathered the most engaged-with articles, which collectively accounted for at least 80% of all Facebook engagement each week. These articles were then compiled into a single corpus for every six-month period, resulting in eight corpora spanning the four years.

This collection of high-engagement content includes 265,812 articles that generated 6,033,366,172 interactions on Facebook between 2017 and 2020, with each article receiving more than 22,000 interactions on average. It includes all the stories that attracted the most audience attention on the political right throughout the first Trump administration. Table A.2.2 in the appendix lists the number of high-engagement articles for each outlet each year.

So, what were the topics that right-wing media audiences engaged with? I applied a structural topic model (STM) to the headlines and the summaries in each corpus. STM is an advanced statistical method used in text analysis to uncover latent topics within a collection of documents while simultaneously examining how those topics relate to document-level metadata (such as publication dates or other attributes). Each STM in my analysis includes the name of media outlets and day as covariates to influence topic proportions.[22] Details on model selection and validation can be found in the appendix.

Figure 2.3 shows the most prominent five topics and their topic proportions for each six-month period. The x-axis indicates topic proportion. For example, a topic with a score of 0.02 means that 2% of the corpus was assigned to the topic by the structural topic model. The y-axis is a summary of the topics based on top words associated with each topic. Topics that are known to be disinformation campaigns are in black, and others are in gray. Table A.2.6 in the appendix shows the top words for each topic.

Notably, "Trump related discourses," including statements both by Trump and about Trump, consistently featured prominently every year. Many articles classified under this topic repeated Trump's

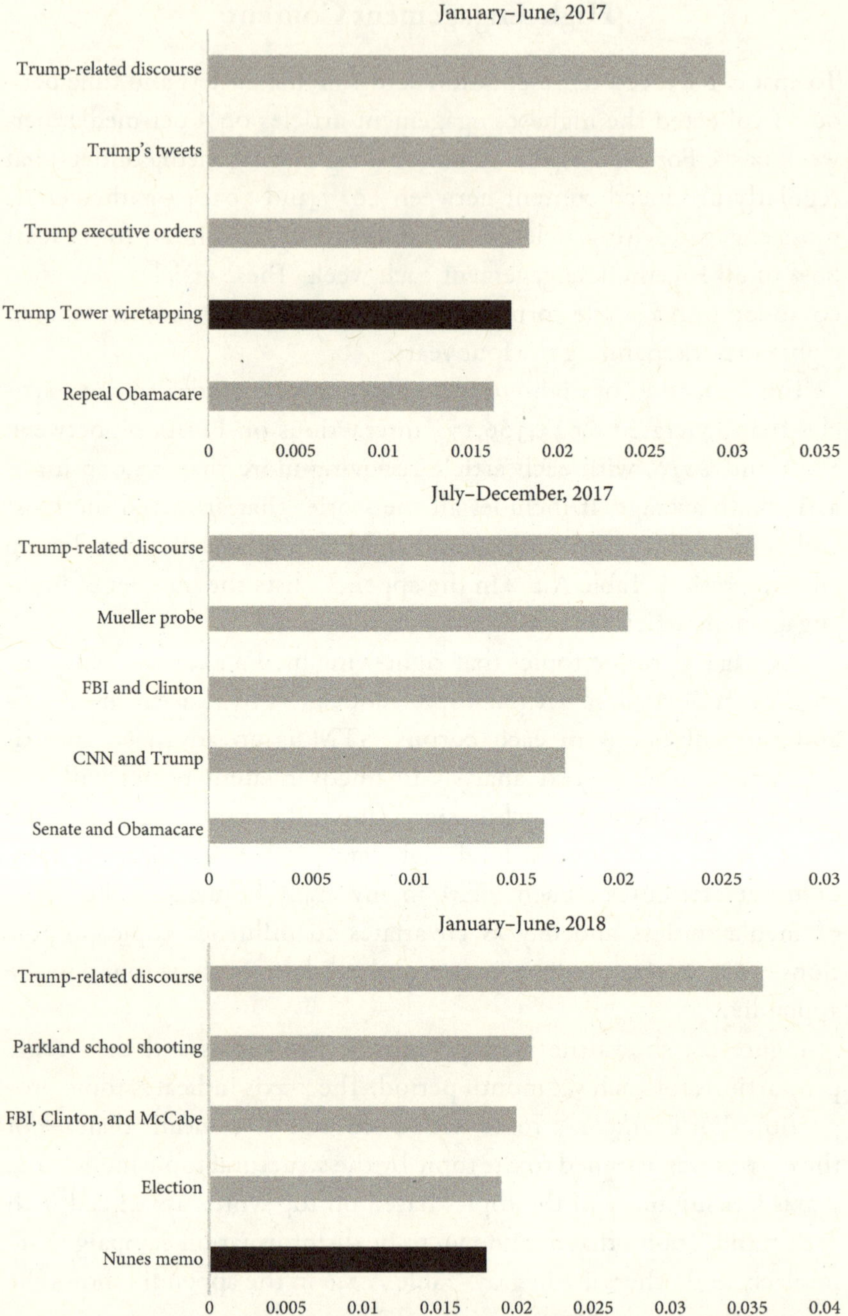

FIGURE 2.3 The most prominent five topics in high-engagement right-wing media content between 2017 and 2020.

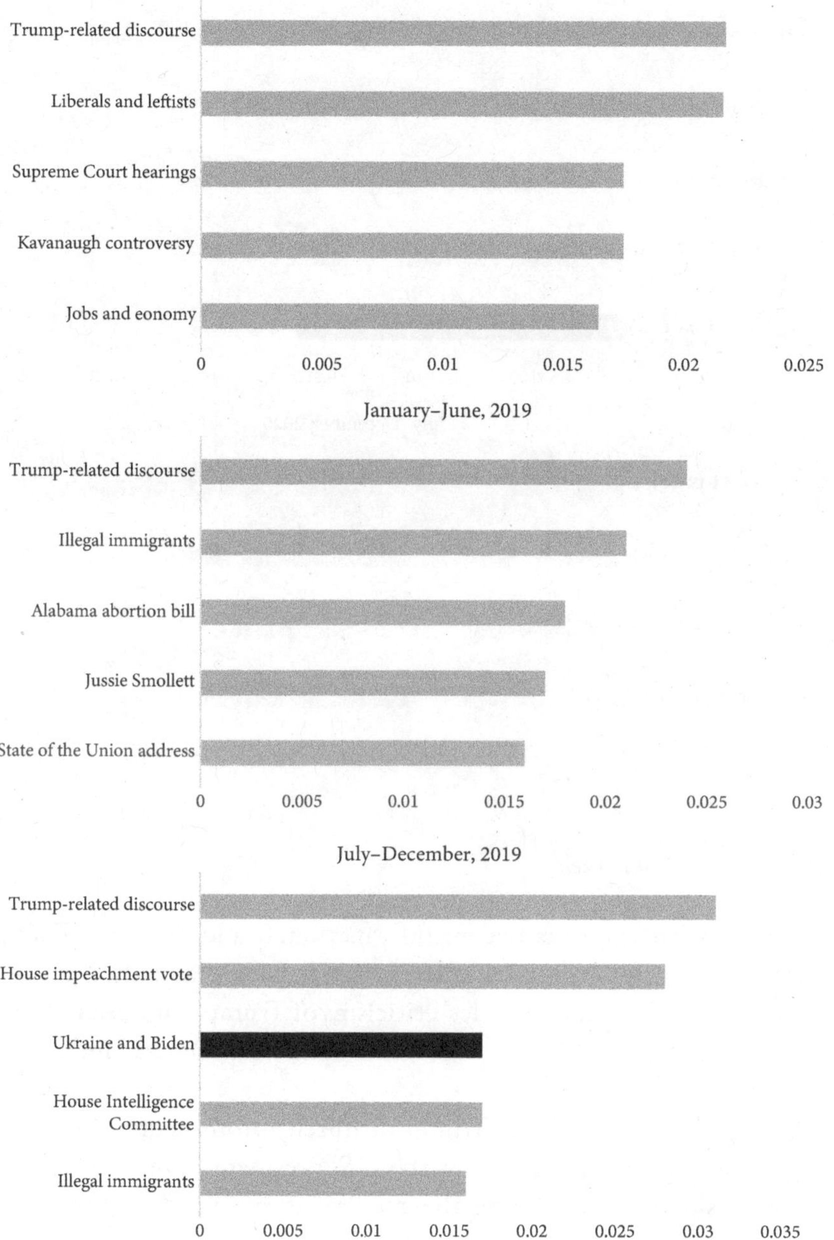
July–December, 2018
Trump-related discourse
Liberals and leftists
Supreme Court hearings
Kavanaugh controversy
Jobs and eonomy
0
0.005
0.01
0.015
0.02
0.025
January–June, 2019
Trump-related discourse
Illegal immigrants
Alabama abortion bill
Jussie Smollett
State of the Union address
0
0.005
0.01
0.015
0.02
0.025
0.03
July–December, 2019
Trump-related discourse
House impeachment vote
Ukraine and Biden
House Intelligence Committee
Illegal immigrants
0
0.005
0.01
0.015
0.02
0.025
0.03
0.035

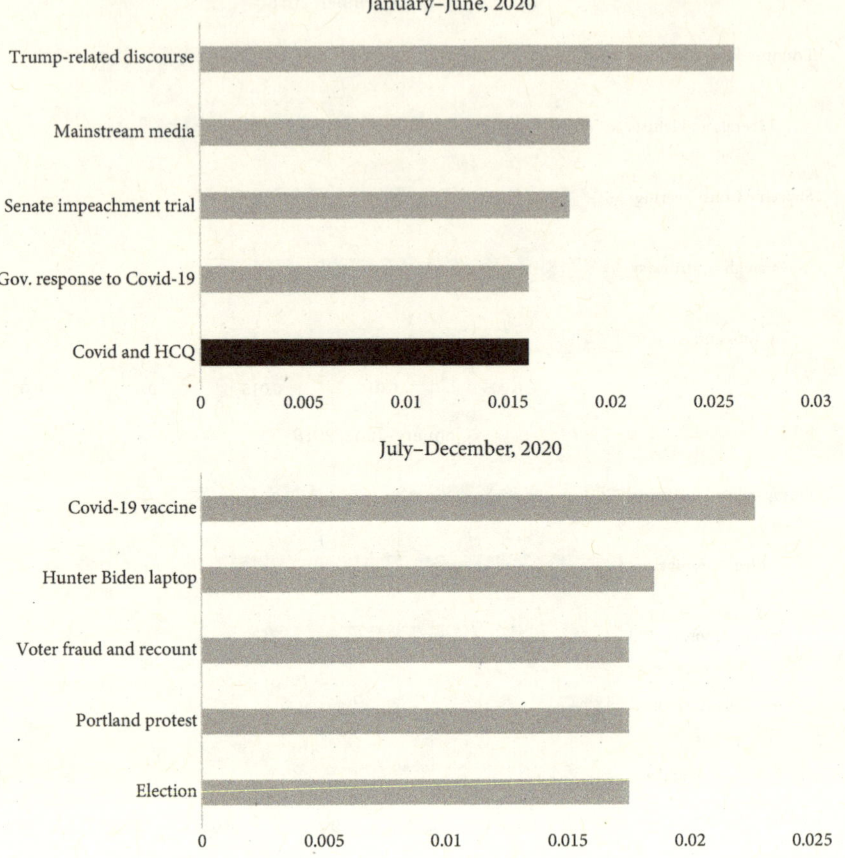

FIGURE 2.3 *Continued*

words, which often contained misinformation. In addition, the "Trump related discourses" topic includes many articles that either praised Trump or covered other peoples' criticisms of Trump—for example, by Democrats, Hollywood celebrities, the mainstream media, and sports figures.

It is no surprise that Trump featured prominently in high-engagement articles: Trump was the U.S. president—one who is particularly skilled at capturing the media's attention. This pattern is consistent with previous work, which noted the close link between mentions of Trump and audience engagement. Fox producers, for instance, noticed that criticizing Trump would negatively impact the network's ratings.[23] On the flip side, covering the criticisms of Trump from out-groups, such as the Democrats, reinforces the "us versus them" narrative, fueling outrage and therefore increasing audience engagement as well.[24]

For the billionaires on the political right, Trump's popularity among right-wing media audiences is a double-edged sword. On one hand, Trump is a useful means to an end. In addition to driving ratings, Trump effectively fulfilled many ideological agendas for them during his tenure as the U.S. president, including cutting corporate taxes, withdrawing from the Iran nuclear deal, appointing conservative judges, and imposing a ban on foreign nationals from seven majority-Muslim countries entering the United States.[25]

However, Trump's popularity can also pull right-wing media into a direction where the billionaires were initially unwilling to go. For example, Rupert Murdoch thought Trump would concede to Biden in the 2020 election. Yet, when Trump and his allies spread the lie that the Dominion voting machine had switched votes to Biden, many Fox executives and hosts felt compelled to go along with it even though they knew it was baseless.

While acknowledging Trump's significant influence, it is important to note that focusing solely on him would overlook broader patterns within the right-wing media sphere. The task for this chapter is understanding how media and political elites on the right weaponized journalism to spread disinformation.

Weaponization of Journalism

To examine the patterns of the weaponization of journalism, I turn to the four disinformation stories highlighted in black in Figure 2.3:

The Trump Tower wiretapping story (2017): This narrative alleged that Barack Obama secretly wiretapped Trump's phone at Trump Tower during the 2016 campaign.

The Nunes memo (2018): This story involved the release of a memo by former Republican Congressman Devin Nunes, which suggested that the Federal Bureau of Investigation (FBI) sought a Foreign Intelligence Surveillance Act (FISA) warrant to spy on Trump's former advisor, Carter Page, as part of a politically motivated conspiracy.

The Ukraine–Biden conspiracy theory (2019): This narrative claimed that Joe Biden engaged in corrupt activities to protect his son's interest in the Ukraine energy company Burisma.

The hydroxychloroquine (HCQ) story (2020): This story promoted the notion that the anti-malaria drug HCQ can effectively treat Covid-19.

While these four stories represent only a fraction of the overall scale of right-wing disinformation during the given period, they were highly popular—and thus "successful." They offer valuable insights into how media and political elites can successfully weaponize journalistic practices to advance their strategic political goals. Table A.2.7 in the appendix shows the number of articles each media outlet published on these four stories. In examining these disinformation stories, I identified four tactics:

Manufacturing lies: Right-wing media fabricate baseless claims. This proactive approach, which Steve Bannon referred to as "flooding the zone with shit," involves the intentional creation and dissemination of false information.

Repeating lies: Right-wing media repeat and amplify false statements made by media or political elites.

False balance: Right-wing media present facts and falsehoods in a false balance.

Lack of context: Right-wing media cover events or public opinion without providing proper context, which can contribute to the spread of disinformation when those events or public opinion are a result of a disinformation campaign.

While "manufacturing lies" represents a deliberate weaponization of journalism by media elites, the remaining three tactics—repeating lies, false balance, and lack of context—reflect dysfunctional forms of journalism that political elites exploit to spread disinformation. However, these tactics do not separate right-wing media outlets into distinct categories. Media outlets of various sizes and journalistic orientations, such as Fox, Breitbart, and Zero Hedge, could engage in all of these tactics.

In the following analyses, I explore how right-wing media covered the four disinformation stories. Specifically, I examine whether each article independently fact-checked false claims. Additionally, I compare the tactics employed by Fox News, Breitbart, and Zero Hedge—three media outlets that, arguably, could not be more different from one another. Despite their differences, I demonstrate that all three have utilized or been influenced by all four tactics.

The Trump Tower Wiretapping Story in 2017

On November 7, 2016, the Murdoch-owned right-wing site Heat Street published an article alleging that the FBI sought a FISA warrant to examine the email exchange between U.S. persons, including Trump himself and two foreign banks, in its investigation of a computer server in Trump Tower in October 2016. On March 2, 2017, the right-wing talk radio host Mark Levin suggested that Obama was conducting a silent coup against Trump—for example, by intercepting Trump's phone calls. Levin's baseless allegation became the subject of a Breitbart article the following day, which added that the Obama administration sought the FISA warrant to "wiretap" a computer server in Trump Tower. The article caught the attention of Donald Trump, who sent out a series of tweets on March 4, alleging that Barack Obama was tapping his phone in Trump Tower in October 2016.[26] By then, nearly every major right-wing media outlet had picked up the story.

The fact is that there were two FISA warrants granted in October 2016; both differed significantly from the account presented in the Heat Street article. One warrant, which requested the interception of electronic records from two Russian banks, only covered foreign citizens and entities.[27] The other warrant specifically targeted Trump's former advisor Carter Page.[28] There was no evidence to support the claim that Obama ordered wiretapping of Trump or Trump Tower.[29]

The Trump Tower wiretapping story is an example of the classic propaganda technique "trading up the chain."[30] It usually starts with a false story, first planted at a small publication. Then, it gets picked up by organizations or people with larger audiences or more credibility. Once it gains enough traction, most media outlets will have to cover it.

Table 2.1 Three Headlines About the Trump Tower Wiretapping Story

Media	Article Headline	Tactics
Breitbart	Mark Levin to GOP: Investigate Obama's "Silent Coup" vs. Trump	Manufacturing lies Repeating lies
Fox	Obama Says Trump Claim He Ordered Trump Tower Wiretapped Is False	False balance
Zero Hedge	This Is Watergate: Trump Accuses Obama of Wiretapping the Trump Tower	Repeating lies

Twenty-nine right-wing media outlets published 175 articles under the "Trump Tower wiretapping" topic. Yet, none of those articles independently fact-checked the baseless allegations made in the Heat Street article.[31] While some outlets such as Fox balanced the disinformation with the denials from Obama and other officials, many others such as Breitbart and the Gateway Pundit simply repeated the lies. Table 2.1 shows the article headlines from Fox, Breitbart, and Zero Hedge as well as their tactics to spread disinformation.

The Breitbart article first repeated Heat Street's misleading claim that the Obama administration sought a FISA warrant in its investigation of a server in Trump Tower. Then, it manufactured the lie that there was wiretapping involved, a term that was not used by the original Heat Street article to describe the FISA warrant. The Breitbart article received a four Pinocchios rating by the *Washington Post*'s fact-check team for being flat-out untrue.[32]

The Fox News article took the "false balance" approach by presenting the story as a "he says, she says" controversy. Citing Trump's misleading tweets in the report, the article also included Obama's denial of Trump's accusation. It also provided a link to the debunked Breitbart article without fact-checking its claims.

The Zero Hedge article repeated lies from Trump. It reposted Trump's misleading tweet—"Terrible! Just found out that Obama had my wires tapped in Trump tower just before the victory." In addition, it provided a link to the Breitbart article and speculated that Trump's tweet was based on an internal government report.

The Nunes Memo in 2018

On February 2, 2018, Devin Nunes, chair of the House Intelligence Committee, released a four-page memo[33] alleging that the FBI sought a FISA warrant on Trump's former advisor Carter Page based on a politically motivated source—the Steele dossier.[34] While the memo contained a certain amount of truth—for example, there were indeed errors in the FBI's FISA application[35]—it created the misleading impression that the FBI did not disclose the role of political actors in funding Steele's efforts.[36] It also omitted the fact that the FBI did treat the Steele dossier with skepticism.[37] Due to its sensitive nature, the memo was first blocked from release. After the memo was eventually released, the FBI issued a statement expressing grave concerns about the accuracy of the memo. Democrats on the House Intelligence Committee also released their own memo as a rebuttal shortly after.

The memo's distortion and omission of facts served a larger purpose, which was to cast doubt on the entire FBI investigation of Trump's ties to Russia.[38] The memo was a crucial step in a sustained disinformation campaign to portray the entire Russia probe led by Robert Mueller as a politically motivated witch hunt.[39] Trump, who pressed for the release of the memo, saw it as a key piece of evidence to discredit the ongoing Mueller investigation.[40] In 2021, Trump awarded Nunes the Presidential Medal of Freedom, praising Nunes for uncovering the "greatest scandal in American history," a reference to Nunes's investigation. Later that year, Nunes resigned from Congress and became the CEO of Trump Media & Technology Group. The Nunes memo represents another type of disinformation campaign. Unlike the trading-up-the-chain approach, this disinformation originated from political elites who were in a privileged position to shape the news. When official sources operate in bad faith—deliberately lying, for example—right-wing media run the risk of repeating and amplifying disinformation.

There are 486 articles in the "Nunes memo" topic, published by 28 media outlets. Only five articles raised concerns about the flaws of the memo: one from the *Washington Examiner*, two from the *National Review* (both authored by David French), and two from Hot Air.

Table 2.2 Three Headlines About the Nunes Memo Story

Media	Article Headline	Tactics
Breitbart	Worse Than Watergate: Shocking House Intel Memo Reveals FISA Abuse by Senior DOJ and FBI Officials	Repeating lies
Fox	Nunes Calls Media's Biased Coverage of Memo "Embarrassing"	Repeating lies
Zero Hedge	Democrats Draft "Counter-Memo" to Refute Bombshell FISA Report	False balance

Most articles repeated and amplified the words from Nunes and his political and media allies. Table 2.2 shows three headlines from Fox, Breitbart, and Zero Hedge.

The Breitbart article was published on January 18, about two weeks before the release of the Nunes memo. It cited eight sources in total, all staunch Trump allies: Mark Meadows, Matt Gaetz, Steve King, Ron DeSantis, Scott Perry, Jim Jordan, Carter Page, and Lee Zeldin. These sources repeated the same talking points, calling the memo "shocking," "jaw-dropping," "sickening," and "worse than Watergate." Ron DeSantis, for example, was quoted saying that this memo raises serious questions about the Russia investigation. Besides repeating DeSantis's misleading statement, the article also linked the Nunes memo to the previous Trump Tower wiretapping disinformation story, creating the impression that it was part of Obama's scheme to spy on Trump. Given its timing, this Breitbart article could be considered part of a pressure campaign to force the release of the Nunes memo.

The Fox article was an excerpt from Sean Hannity's program on February 5. In the program, Hannity invited multiple guests, including Sara Carter, Mark Levin, and Devin Nunes, to comment on the memo. No Democrats or FBI officials were invited. The article repeated Nunes's claim that Hillary Clinton's campaign colluded with the Russians to get dirt on Trump and feed it to the FBI. The claim received four Pinocchios by the *Washington Post* for being totally untrue.[41]

The Zero Hedge article covered both the Nunes memo and the Democrats' counter-memo. While it repeated the misleading claim that the Nunes memo uncovered a conspiracy theory involving the FBI, the Department of Justice (DOJ), the Obama administration, and the Clinton campaign, it also quoted the Democratic ranking member of the House Intelligence Committee Representative Adam Schiff's announcement that the counter-memo was about "setting out the relevant facts and exposing the misleading character of the Republicans' document so that members of the House are not left with an erroneous impression of the dedicated professionals at the FBI and the DOJ."

The Ukraine–Biden Conspiracy Theory

The Ukraine–Biden conspiracy theory, designed to harm Democratic hopeful Joe Biden in the 2020 election, claimed that then-Vice President Joe Biden engaged in corrupt activities— namely, pressuring Ukraine to fire its prosecutor general, Viktor Shokin, for investigating Burisma to protect his son Hunter Biden, a former board member of Burisma.[42] Other related disinformation narratives,[43] manufactured by a variety of political actors, such as Rudy Giuliani, John Solomon, and Donald Trump, claimed that Joe Biden was paid $900,000 by Burisma and that Joe and Hunter Biden were involved in money laundering in Ukraine. Table A.2.8 in the appendix shows examples of false or unverified claims about the Ukraine–Biden conspiracy theory.

The fact is that Joe Biden, in coordination with the European Union and the International Monetary Fund, urged Ukraine to fire Shokin because of his failure to fight corruption in Ukraine, not because of his investigation of Burisma or Hunter Biden.[44] There is no evidence that Joe Biden engaged in corruption (e.g., by selling out national security for personal gain).

Most articles in the Ukraine–Biden conspiracy theory topic failed to set the record straight. Among the 293 articles published by 27 right-wing media outlets on this topic, only three stated this fact. One hundred and forty articles, published by 25 right-wing media outlets (the exceptions were Real Clear Politics and Free Beacon), contained at least one false, debunked, or unverified claim. Another 60 articles covered public misbeliefs (e.g., poll numbers showing most Americans believed that Biden was corrupt) and events (e.g., Lindsey Graham requesting

Table 2.3 Three Headlines About the Ukraine–Biden Conspiracy Theory

Media	Article Headline	Tactics
Breitbart	Lindsey Graham Launches Senate Probe into Bidens' Burisma Actions	Lack of context
Fox	Joe, Hunter Biden Seen Golfing with Ukraine Gas Company Exec Back in 2014, Photo Shows	Manufacturing lies
Zero Hedge	Ukrainian Indictment Reveals Hunter Biden Group Made $165 Million	Manufacturing lies

documents to investigate Joe Biden) without providing proper context. Table 2.3 shows the headlines of three stories from Fox, Breitbart, and Zero Hedge.

The Breitbart article centered on Lindsey Graham, who requested phone call records between Biden and Ukraine's then-president, Petro Poroshenko, to investigate the allegation that Biden pressured Shokin to end the investigation into Burisma. It did not include the context that Graham's investigation was based on a baseless allegation.

The Fox News article centered on a photo of Joe and Hunter Biden golfing with Devon Archer, an American businessman who—like Hunter Biden—served on the board of Burisma. The photo was first unearthed by Fox's former host Tucker Carlson and was later picked up by multiple right-wing media outlets and Donald Trump as evidence of the false allegation that Joe Biden spoke to the CEO or boss of Burisma.[45] Devon Archer was not the CEO or the boss running Burisma. However, the title of the Fox article implied that he was, though Fox did clarify Archer's actual position at the bottom of the article.

The Zero Hedge article falsely claimed that the Ukrainian government just indicted Burisma. The article Zero Hedge cited the Interfax-Ukraine News Agency, which reported that Ukrainian members of parliament held a press conference to demand Ukrainian President Volodymr Zelensky and Trump investigate suspected money laundering involving Burisma. The Interfax article did not say anything about indictment. Zero Hedge made it up.

HCQ as a "Miracle Cure" for Covid-19

The false narrative about HCQ as a Covid-19 treatment originated from a small-n observational study by the French doctor Didier Raoult in early 2020.[46] Despite its significant limitations, the study was picked up by a lawyer and blockchain enthusiast named Gregory Rigano, who later appeared on Fox's *Ingraham Angle* on March 16. During the show, host Laura Ingraham declared HCQ as a game changer. On March 19, Trump openly promoted the drug at a White House briefing. Ingraham later credited herself for bringing HCQ to Trump's attention. In the following months, Trump continued to vouch for the drug—for example, by declaring that he was taking the drug in May. His actions resulted in extensive coverage and circulation of the false narrative.[47] Meanwhile, the disinformation about HCQ also materialized into policy: The Trump administration pressured the Food and Drug Administration (FDA) to give an emergency authorization of HCQ and distributed the strategic national stockpile of HCQ to hospitals and clinical trials.

All of this happened despite the lack of reliable scientific evidence that HCQ could effectively treat Covid-19. Worse yet, if used inappropriately, HCQ may cause heart rhythm problems and kidney injuries. Even though public health experts had warned about the potential risk of using HCQ to treat Covid-19, many right-wing media outlets kept pushing the false narrative about HCQ—and later the antiparasitic medicine ivermectin—as cures for Covid-19.

The false narrative about HCQ as a "miracle cure" was a politically motivated disinformation campaign. It was designed to persuade people to go back to work in the early days of the pandemic, when multiple states had just begun lockdowns. Even though Covid-19 was raging across the country at that time, Trump and his political allies spared no effort to keep the economy open—and later reopen it as soon as possible—with the ultimate goal of solidifying Trump's re-election bid.[48]

Among the 204 articles published by 28 media outlets on this topic, only 20 issued warnings about the risks or danger associated with HCQ as a Covid-19 treatment. The vast majority repeated the misleading narrative, citing patients, doctors, Republican officials, and questionable studies. Events and public policies created based on this disinformation,

Table 2.4 Three Headlines About HCQ and Covid-19

Media	Article Headline	Tactics
Breitbart	French Expert: Second Study Shows Malaria Drug Helps Fight Coronavirus	False balance
Fox	Trump Reveals He's Taking Hydroxychloroquine in Effort to Prevent Coronavirus Symptoms	Lack of context False balance
Zero Hedge	Trump Admits to Taking Hydroxychloroquine with Zinc as Preventative Measure	Lack of context False balance

including Trump taking the drug himself and the FDA's emergency authorization of HCQ, also provided fodder for right-wing media's coverage. Table 2.4 shows three headlines from Fox, Breitbart, and Zero Hedge.

The Breitbart article started with Raoult's controversial claim that his new study showed that HCQ was effective in combating Covid-19. Then, the article cited the critics who cast doubt on the validity of Raoult's findings. Both the Fox News article and the Zero Hedge article covered the news that Trump himself was taking the drug. The Fox News article first balanced Trump's touting of the drug with a study showing that HCQ provided no benefits in treating Covid-19. Then, it cited critics saying that the study was perhaps not vigorous. Overall, it presented the effectiveness of HCQ in treating Covid-19 as an open debate with merits on both sides. Like the Fox article, the Zero Hedge article also engaged in false balance in covering Trump.

Conclusion

The analysis in Chapter 2 shows that the top 10 most engaged topics within the right-wing media sphere included at least one disinformation campaign every year between 2017 and 2020. The prominence of disinformation among the top stories was not a result of only a few fringe sites "flooding the zone with shit." Various right-wing media outlets, ranging from established brands to medium-sized digital sites and blogs, participated in spreading disinformation. This finding points to the sobering reality of the right-wing media sphere: It suffers from systematic breakdowns in information quality when it comes to the most prominent topics that were consumed by most audiences.

Chapter 2's analysis shows that both media and political elites on the right are responsible for weaponizing journalism for political purposes. Right-wing media elites, represented by no less an authority than the former CEO of Breitbart Steve Bannon, who infamously declared his intent to "flood the zone with shit," manufactured factually dubious narratives. While many right-wing media organizations may profess to be factual, some of their biggest stars, such as Sean Hannity, Tucker Carlson, and Laura Ingraham, displayed Bannon's disregard for good-faith journalism.

Republican elites such as Donald Trump and Lindsey Graham also loomed large. The daily supply of lies from Republicans presents a serious challenge for right-wing media to fulfill their journalistic role, as they tend to favor Republican sources or select stories that favor Republicans. The four disinformation stories revealed just how easily Republican elites channeled their lies into right-wing news coverage. Right-wing media amplified these lies by repeating them, presenting them in a false balance with facts, and failing to provide context when covering events and public opinion that were a result of lies.

It is concerning that right-wing media of different kinds, exemplified by Fox, Breitbart, and Zero Hedge, embraced the same tactics in spreading the four disinformation stories. Their decisions likely involved a combination of different factors. First, all of these stories were designed to protect a sitting Republican president against external threats, which could serve as a rallying cry to unite different ideological factions on the right. The Trump Tower wiretapping story and the Nunes memo were used to discredit the ongoing Mueller investigation into then-President Trump, the Biden–Ukraine conspiracy theory was designed to malign Trump's Democratic opponent in the 2020 election, and the HCQ disinformation story was used to help with Trump's re-election bid. Although the right is often divided on certain issues—a topic explored in Chapter 3—right-wing media consistently rallied when Trump faced trouble.

Moreover, all four cases involved prominent Republican elites making public statements about or taking actions upon the misleading narratives, which created news hooks for right-wing media. The Nunes memo came directly from the Republican committee chair in Congress, the Ukraine–Biden conspiracy theory involved Lindsey Graham launching a congressional investigation, the HCQ story involved the Trump administration distributing stockpiles of HCQ, and the Trump Tower wiretapping story involved Trump publicly endorsing the narrative on Twitter. When Republicans create news based on factually dubious narratives, right-wing media—even those that operate more like traditional forms of partisan journalism—might find it too hard to not cover the story.

However, the fact that many right-wing media organizations promoted these four high-profile disinformation stories does not mean that they are homogenous or operate like a mindless automaton for the GOP. The next chapter shows how ideological fissures on the right can give rise to a unique political organizing dynamic within the right-wing media sphere.

3

Divided We Fall

IN LATE JULY 2017, PRESIDENT Trump's national security advisor, H. R. McMaster, a three-star lieutenant general, fired several self-branded "anti-establishment" National Security Council officials who were Steve Bannon's allies while he served as chief strategist for the Trump administration. The general soon became the target of a Breitbart-led campaign that demanded Trump remove McMaster from office. The campaign quickly garnered wide support from pro-Trump media, right-wing pro-Israel groups, and anti-Islam organizations funded by Paul Singer, Robert Mercer, and Sheldon Adelson. However, it also triggered a public backlash from a different group of right-wing media outlets funded by Philip Anschutz, Charles Koch, and the Ed Uihlein Family Foundation. By August 6, Trump had to step in and issue a public statement to defend McMaster: "General McMaster and I are working very well together," Trump said in a public statement. "He is a good man and very pro-Israel. I am grateful for the work he continues to do serving our country."

Trump's intervention did little to quell the uprising from the anti-McMaster wing of right-wing media. In the following days, Breitbart accused Trump of defying his base, the *Conservative Review* called Trump's support of McMaster indefensible, and the Washington Free Beacon even warned that Trump would have to face consequences if he continued to support McMaster.

Weapons of Mass Deception. Yunkang Yang, Oxford University Press. © Yunkang Yang (2025).
DOI: 10.1093/9780197820339.003.0004

We have long been told that right-wing media are a propaganda arm for Republican politicians. David Brock, the founder of Media Matters for America and a one-time right-wing hitman himself, chronicled the right-wing media's fealty to the GOP and referred to them as the GOP's noise machine.[1] The work of investigative journalist Lee Fang showed that right-wing media outlets served as a channel for GOP politicians to coordinate with conservative grassroots movements.[2] *The New Yorker*'s investigative journalist Jane Mayer, after examining Fox's history with Trump, suggested that Fox functioned as an extension of the Trump White House.[3]

The campaign against McMaster suggests a more complicated story. Not only did many right-wing media outlets try to push out a key senior aide in a Republican administration, but they also defied a sitting Republican president. Trump, despite his significant influence over the Republican base, does not have full control over right-wing media.

Owned by billionaires on the political right, right-wing media's loyalty does not lie with the GOP. Although Fox News, Breitbart, and the Daily Caller may come to the rescue of Republicans, it would be a mistake to regard right-wing media simply as a mouthpiece for the Republican Party or a Republican administration. Unlike the 19th-century partisan newspapers, which were heavily subsidized by political parties, today's right-wing media are controlled by private individuals with deep ties to an army of think tanks, activists, and campaign organizations. Drawing on this powerful political network, many right-wing media outlets possess the power to challenge the Republican establishment.

The campaign against McMaster also suggests that the right-wing media sphere does not always operate as an ideological echo chamber[4] or a network propaganda sphere[5] that echoes, repeats, and amplifies the same partisan narratives. Prior scholarship might have overestimated the coherence of the right-wing media sphere. As this chapter will show, right-wing media were divided in the McMaster controversy. While Breitbart and the Free Beacon attacked McMaster, the *Weekly Standard* and the *National Review* defended him.

The divide within the right-wing media sphere reflects deep ideological fault lines among different right-wing factions. Although Trump's political coalition helped him win the 2016 election, it was also fraught with internal strife over issues such as foreign policy. The ideological disagreement between the McMaster wing and the Bannon wing was initially managed internally through a balance of power within the White House. However, when McMaster fired Bannon's political allies, he tipped the delicate balance, resulting in divergent reactions in the right-wing media sphere, with one camp attacking McMaster and the other defending him.

This chapter reveals the first organizing mechanism of the right-wing media sphere: ideologically contested political organizing. Using the McMaster controversy as a case, it shows that ideological contestation among warring right-wing factions can drive the political organizing activities of right-wing media. To understand how ideologically contested political organizing works, we must first recognize that the right-wing media sphere is not politically or ideologically homogeneous.

A Media Sphere in Turmoil

After an agonizing one-year partnership with President Trump, Republican House Speaker Paul Ryan decided that he would not seek re-election in 2018. After stepping down in January 2019, Ryan told *Politico* journalist Tim Alberta that he had lost the battle within the GOP to the Trump wing:

> "I'm a traditional conservative, and traditional conservatives are definitely not ascendant in the party right now," Ryan said, continuing, "the Reagan Republican wing beat the Rockefeller Republican wing and now the Trump wing beat the Reagan wing."[6]

For more than 30 years, the GOP was rooted in Reagan conservatism, which forged a winning Republican coalition in the 1980s. This coalition consisted of social conservatives that believed in Christian values, fiscal conservatives who favored tax cuts and government deregulation, and foreign policy hawks who wanted to project American values around the world. Supported by these three key constituents, mainstream Republicans advocated free trade, foreign intervention, and even an "amnesty" for immigrants.[7]

During this time, the conservative media establishment consisted of only a handful of media outlets. Fox News host Sean Hannity and Rush Limbaugh both proudly identified themselves as Reagan conservatives at that time, stressing that it was Reagan who brought an end to the Cold War, restored America's leadership in the world, and revived the American economy through "trickle-down" economics. As political scientists Kathleen Jamieson and Joseph Cappella described, right-wing media were "cousins with a shared commitment to Reagan conservatism, a common ideological ancestry, and a network of related kin";[8] it was their shared embrace of the tenets of Reagan conservatism that unified these diverse media figures and outlets into a cohesive conservative media establishment.[9]

After Trump took office, he shook the ideological foundation of the Republican Party. While he still had to rely on social conservatives and fiscal conservatives to win the 2016 election, he built his political momentum on the anti-establishment nationalist movement, occasionally drawing energy from white supremacists, neo-Nazis, conspiracy theorists, and the manosphere. As he brought the anti-establishment wing into the Republican Party in 2017, he challenged the orthodoxy of Reagan conservatism on trade, immigration, and foreign policy. On trade, Trump imposed massive tariffs on America's major trading partners; on immigration, Trump imposed the 2017 "Muslim travel ban" and the "zero tolerance" policy, which resulted in the separation of children from their families; and on foreign policy, Trump threatened to withdraw from NATO and proposed massive cuts to the U.S. foreign aid.

However, the first Trump administration could not rely solely on its anti-establishment wing. While the nationalists were useful in energizing his base, few had much experience in government. To accomplish his goals, Trump needed experienced career officials who were well-versed in Washington politics. Hence, not only did he bring the anti-establishment firebrand Steve Bannon into the White House, but he also installed John Kelly as his chief of staff and H. R. McMaster as his national security advisor, whose political views were more in line with those of the GOP establishment.

At the start of Trump's first term, fierce disagreements were already emerging between Bannon's nationalist wing and more moderate White House officials. Bannonites opposed the North American Free Trade Agreement (NAFTA), the Iran nuclear deal, America's military involvement in Afghanistan, and tax cuts for the rich. Some of the disagreements were resolved through compromise. However, constant infighting among Trump's officials resulted in an extraordinary number of leaks, firings, and resignations during Trump's first term. In Bannon's own words, he engaged "in a fight every day," clashing with the national economic council director Gary Cohn over trade, Trump's senior advisor Jared Kushner over healthcare reform, and National Security Advisor H. R. McMaster over Afghanistan.

The right-wing media sphere mirrored these developments in the political world. On the one hand, there was still the "old guard"—traditional, center-right conservative publications such as the *Weekly Standard* and the *National Review* in 2017; on the other hand, Breitbart, the anti-establishment beachhead, was gaining momentum during the 2016 Trump campaign, drawing support from Infowars, Zero Hedge, and the Gateway Pundit. Among the 46 right-wing media outlets discussed in the book, 31% described themselves as conservative media outlets on their websites' About page, and 24% said they defied the left and right cleavage, instead positioning themselves as alternatives to the establishment media.

There was no shortage of vitriol between these two camps. While the *National Review* called Breitbart a dangerous, malignant, and malicious apologetic for the alt-right, Breitbart referred to the *National Review* as one of the most hypocritical, anti-intellectual, feelings-first, and unethical troll sites and called the *Weekly Standard* a hysterical voice of pompous bitterness directed towards those who dared not share its desire to hold on to its failed ideas about Middle East wars, immigration, trade, and rolling over for the establishment media. The right-wing media sphere was no longer the "conservative media establishment" that previous scholars declared more than a decade ago. It was fraught with simmering ideological tensions. For an infighting to begin in earnest, all that was needed was a triggering event.

The Triggering Event

In late July 2017, McMaster fired three national security officials, Rich Higgins, Derek Harvey, and Ezra Cohen-Watnick, who were allies of Bannon.[10] According to McMaster's own account, the personnel changes were meant to ensure President Trump had the best staffers.[11] Yet, this series of firings was seen as a showdown between McMaster's wing and Bannon's anti-establishment wing, who had been fighting over foreign policies in the Middle East and Afghanistan since April 2017. Backed by powerful right-wing pro-Israel groups such as the Zionist Organization of America (ZOA), the anti-establishment wing fought back in the aftermath of the firings and launched a coordinated campaign to oust McMaster. In the two weeks after the initial firing of Rich Higgins on July 21, multiple leaks targeting McMaster appeared almost simultaneously on media sites such as Circa, Breitbart, and the Free Beacon. Meanwhile, numerous opinion pieces penned by right-wing pro-Israel and anti-Islam groups quickly circulated through anti-establishment right-wing media.[12]

The open conflict between McMaster and Bannon was fueled by a longstanding, ideological tension around foreign policy. Bannon's anti-establishment faction championed the so-called America First agenda, which took an isolationist and protectionist approach to international affairs that dates to the paleoconservative Pat Buchanan in the 1990s.[13] This faction harbored skepticism toward transnational organizations like NATO, free trade agreements such as NAFTA, and military interventions such as the wars in Iraq and Afghanistan.

In contrast with the views of the anti-establishment wing, McMaster's approach to foreign policy was more in line with the established practices of previous administrations. His conflict with Bannon centered on three issues: the war in Syria, the war in Afghanistan, and the Iran nuclear agreement (i.e., the Joint Comprehensive Plan of Action).

Their earliest dispute dated back to April 7, 2017, when Trump decided to launch missile strikes in Syria in response to the Syrian government's use of chemical weapons against civilians. McMaster advocated the missile strikes, while Bannon opposed them on the grounds that such a reaction would betray Trump's America First campaign pledge. Trump sided with McMaster, who removed Steve Bannon from the National Security Council shortly thereafter. This action reportedly antagonized Bannon and his political allies, including Jack Posobiec, Lee Stranahan, Mike Cernovich, and Alex Jones, who started an online campaign with the hashtag #FireMcMaster in April.

Removed from the National Security Council, Bannon continued to clash with McMaster on two other foreign policy issues. Regarding the war in Afghanistan, Bannon pushed for a withdrawal of troops, while McMaster convinced Trump to commit more troops to stabilize the region. They reportedly shouted at each other during a meeting in the White House.[14] On the issue of the Iran nuclear agreement, Bannon wanted a complete withdrawal, whereas McMaster successfully dissuaded Trump from completely jettisoning the agreement.

Even though the power struggle between McMaster and Bannon within the Trump administration was largely driven by ideological differences over Syria, Afghanistan, and the Iran nuclear agreement, many anti-establishment media outlets did not entirely focus on policy differences in their campaign against McMaster. Instead, they framed the conflict through three themes: McMaster was globalist, anti-Trump, and anti-Israel. These three core narratives, which were later confirmed by McMaster's 2024 memoir *At War with Ourselves*,[15] were likely designed to mobilize a broader political coalition against McMaster.

Framing the Conflict

The first major organizing theme was that McMaster was a globalist. Popularized by Breitbart to denigrate political opponents, the term "globalist" was a veiled reference to a right-wing anti-Semitic conspiracy theory about rich Jewish bankers working behind the scenes to control the world.[16] The most vilified target of this right-wing conspiracy theory was George Soros, a billionaire who funded many liberal causes. Used as a strawman to attack Democrats, Soros was accused of many things, including controlling Barack Obama and paying women on Hillary Clinton's behalf to fabricate sexual assault allegations against Trump. The anti-establishment right-wing media employed the same trope in their attack against McMaster. For instance, Mike Cernovich, an alt-right political operative known for promoting the Pizzagate conspiracy theory, reportedly set up the website McMasterleaks.com, where a cartoon of a Jewish banking family, the Rothschilds, controlled a George Soros puppet, which in turn controlled a McMaster puppet; Breitbart claimed that McMaster worked at a think tank funded by George Soros. By tapping into anti-Semitic tropes and associating McMaster with the familiar villain George Soros, anti-McMaster media sites were trying to depict McMaster as a common enemy of the political right.

The second theme portrayed McMaster's firings as a subversive act against Trump. This included referring to the officials fired by McMaster as Trump loyalists, implying that McMaster secretly helped Trump's political opponent Susan Rice, and claiming that McMaster's agenda was at odds with that of Trump. This narrative was likely designed to create a schism between McMaster and Donald Trump. It was also aimed to mobilize support from pro-Trump media outlets such as Infowars, whose audience may not be interested in the minute details of foreign policy.

The third major theme was that McMaster was anti-Israel. Right-wing pro-Israel groups had long lobbied against the Iran nuclear deal before Trump became president in 2016. An anti-Israel angle was useful for Bannon to mobilize the powerful pro-Israeli network, which he had long been cultivating at Breitbart. Despite its cynical use of anti-Semitic tropes to attract readers,[17] Breitbart started out as an unabashedly pro-Israel website, with its founder, Andrew Breitbart, stating in 2012 that one of its goals was advocating for Israel.[18] When Bannon took the helm of Breitbart, he courted right-wing pro-Israel individuals and groups such as Pamela Geller, David Horowitz, and the ZOA. By tying the anti-McMaster campaign to a pro-Israel stance, Bannon gave the Israeli right-wing network a reason to join his fight.

Mobilizing Resources

The anti-establishment wing of the right-wing media sphere demonstrated a remarkable ability to mobilize resources both inside and outside the Trump White House. In the immediate aftermath of McMaster's firing of Cohen-Watnick on August 2, multiple anonymous sources inside the White House leaked damaging information depicting McMaster as an anti-Trump official to five leading anti-McMaster media outlets. Table 3.1 lists the top-five most-linked stories published by anti-McMaster media outlets.

As Table 3.1 shows, one day after the firing of Cohen-Watnick, five different reports emerged from five outlets, all citing anonymous sources within the White House. The most linked story, Circa's "A

Table 3.1 Sources for Most Linked Anti-McMaster Stories

Title	Date	Media	Source
1. "A Letter from H. R. McMaster Said Susan Rice Will Keep Her Top-Secret Security Clearance"	August 3, 2017	Circa.com	Anonymous "White House officials," including "a senior West Wing official" and "an intelligence official"
2. "McMaster Has 'List' of White House Officials He Plans to Fire. They're All Key Trump Allies"	August 3, 2017	Freebeacon.com	More than six anonymous "Trump administration insiders"
3. "NSC Purge: McMaster 'Deeply Hostile to Israel and to Trump'"	August 3, 2017	Breitbart.com	Anonymous "senior officials"
4. "Exclusive: Trump Loyalist Ezra Cohen-Watnick Fired from National Security Council, Sources Say"	August 2, 2017	Conservative review.com	Two anonymous "senior administration officials who are not authorized to discuss personnel matters"
5. "Exclusive: Everything the President Wants to Do, McMaster Opposes, Former NSC Official Says"	August 3, 2017	Dailycaller.com	Two anonymous "senior NSC officials"; BuzzFeed, Politico, *The Atlantic*, and the *Weekly Standard*

Source: Media Cloud. Media Cloud is an open-source, online news analytics tool developed by the Berkman Klein Center for Internet & Society at Harvard University in 2011. It tracks over 60,000 media sources globally. For more details, see http://www.mediacloud.org.

Letter from H. R. McMaster Said Susan Rice Will Keep Her Top-Secret Security Clearance," was likely the product of a coordinated effort between Circa and Cohen-Watnick, the anti-establishment official who had just been fired by McMaster.[19] After being fired, Cohen-Watnick reportedly leaked to Circa a pro forma letter that McMaster sent to Obama's national security adviser, Susan Rice,[20] notifying her of the extension of her security clearance; this, Circa noted, implied that McMaster gave Trump's political opponent unfettered access to classified information.[21] This misleading story, which circulated among more than 20 right-wing media outlets, became the single most cited piece of evidence in support of the narrative that McMaster was anti-Trump. The other four top stories exhibited the same pattern of one-sided talking points. As their titles suggest, these articles all strategically framed the officials fired by McMaster as Trump loyalists instead of as Bannon's allies.

Not only did anti-establishment media outlets coordinate with their allies within the White House, but they also mobilized various right-wing political groups funded by the same network of donors. Breitbart, in particular, gave its platform to at least five right-wing political groups to publish their anti-McMaster materials and talking points. Table 3.2 lists the quotes from seven political groups that were cited by anti-McMaster media.

As the quotes in Table 3.2 show, some of the groups threatened Trump and demanded that he fire McMaster. These groups had a significant influence on American right-wing politics. Funded by powerful donors such as the Mercer family, the Adelson family, and the Scaife family, they held significant sway over Donald Trump's political appointments and policy initiatives. For instance, Michael Flynn, McMaster's predecessor, was a former board member of Act for America, and John Bolton, McMaster's successor, was a former chairman of the think tank the Gatestone Institute and a board member of Secure America Now.

The appointment of McMaster, who was recommended by establishment GOP politicians such as John McCain, frustrated right-wing political groups that had reservations about McMaster's approach to the Middle East. In the McMaster controversy, media sites such as Breitbart mobilized these powerful groups, providing them with publicity to unite in opposition to McMaster and exert pressure on Donald Trump.

Table 3.2 Right-Wing Political Groups Cited by Right-Wing Media

Quotes	Groups	Funders
"If the president does not take some action against McMaster, given everything that's come out, then the president owns everything that he is doing." (Richard Manning on freebeacon.com)	Americans for Limited Government	Howard Rich and others
"If McMaster isn't fired after all that he has done and all that he will do, we're going to have to reconsider Trump's foreign policy." (Caroline Glick on Breitbart)	Center for Security Policy	The Scaife Foundation, the Bradley Foundation, Becker Foundations and Charitable Trust, Fairbrook Foundation, William Rosenwald Fund, Middle Road Foundation, Abstraction Fund, and Alan and Hope Winters Family Foundation
"National security advisor McMaster opposes Trump's anti-Iran, pro-Israel, radical-Islamist-terrorism-fighting policies; he should be reassigned to a position unrelated to these vital issues." (ZOA report on Breitbart)	Zionist Organization of America	Sheldon Adelson and others
"The National Security Council is becoming a national security threat." (Daniel Greenfield on frontpagemag.com)	Freedom Center	The Olin Foundation, the Bradley Foundation, the Scaife Foundation, Becker Foundations and Charitable Trust, Fairbrook Foundation, William Rosenwald Fund, Middle Road Foundation, and Abstraction Fund

Continued

Table 3.2 *Continued*

Quotes	Groups	Funders
"You have a situation where the president's policies are not being put forth by the national security adviser." (Allen Roth on Breitbart)	Secure America Now	Robert Mercer, Brad Anderson, Richard Schulze, and Ronald Lauder
"[McMaster's refusal to] condemn radical Islamic terrorism by name is a threat to our national security." (Steve Emerson on Breitbart)	Investigative Project on Terrorism	The Bradley Foundation, Richard Mellon Scaife, Becker Foundations and Charitable Trust, Fairbrook Foundation, William Rosenwald Fund, Middle Road Foundation, and Abstraction Fund
"The president would do well to re-examine whether his national security advisor is serving either his interest or those of the United States." (wnd.com)	Gatestone Institute	Robert and Rebekah Mercer
"It is very clear that McMaster is on a completely different track than what President Trump promised the American public." (Brigitte Gabriel on Breitbart)	Act for America	Fairbrook Foundation, Becker Foundations and Charitable Trust, and the Alan and Hope Winters Family Foundation

Backlash

Anti-establishment right-wing media's attacks on McMaster provoked a backlash from the *National Review*, the *Weekly Standard*, and Real Clear Politics. The strongest reaction came from David French at the *National Review*, who not only defended McMaster but also called for Bannon's removal. The *Weekly Standard* exposed the coordination between Circa and Cohen-Watnick in leaking damaging information about McMaster and called Breitbart's articles "opposition research." Real Clear Politics proclaimed that McMaster was a rare asset for Trump, and defended his move to fire Bannon's allies, calling it "process-driven rather than ideological."

Figure 3.1 plots each right-wing media outlet's stance on McMaster on the x-axis[22] and the number of unique media in-links it received on the y-axis. "Stance on McMaster" was scored based on an analysis of 226 articles published by 38 right-wing media outlets.[23] It ranged between −1 and 1. A −1 score for a media outlet indicates that all of the outlet's articles about McMaster were negative, a 1 score indicates all of the articles were positive, and a 0 score means the overall stance was neutral.

The six top anti-McMaster sites, including Circa and the Free Beacon, were highly influential: Each received links from no fewer than 10 unique right-wing media outlets. With firsthand access to exclusive sources, including White House officials and right-wing political groups, these six top sites mobilized a great deal of anti-McMaster materials and disseminated them to smaller sites such as the Gateway Pundit, Western Journal, and the Daily Wire.

The pro-McMaster media sites, however, were outnumbered by the anti-McMaster sites. They also published fewer articles, most of which were opinion pieces penned by their own contributing writers with few sources from the White House or right-wing political groups. They received far less attention than the six most cited anti-McMaster sites within the right-wing media sphere.

Ideologically Contested Political Organizing

Figure 3.2 shows the hyperlink network of right-wing media's coverage of the McMaster controversy between July 21 and August 18. Node

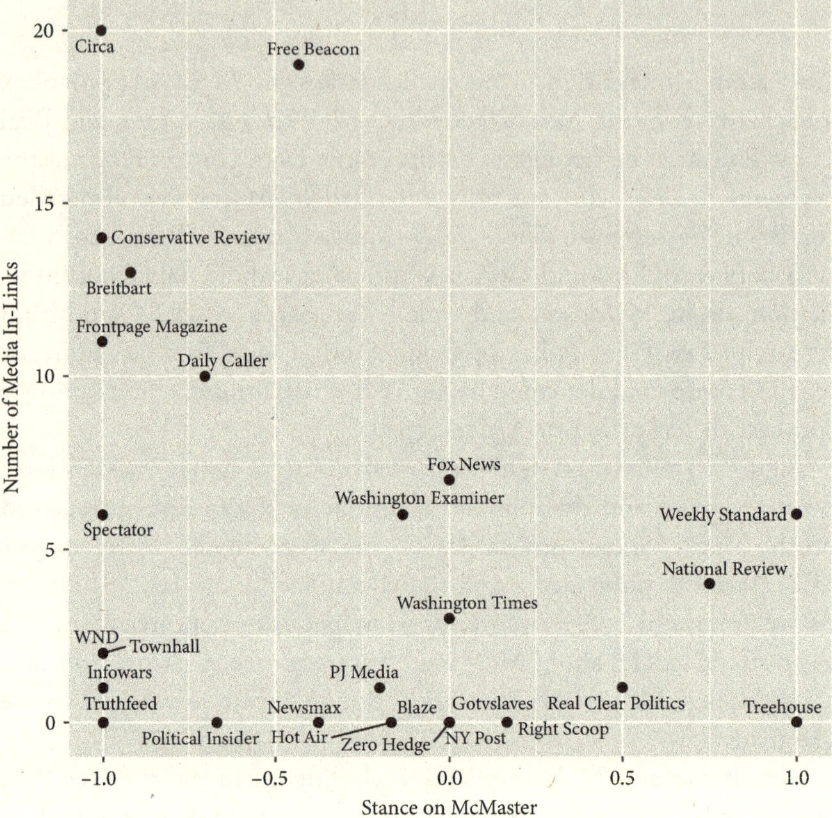

FIGURE 3.1 Right-wing media's stance on McMaster.

Note: For visualization purposes, certain data points were removed from the graph due to overlaps.

Source: Media Cloud

label size is proportional to the number of unique media in-links, and arrows point to the origin of hyperlinked stories.

Free Beacon, Circa, Daily Caller, Breitbart, Conservative Review, and FrontPage Magazine emerged as the leading anti-McMaster media outlets. As I previously showed, these six media outlets mobilized a number of information resources at the White House and various think tanks. Their visibility in the network was boosted by smaller sites such as PJ Media, which repeated and amplified those materials. The six leading anti-McMaster media outlets received 87 story in-links in total, approximately three times the number for all other right-wing media combined. By comparison, the pro-McMaster and

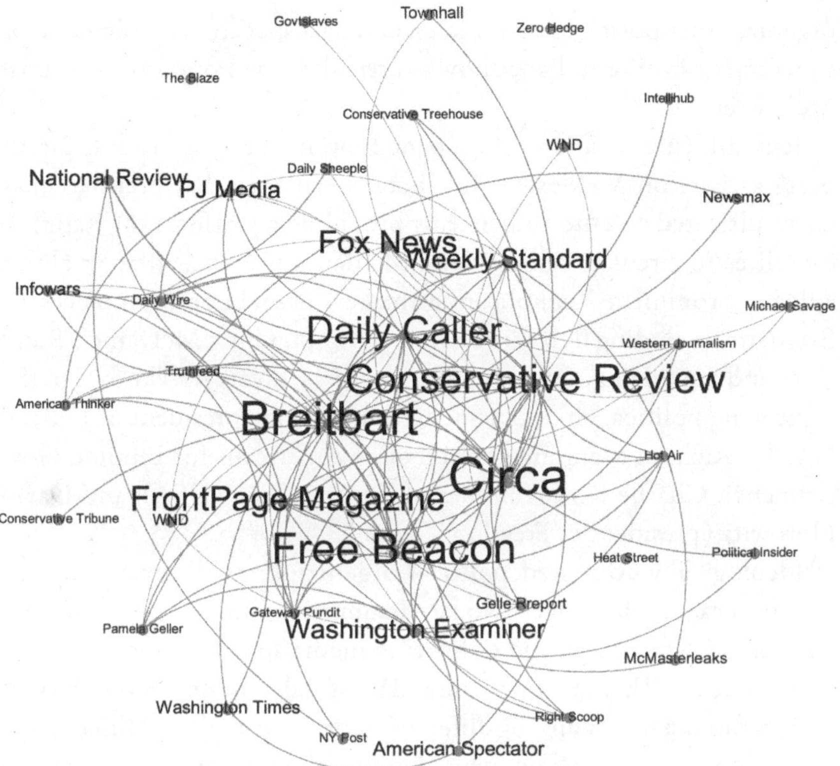

FIGURE 3.2 Hyperlink network of right-wing media's coverage of the McMaster controversy between July 21 and August 18.

neutral media outlets received much less attention. With the six anti-McMaster media outlets taking the lead, much larger outlets receded into the background. Fox was linked by only five media outlets.

It is worth noting that the McMaster story was not a high-engagement story on Facebook. On average, the 226 articles about the story generated 1550 user interactions, whereas articles in the high-engagement corpus between July and December 2017 generated 9778 interactions on average. It stands to reason that the McMaster story may not be particularly popular among ordinary conservative news consumers on Facebook. After all, the average Republican primary voter may not care much whether McMaster stays in power. However, Breitbart, for example, still published a significant number of articles belaboring McMaster's background, affiliation with various organizations, positions on policies, and past speeches. It seemed to be signaling to an elite audience how to articulate their opposition against McMaster.

It is difficult to know who spent how much time reading Breitbart's articles on McMaster. But there is evidence that Breitbart may have cultivated an elite audience by providing a platform for Republican elites to circulate policy ideas. My data show that in 2017 alone, a dozen prominent Republican lawmakers penned opinion pieces on Breitbart, including Ted Cruz, Marco Rubio, Chris McDaniel, Rand Paul, and Steve King. Other opinion writers who are well known in the right-wing political circles included Tom Fitton (president of Judicial Watch), Richard Manning (president of Americans for Limited Government), Charlie Kirk (founder of Turning Point USA), and David Horowitz (president of Freedom Center).

Ideologically contested political organizing, as illustrated by the McMaster case, challenges two key assumptions about right-wing media. First, it shows that the right-wing media sphere is not politically homogeneous. There are important ideological fault lines around issues such as foreign policy among different right-wing media. Political organizing can take place along these ideological fault lines, which may result in conflicts. Second, right-wing media are not simply a propaganda arm for the GOP or the Republican administration. Owned by rich individuals who have personal ideological agendas, many right-wing media can mobilize their resources to contest the power of Republican officials.

4

In GOP We Trust

IN JULY 2018, THE RETIREMENT of Supreme Court Justice Anthony Kennedy—who was known as a swing vote on the court—gave Republicans in the Republican-controlled Senate a chance to tilt the U.S. Supreme Court to the right. However, their time to confirm Trump's nominee, Brett Kavanaugh, was short: The 2018 midterm elections were only four months away. Given the prospect that Democrats might retake the U.S. Senate, Republicans needed the confirmation to be completed before the election.

As Senate Republicans rushed through Kavanaugh's confirmation hearing in September, a woman named Christine Blasey Ford alleged that Kavanaugh attempted to rape her when they were high school students. Democrats immediately called for a suspension of the confirmation hearing until a thorough investigation into the alleged sexual assault could be conducted. Kavanaugh's confirmation, which had once seemed all but certain to succeed, suddenly hung in the balance.

The stakes could not have been higher. Not only could Ford's allegation of sexual assault cost Republicans the chance to tip the ideological balance of the U.S. Supreme Court, but it might also push women voters away from the GOP in the upcoming elections if not handled properly.

Weapons of Mass Deception. Yunkang Yang, Oxford University Press. © Yunkang Yang (2025).
DOI: 10.1093/9780197820339.003.0005

As expected, nearly all major right-wing media outlets rallied around Kavanaugh in the wake of Ford's allegations. They vouched for Kavanaugh's character and blamed Democrats for exploiting the controversy for partisan gain. Nevertheless, right-wing media's coverage of this event largely avoided attacking Christine Blasey Ford. Some articles from Fox News and the Daily Wire even struck a compassionate tone toward her.

The outrage-stoking industry of right-wing media is not known for pulling punches. For years, they pursued the politics of personal destruction, including going after private individuals. Why, then, did outlets such as Fox and the Daily Wire hold back on attacking Christine Ford when it had all seemed a good strategy to defend Kavanaugh by calling her a liar?

It turns out that most right-wing media articles took their cue from GOP elites, primarily Republican senators who did not want to humiliate an alleged victim of sexual assault in public during the "Me Too" era. With the midterm elections approaching, many Republican politicians were worried that openly questioning Ford's credibility would drive away women voters. Therefore, throughout the controversy, Republican senators focused on defending Kavanaugh and attacking Democrats. When commenting on Ford, they claimed that they believed Ford was a victim of sexual assault but did not concede that Kavanaugh was her attacker. This strategy allowed Republican politicians to protect Kavanaugh without offending women voters in the 2018 midterm elections.

To be sure, right-wing media were not directly controlled or managed by GOP politicians. Rather than dictating to right-wing media an official line, Republican elites became narrative guiding agents by virtue of simply being the most prominent source in the story. As Republicans stayed on message and refrained from attacking Ford, right-wing media, which relied on Republicans as sources, had fewer opportunities to attack Ford as well.

This chapter conducts a four-part analysis of the Kavanaugh–Ford controversy to show how politician-led political organizing works in the right-wing media sphere. It will first show that most right-wing media coverage refrained from personally attacking Ford. Then, it will show that the most cited sources in right-wing media reports were Republican politicians. Next, using a multilevel logistic regression model, this chapter will demonstrate that the right-wing media's use of sources is associated with their stance on Ford: The more GOP sources an article used, the less likely it was to attack Ford. Last, based on a qualitative analysis of the quotes of top GOP sources in right-wing media reports, it will show the way Republican elites' talking points influenced right-wing media's stance on Ford.

The data were based on a 10% random sample of 3,876 articles published by 31 top right-wing media outlets[1] between September 16, when Ford went public with her allegation, and October 6, 2017, when Kavanaugh was confirmed to the U.S. Supreme Court. The articles were collected from Media Cloud and manually coded.

To Attack or Not to Attack

Ford's allegation looked credible. She had mentioned the sexual assault, although without identifying the name of the perpetrator, to her husband, therapist, and friends long before Kavanaugh was nominated by Donald Trump. She also passed a lie detector test in July 2018 and named several potential witnesses. However, as is common with most sexual assault survivors, there were significant gaps in Ford's memory. For instance, she could not remember where the assault took place and how she made it home after the assault happened.

Throughout the controversy, two diverging approaches emerged on the political right. The first approach was to attack Ford's credibility. The logic here was that Kavanaugh was innocent because his accuser was a liar. The second approach was to acknowledge Ford as a true victim of sexual assault but to deny that Kavanaugh was her attacker. In this case, both Ford and Kavanaugh are victims. Ford is a victim of sexual misconduct who misidentified the perpetrator, and Kavanaugh is a victim of Democrats' ploy to derail his confirmation for the Supreme Court.

Many content producers, from fringe conspiracy sites, social media platforms, and right-wing nongovernmental organizations (NGOs), pursued the personal attack strategy. For instance, whatdoesitmean.com conjured up the theory that Ford was a CIA operative acting on behalf of the deep state to undermine Trump. Grabien, another conspiracy site, falsely claimed that Ford was an angry and troubled professor. On social media, some falsely claimed that Ford had a personal vendetta against Kavanaugh, whose mother allegedly foreclosed Ford's parent's house; others declared that Ford was paid by the abortion pill industry to block a pro-life judge; and still others promoted the falsehood that Ford hypnotized herself into having false memories. While fringe sites and social media users pushed out various disinformation narratives to discredit Ford, some right-wing NGOs penned op-eds to question her credibility too. For instance, Lisa Boothe from the conservative NGO Independent Women's Voice seized upon minute inconsistencies in Ford's account and argued that Ford could therefore not be trusted.

Concerned that attacking Ford might hurt the GOP in the midterm elections, prominent Republican senators and the Trump White House pursued the "no attack" strategy. White House counselor Kellyanne Conway explicitly told President Donald Trump that "you cannot—absolutely cannot—attack Christine Blasey Ford."[2] Likewise, Republican senators were careful in their response to Ford. Once Ford's allegation was out, nearly all Republican members of the Senate Judiciary Committee said that they wanted to hear Ford out. To avoid the optics of having the victim interrogated by a few old White male politicians, the Republican-controlled Judiciary Committee hired a female prosecutor to ask Ford questions during her testimony. After Ford's testimony, nearly all Republican Senators on the Judiciary Committee described her as credible, believable, or sincere. Even President Trump—who was known for his penchant for personal attacks—stayed on message at first, calling Ford's testimony compelling and credible. When he later mocked Ford during a rally on October 2, many Republican senators immediately criticized his behavior.

How did right-wing media react to Christine Ford? Ultimately, 85% of right-wing media articles (n=388) did not attack Ford's credibility or motives.[3] Figure 4.1 plots the percentage of "attack articles" and the total number of articles published by each right-wing media outlet.

In Figure 4.1, right-wing media outlets where more than 50% of articles had a critical tone were mostly fringe, conspiratorial, or far right online publications such as Infowars, Big League Politics, and

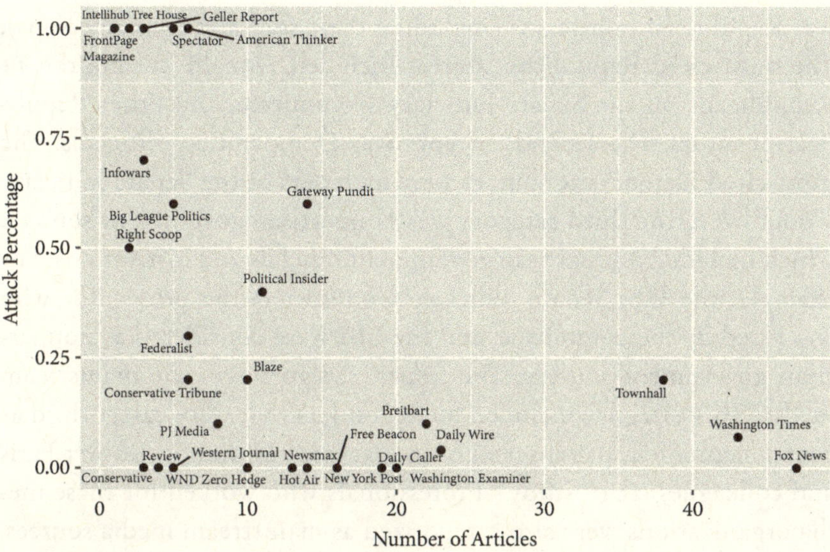

FIGURE 4.1 Right-wing media's stance on Ford.

Note: For visualization purposes, certain data points were removed from the graph due to overlaps.

Source: Media Cloud

the Gateway Pundit. Outlets where less than 50% of articles had a critical tone consisted of more established brands such as the *Washington Times*, Fox News, the Daily Caller, and the *Washington Examiner*, as well as some fringe sites such as Zero Hedge and WorldNetDaily (WND). As Figure 4.1 shows, for most right-wing media, less than 50% of their articles engaged in personal attacks. In addition, less than 25% of the articles from the three most prolific right-wing media—Townhall, the *Washington Times*, and Fox News—were "attack articles." This suggests that the lack of attack on Ford in right-wing media's coverage was a result of two factors: Most right-wing media did not focus on personal attacks, and the most prolific right-wing media did not focus on personal attacks.

Sourcing Information from the GOP

There were 10 major types of original source[4] in the right-wing media's coverage of the Kavanaugh–Ford controversy. The first source category was Republican politicians (including their staff and spokespersons). The most-cited Republican sources included Donald Trump, the 11 Republicans on the Senate Judiciary Committee, and other Republican senators. The second category was Democratic politicians. The most-cited Democratic sources were members of the Senate Judiciary Committee. The third category was nonpartisan government sources, which included nonpartisan government officials and institutions. For example, the U.S. Senate Judiciary Committee, the prosecutor who was hired by the committee, and the FBI were considered as nonpartisan government sources. The fourth category was the mainstream media. This category included media outlets that were categorized as center, center left, or center right in Harvard researchers Robert Faris and colleagues' 2017 study.[5] Professionals who worked for these media organizations were also categorized as mainstream media sources. The fifth and sixth categories were right-leaning media and left-leaning media, respectively, according to Faris and his colleagues' 2017 study. The seventh category was NGOs, including right-wing think tanks, political action committees (PACs), and grassroot organizations such as Turning Point USA. The eighth category was social media users, including Twitter users who were not associated with any organizations as discernible in their Twitter profiles. The ninth category was "involved parties," which included Ford and Kavanaugh's past or present romantic partners, friends, classmates, schoolmates, and colleagues. The tenth category was other, which included former politicians and elected officials, protesters, former law enforcement officials, political candidates for office, and voters.[6]

Table 4.1 displays the count of source types at the article level. This shows that Republican politicians were the most prominent source in right-wing media reports. They accounted for approximately 40% of all sources, with each article citing one Republican politician on average. Democratic politicians were the second most cited source, but they accounted for only 15% of all sources. Right-wing media ranked in a distant seventh place,

Aggregated at the media level, the count data show that 63% of right-wing media coverage used GOP politicians as its primary information source. Moreover, right-wing media coverage that focused on attacking Ford exhibited a different sourcing pattern than coverage that did not.

Table 4.1 Count of Original Sources at the Article Level (n = 388)

Source types	Range	Mean	SD	Count Total
GOP	(0,6)	0.93	1.25	356 (40%)
Democrats	(0,4)	0.35	0.66	135 (15%)
Government	(0,2)	0.08	0.3	32 (4%)
Mainstream media	(0,6)	0.23	0.59	88 (10%)
Right-wing media	(0,5)	0.12	0.42	45 (5%)
Left-wing media	(0,1)	0.02	0.15	6 (1%)
Involved parties	(0,7)	0.19	0.7	73 (8%)
NGOs	(0,1)	0.02	0.15	9 (1%)
Social media	(0,5)	0.09	0.47	34 (4%)
Other	(0,6)	0.27	0.68	104 (12%)

None of the "mostly attack" media outlets used GOP politicians as their primary source, but 90% of those that did not attack or only occasionally attacked Ford did use such sources. This suggests that there might exist a relationship between right-wing media's use of GOP sources and their articles' stances on Ford. The next section uses a statistical model to explore this relationship.

Modeling the Influence of GOP Sources

The relationship between the stance on Ford and the use of GOP sources was modeled at the article level for two reasons. First, given that media sites publish information in articles, the article is a natural unit of observation. Second, one should consider selecting the unit of analysis at a lower level if the number of observations at the higher level is too small to generate enough statistical power.[7] Modeling the relationship at the article level (n=388) generates more statistical power than modeling the relationship at the media site level (n=31).

A logistic regression model was used to estimate the effect of GOP sources in an article on the probability that the article attacks Ford. Also included in the model are the nine other source types, as well as a binary control variable—namely, whether the article was written in the format of straight news or an opinion article. The control variable was included because the article format was associated with both stance on Ford and the number of GOP sources.[8]

Since the data have two levels, with articles at the individual level and media sites at the group level, a multilevel model is most appropriate. I fitted the data with a multilevel logistic regression model where I set random intercepts for each media site to account for group-level variation in estimating individual-level coefficients. In other words, I constructed a logistic regression model with 388 data points predicting the probability of an article attacking Christine Ford given individual-level predictors in the article and with an intercept that can vary by media site. The following equation demonstrates the formula:

$$\Pr\left(y_i = 1\right) = \text{logit}^{-1}\left(a_{j[i]} + b_1X_{1i} + b_2X_{2i} + \ldots + b_{11}X_{11i}\right), \quad \text{for } i = 1, \ldots, n$$

$$a_j \sim N\left(m_a, s^2_{\text{media}}\right), \quad \text{for } j = 1, \ldots, 30$$

where $\Pr(y_i{=}1)$ is the probability of the presence of personal attacks; n is the number of articles, and j is the number of media sites; $X_1, X_2, X_3, X_4, X_5, X_6, X_7, X_8, X_9$, and X_{10} are the count of GOP politicians, Democratic politicians, nonpartisan government sources, mainstream media, right-leaning media, left-leaning media, social media users, NGOs, involved parties, and other sources; X_{11} is the control variable article format; and a_j is the varying intercept for media sites, which follows a normal distribution with mean m_a and standard error s.

The results show that the more times an article cites Republican politicians the less likely it is to engage in personal attacks against Ford. They also show that the use of right-leaning media as original sources had an opposite—although less certain—effect. Figure 4.2 shows two plots of predicted probabilities with 95% confidence intervals to quantify the effects of GOP sources on the probability that right-wing media attack Ford. The effect of rightwing media sources is also included to provide a point of reference. The left graph shows the sources' marginal effects in opinion pieces, and the right graph shows the effects in articles written in the straight news format. The y-axis indicates the probability of personal attacks, while the x-axis shows

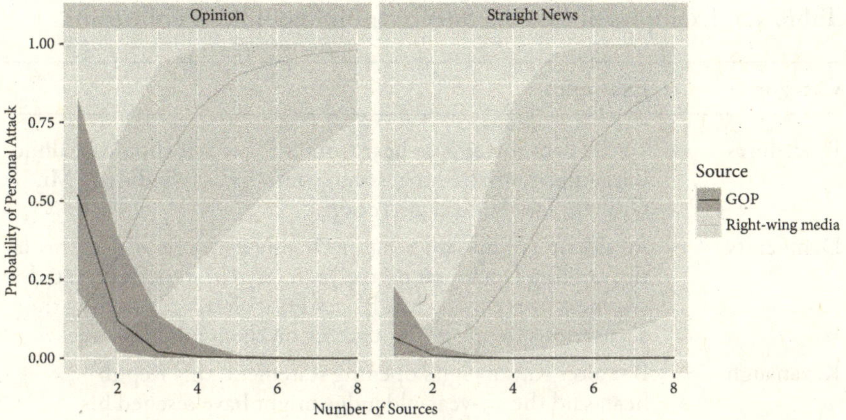

FIGURE 4.2 Plots showing predicted probabilities for articles with varying numbers of sources holding all other variables at the sample means. The graph includes 95% confidence intervals for the marginal effects using the methods and tools described in Adolph (2016).

the number of sources cited. For details on the regression coefficients, see Table A.4.1 in the appendix.

As shown in the left graph in Figure 4.2, if an opinion piece uses no GOP sources, the probability of it attacking Christine Ford is roughly 50%. However, adding one GOP source significantly reduces the probability to 12.5%, and adding one more reduces it to almost zero. If an article is written in a straight news format, the probability of it attacking Ford remains very low. Adding one GOP source reduces the probability to almost zero. The effect of citing right-wing media on the probability of personal attacks is positive but less certain, as it is characterized by wider confidence intervals.

How Republicans Shaped Right-Wing Media Coverage

Quotes from Republican politicians in right-wing media reports focused on four main areas: providing updates on procedures, attacking Democrats, defending Kavanaugh, and evaluating Ford. First, Republicans were quoted on procedures, including how the Senate Judiciary Committee would investigate Ford's claims, how it would arrange hearings for Kavanaugh and Ford, how the confirmation process would

Table 4.2 Examples of Quoted Speech from Republican Politicians

Categories	Examples
Procedures	"If the committee is to hear from Ms. Ford, it should be done immediately so the process can continue as scheduled," Mr. Graham said Sunday afternoon.
Democrats	President Trump said Senator Dianne Feinstein of California, the ranking Democrat on the Judiciary Committee, created the mess by receiving Ms. Blasey Ford's letter containing the accusations in July but not acting on them until last week.
Kavanaugh	But after Kavanaugh's opening statement, this Republican said the 53-year-old judge might have rescued his confirmation, proclaiming, "He's knocking it out of the park."
Ford	Mr. Trump said he watched her testimony to the Senate Judiciary Committee and felt she was "a very fine woman, a very credible witness."
Others	"You're talking about history," Graham said. "We're not looking back. We're looking forward."

proceed, and how Republicans senators would vote. Second, they criticized Democrats. Third, they defended Kavanaugh, which included praising his qualifications, vouching for his integrity, or sympathizing with the trouble he experienced during the controversy. Finally, they evaluated Ford's allegation and her testimony. Table 4.2 shows an example for each category.

Fifty articles that mentioned at least three unique GOP sources were randomly sampled. They contained 243 sentences quoting GOP sources. The sentences were manually coded in terms of the categories identified above. Fifty-eight percent of quoted speech from Republicans focused on procedures, 13% on Democrats, 10% on Ford, 10% on Kavanaugh, and 9% on other topics. Figure 4.3 shows the subjects on which the top 18 most frequently quoted Republican sources (including an anonymous source) spoke.

Figure 4.3 shows that the most cited Republican sources are U.S. President Donald Trump, Republican members of the Senate Judiciary Committee (e.g., Chuck Grassley, Lindsey Graham, and Bob Corker), and Republican senators who were considered swing votes (e.g., Jeff Flake, Susan Collins, and Lisa Murkowski). Quotes from Republican

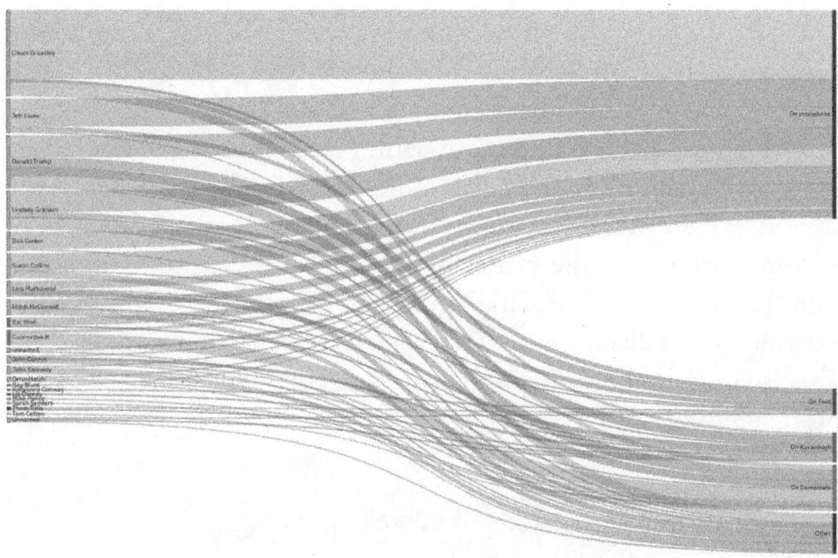

Figure 4.3 Top Republican sources and their quoted speech at the sentence level (n=243).

members of the committee and swing vote Republicans overwhelmingly focused on procedures, while those from Donald Trump were split among procedures, Ford, Democrats, and Kavanaugh. As right-wing media quoted Republicans, they paid less attention to Ford than to updates on procedures and talking points about Democrats.

Politician-Led Political Organizing

Chapter 4 reveals the mechanism that brought organizational coherence to the right-wing media sphere: politician-led political organizing. It shows that when a crisis threatens the collective interests of the political right, the right-wing media sphere can cohere around GOP politicians' message. Yet, this process, as shown in the Kavanaugh–Ford controversy, took a more subtle form than GOP elites dictating a line to right-wing media. It primarily involved more established media outlets that relied on Republican elites as sources and produced an overwhelming majority of media coverage that dominated the right-wing media sphere.

Figure 4.4 shows the hyperlink network of the Kavanaugh–Ford controversy between September 16 and October 6. Node label size is proportional to the number of unique media in-links.

As Figure 4.4 shows, attention within the right-wing media sphere was distributed to Fox and other more established outlets such as the *New York Post*, Real Clear Politics, and the *Washington Examiner*. To be sure, Fox was at the center of the network, getting more attention than any other right-wing media. But the network overall was not extremely centralized—with the Freeman centralization score at 0.77.[9] This is largely because Republicans—not Fox News—were the most prominent source in the story.

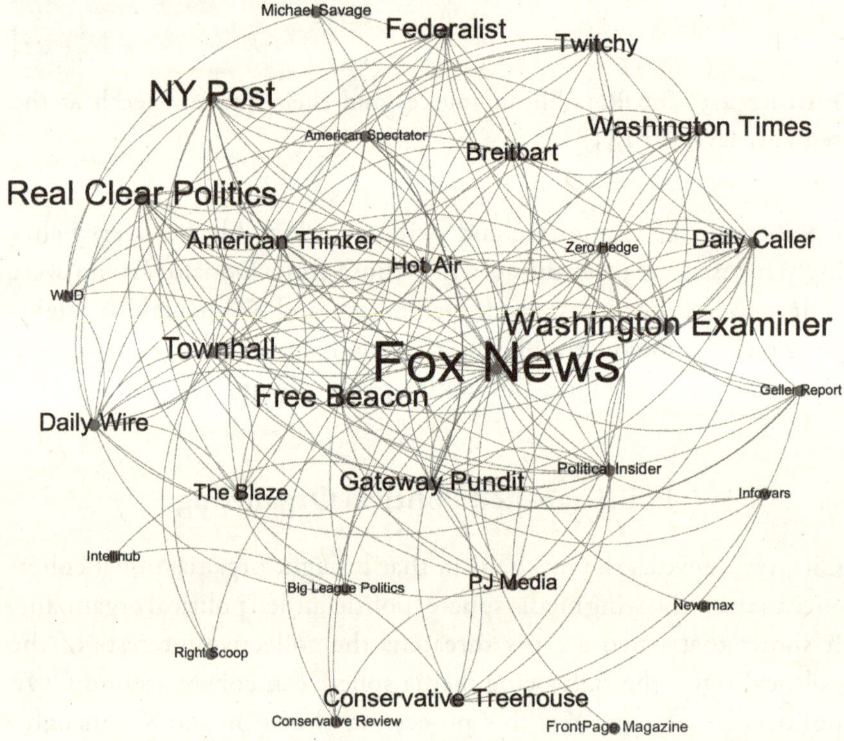

FIGURE 4.4 Hyperlink network of the Kavanaugh–Ford controversy (9/16–10/6).

In the contemporary United States, the GOP does not directly control right-wing media through ownership. Yet, GOP politicians can exercise their influence by virtue of being the most prominent information source. Although this may not necessarily lead to homogenous news framing within the right-wing media sphere, GOP politicians can still influence important angles of the story.

The context of the Kavanaugh–Ford controversy was particularly conducive to this subtle form of GOP influence. GOP senators held a unique position to offer a steady supply of authoritative information on the controversy. In addition, the public nature of the controversy meant that even right-wing media with limited resources could easily access Republicans' talking points through social media, the mainstream media, and other public channels. As a result, these media outlets extensively used Republican politicians as sources, leading to reports that remained aligned with the party' strategic message.

We can expect politician-led political organizing to occur during public events where GOP politicians share a unified political goal and are in a position to generate the most relevant information in response to the event. The Kavanaugh–Ford controversy shows that many right-wing media—by virtue of citing Republicans—in effect executed a calculated political strategy. However, it is worth noting that politician-led political organizing can also take a dark turn. Right-wing media have also too often repeated Republicans' lies, serving as instruments of disinformation campaigns.

The next chapter introduces the third organizing mechanism, demonstrating that a leading right-wing media outlet such as Fox that commands attention, can rally the right-wing media sphere around a strategic narrative designed to advance a tangible political objective.

5

The Fox "News" Effect

ON MAY 17, PRESIDENT DONALD TRUMP suddenly found himself in serious trouble when Attorney General Jeff Sessions informed him that a special counsel was being appointed by Deputy Attorney General Rod Rosenstein to investigate the link between Russia and the 2016 Trump campaign. This meant that Trump could no longer, as he did before, influence the ongoing Russia probe.

"Oh my God. This is terrible. This is the end of my presidency. I am fucked," Trump said in disbelief. As he slumped back in his chair, Trump pointed his finger at his attorney general, who had recused himself from the investigation. "How could you let this happen?" Trump asked. "You were supposed to protect me."[1]

While the attorney general had stepped aside, Fox News stepped in. By May 17, when Trump heard the devastating news, Fox had already come to his rescue with a made-up story designed to distract the public from the ongoing political crisis.

On May 15, the Fox affiliate Fox 5 DC claimed that it had found evidence that it was a Democratic National Committee (DNC) staffer named Seth Rich—not Russian hackers—who had delivered the DNC emails to WikiLeaks. The logic behind the story was simple: If Russia did not hack the DNC, then there was no collusion between the Trump campaign and Russia.

Weapons of Mass Deception. Yunkang Yang, Oxford University Press. © Yunkang Yang (2025).
DOI: 10.1093/9780197820339.003.0006

The Fox 5 DC story, likely based on fabricated sources, was repeated by foxnews.com and various on-air personalities at Fox the following day. By May 17, Fox's false narrative had been covered by almost every major right-wing media outlet, including Breitbart, the *New York Post*, the *Washington Times*, The Blaze, the *Washington Examiner*, and Newsmax. The right-wing media sphere was quickly mobilized to spread the disinformation narrative designed to protect Donald Trump in anticipation of the greatest crisis in his early presidency.

How did various right-wing media controlled by different owners and managers rally behind this common disinformation narrative? This chapter reveals "media-led political organizing," in which a top right-wing media outlet that commands attention takes the lead in concocting and spreading a narrative that is shared, repeated, and amplified by other right-wing media outlets.

Fox was not the first media organization to spread the Seth Rich conspiracy theory, which had originated on social media nearly 10 months earlier. As this chapter will show, WikiLeaks, Heat Street, and Infowars had all spread various versions of this conspiracy theory before. However, none of them was able to elevate it to such a scale as Fox did in May 2017. What made the difference?

Tracking the development of the Seth Rich conspiracy theory from July 2016 to May 2017, this chapter shows two key conditions that enabled large-scale "media-led political organizing" within the right-wing media sphere. First, it was initiated by Fox News, the leading media outlet that commanded attention. This means that other right-wing media outlets could quickly notice the spread of (dis)information when it came from the center of the right-wing media sphere. Second, disinformation regarding Seth Rich became a politically useful narrative for dealing with an emerging political crisis that threatened a partisan agenda widely shared among different right-wing media outlets—namely, protecting Donald Trump.

The Seth Rich Conspiracy Theory

In late June 2016, the Russian Chief Intelligence Office (the GRU) transferred the stolen DNC emails to WikiLeaks.[2] To achieve maximal political impact, WikiLeaks dumped more than 20,000 DNC emails on July 22, only three days before the 2016 Democratic National Convention. This series of events prompted the DNC and the FBI to initiate an investigation in June 2016, which found that Russian intelligence was behind the cyberattack on the DNC.

On July 10, 2016, the DNC staffer Seth Rich was killed in a botched robbery in Washington, D.C. His death immediately spawned various conspiracy theories online in mid-July 2016, most of which linked Rich's death to Hillary Clinton. For instance, one conspiracy theory claimed that Rich was killed because he was about to inform the FBI of voter fraud committed by Hillary Clinton. Another claimed that Rich was a Bernie Sanders supporter and that he was killed because he opposed the Clinton campaign's use of a voter database that targeted Sanders's supporters.

Seeing Rich's death as an opportunity to undermine Hillary Clinton's campaign, various domestic and foreign political operatives, including Russian intelligence agents, promoted these conspiracy theories in the following month. For instance, the Russian Foreign Intelligence Service (the SVR) reportedly circulated a fake intelligence report on July 13 to support the narrative that Hillary Clinton had ordered Rich's assassination.[3]

On August 9, 2016, approximately one month after Rich's death and two weeks after WikiLeaks' release of the stolen DNC emails, WikiLeaks publicly suggested that Rich could be its source. It also announced a $20,000 reward for information about Rich's death. WikiLeaks's announcement fueled a new version of the conspiracy theory: that Rich was assassinated at the order of the DNC or the Clinton campaign for leaking DNC emails to WikiLeaks. This false narrative not only undermined the Clinton campaign but also provided political cover for WikiLeaks and Russia. Hence, the story was later aggressively promoted in 2016 by Russia's troll farm, the Internet Research Agency; Russia-backed media outlets; political operatives such as Roger Stone; and right-wing media such as Infowars.[4]

However, despite sustained efforts by foreign and domestic political operatives to promote the Rich conspiracy theory, societal attention to Rich's story tailed off over the following 10 months after his

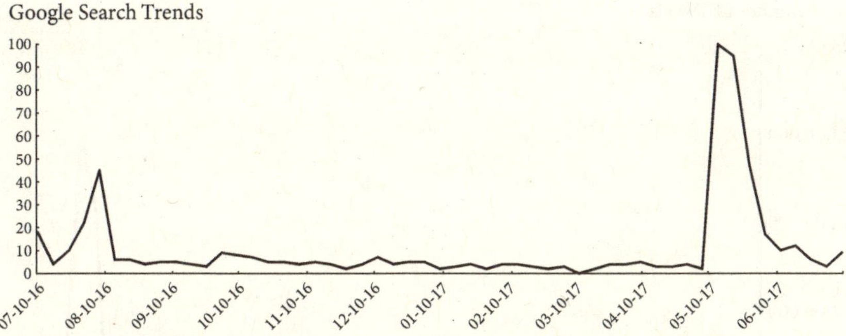

FIGURE 5.1 Google search trends in the United States about Seth Rich.

Note: Google Trends indicates search interest in Seth Rich on a 100-point scale. The numbers are normalized to represent search interest relative to 100—the maximum search interest for a certain topic during a given time period. The search string was "Seth AND Rich."

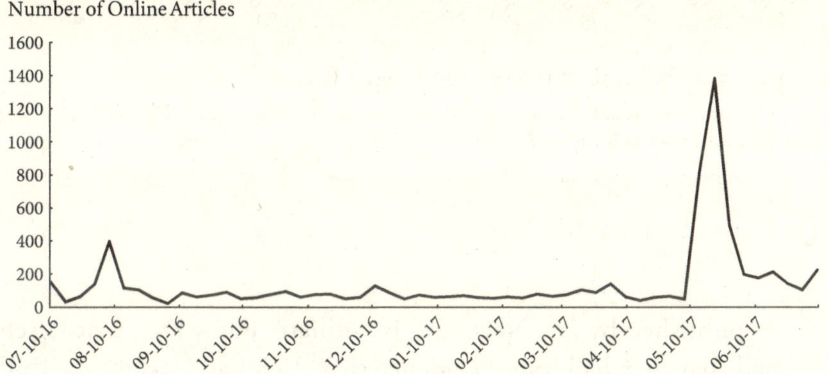

FIGURE 5.2 Number of online articles about Seth Rich.

Note: I tracked the number of online articles published by approximately 70,000 media sources that were included in Media Cloud's 2016 U.S. election collection used by Benkler et al., (2018) to study election coverage in 2016.

Source: Media Cloud

death. As Figure 5.1, Figure 5.2, and Figure 5.3 show, Google search trends, the volume of online articles, and user activities on Twitter between July 2016 and July 2017 all point to a common pattern: The attention to Seth Rich gradually declined after an initial spike at the time of WikiLeaks's announcement until mid-May 2017, when it suddenly peaked.

Public attention to Rich resurged in mid-May 2017, almost 10 months after his death. This was due to a series of disinformation

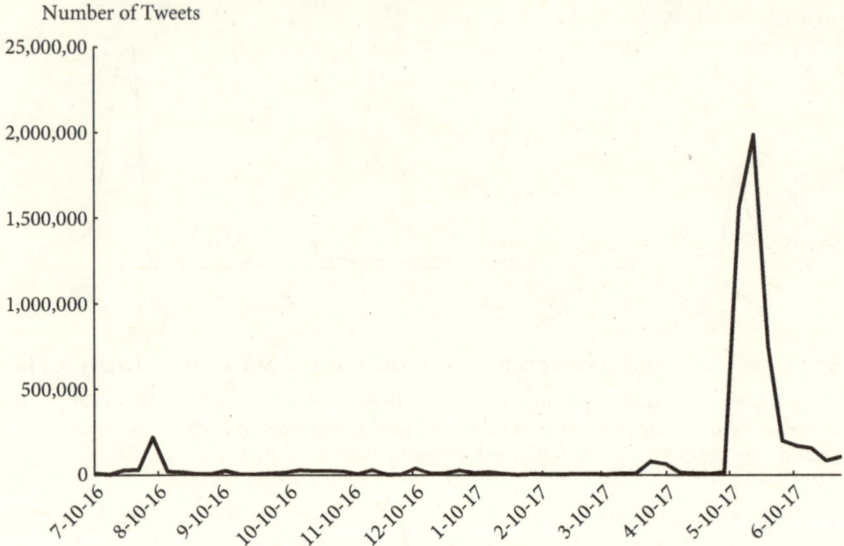

FIGURE 5.3 Volume of tweets about Seth Rich.

Note: The data came from Crimson Hexagon with the search string "Seth" AND "Rich." Crimson Hexagon, now known as Brandwatch, was a digital analytics tool that collected Twitter data.

Source: Crimson Hexagon (Brandwatch)

stories published by Fox News and its affiliate, Fox 5 DC, that falsely claimed that they had found evidence that Rich had leaked the DNC emails to WikiLeaks. Fox News's false stories quickly spread to most right-wing media outlets in a matter of days, despite being immediately debunked by both government authorities and the mainstream media. Fox News eventually retracted these stories on May 23, 2017, but its short-lived nine-day disinformation campaign mobilized societal attention on a massive scale that was unparalleled in the previous 10-month period.

The two peaks of public attention to Rich—one around August 9, 2016, when WikiLeaks announced the $20,000 reward, and the other around Fox's disinformation campaign in mid-May 2017—divides the life span of the Seth Rich conspiracy theory into three phases: the pre-WikiLeaks period (July 10–August 8, 2016), the WikiLeaks disinformation campaign (beginning August 9, 2016), and Fox News's disinformation campaign (May 15, 2017–May 23, 2017). The following analysis tracks 46 right-wing media outlets' changing reactions to the Seth Rich conspiracy theory over these three distinct periods.

The Pre-WikiLeaks Period

Conspiracy theories about Rich's death emerged on Twitter as early as July 11, one day after Rich's death. They focused on the cause of death, suggesting that he was assassinated on the orders of Hillary Clinton. The following two examples came from a comprehensive search of Twitter's historical data through the social media analytic tool Crimson Hexagon, which yielded 57,386 tweets containing the name "Seth Rich" between July 20 and August 8, 2016.[5]

1. "All #HRC's negative ratings'll worsen after ASSASSINAION of #DNC's DIC., VOTER EXPANSION DATA."
2. "Millions of Americans want to see what #SethRich was working on before he was ASSASSINATED. @HillaryClinton@RepDWStweets@TheDemocrats"

On July 12, @HillaryClinton became the second most mentioned Twitter handle in Rich-related tweets. In addition, tweets that linked Rich's death to Hillary Clinton made it onto the top-five retweet lists on the same day. Thus, less than two days after Rich's death, Hillary Clinton was at the center of the Seth Rich conspiracy theory on Twitter.

This conspiracy theory on social media then quickly spread to the right-wing media sphere. An analysis of URLs embedded in the 57,386 tweets and a comprehensive search in Media Cloud's database of online news articles[6] showed that Heat Street, a short-lived media site owned by the Murdoch family, was the first right-wing media outlet to spread the conspiracy theory. At 8 a.m. on July 12, Heat Street published an article titled "Beloved DNC Staffer Seth Rich Shot Dead in the Back in DC, Just Hours After Calling for Dallas Unity; Conspiracy Theories Abound." This article, which cited several July 12 tweets, later fed back into Twitter, pushing @heatstreet to the top-mentions list on July 12.

How far did the conspiracy theory spread within the right-wing media sphere in the first month following Rich's death? And how did various right-wing media outlets cover the Rich story? It turned out that 27% of right-wing media in my sample promoted the disinformation, 17% covered the story focusing on established facts, and 56% ignored the story. Figure 5.4 shows the cumulative percentage of the right-wing media sphere that promoted the conspiracy theories each day.

Figure 5.5 shows the sources of the first Rich articles published by right-wing media sites. The edges show the instance of sourcing, and node label sizes are based on the number of times a source was cited. Black nodes represent right-wing media: Those that did not publish any articles about Seth Rich are on the left; those whose first article about Seth Rich included conspiracy theories are in the middle; and those whose first article about Seth Rich did not include conspiracy theories are in the top-right corner. Gray nodes represent non-right-wing-media sources cited in the stories.

Thanks to Heat Street, by August 8, 2016, the Seth Rich conspiracy theory had spread to 12 other right-wing media sites, including the Gateway Pundit, Conservative Tribune, WorldNetDaily (WND), Infowars, and most noticeable of all, Fox News, which published an article titled "Mysterious Deaths of DNC's Seth Rich and Other

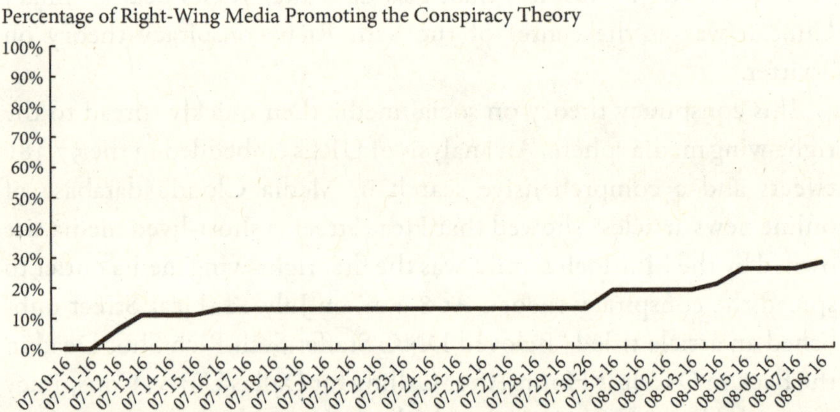

FIGURE 5.4 Propagation of Seth Rich conspiracy theories in the right-wing media sphere.

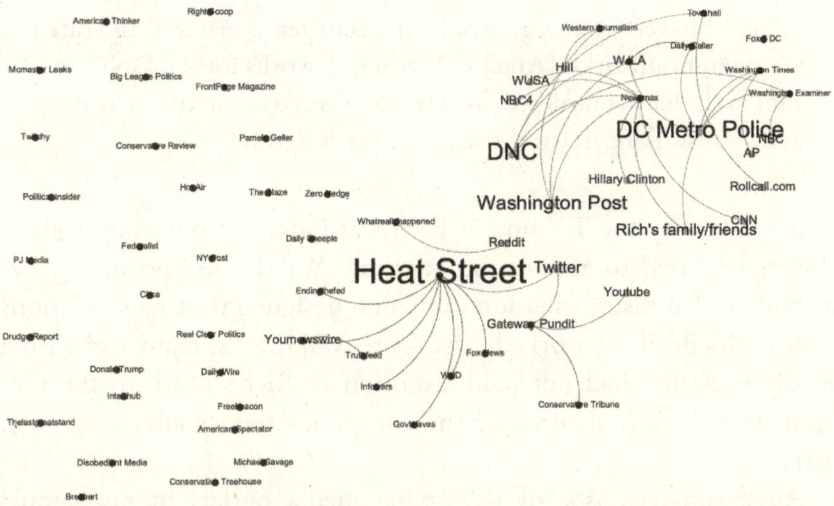

FIGURE 5.5 Sourcing patterns of right-wing media's first articles about Seth Rich. (7/10–8/8, 2016).
Source: Media Cloud

East Coast Politicos Fuel Conspiracy Theories." In this article, Fox cited Heat Street yet stopped short of vouching for the veracity of the conspiracy theory.

Despite the role that Heat Street and, later, Fox played in amplifying the Seth Rich conspiracy theory from social media, most right-wing media outlets ignored it. However, the overall apathy toward the conspiracy theory during the first month ended when WikiLeaks openly suggested that Rich might be its source for the DNC emails.

WikiLeaks's Disinformation Campaign

On August 9, 2016, WikiLeaks announced a $20,000 reward for information about Rich's death on Twitter. However, it also put out a statement in the *Washington Times* that "this should not be taken to imply that Seth Rich was a source to WikiLeaks or to imply that his murder is connected to our publications."[7] On the same day, its founder Julian Assange said the following in an interview with the Dutch TV Nieuwsuur:

> Whistleblowers go to significant efforts to get us material and often very significant risks. [And] a 27-year old, works for the DNC, was shot in the back, murdered just a few weeks ago for unknown reasons as he was walking down the street in Washington.[8]

When asked by the TV host if Rich was indeed WikiLeaks's source, Assange refused to answer the question. WikiLeaks's posturing was a thinly veiled disinformation campaign designed to stir speculations over Rich's death. It worked. Thanks to WikiLeaks, many right-wing media sites that had not paid attention to Rich's death in the previous month started to cover the conspiracy theory after August 9, 2016.

Approximately 65% of right-wing media outlets in my sample responded to WikiLeaks's announcement in the following month. There were two types of responses. The first type (42%), including the responses from Infowars, townhall.com, WND, the Gateway Pundit, Zero Hedge, and Michael Savage, saw WikiLeaks's statement as vindication of the conspiracy theory. They repeated WikiLeaks's message and cited other materials to support it. For instance, Infowars added the Clinton Body Count conspiracy theory to the mix, claiming that Hillary and Bill Clinton ordered the killings of their former aides, and therightscoop.com commented that WikiLeaks's announcement made it believe that the Seth Rich conspiracy theory was true.

The second type of response (23%) provided established facts to counter the conspiracy theory. Fox News, for instance, reacted by reporting on WikiLeaks's announcement of the reward, drawing attention to the counterevidence from the police, and asking the police to comment on WikiLeaks's statement. Hot Air cautioned that WikiLeaks had a history of acting as a propaganda outlet for Russia. The following paragraph is an excerpt from a Hot Air article:

> Assange appears to be capitalizing on a family's personal tragedy to distract from the unpleasant truth that his DNC material was not a leak from an idealistic whistleblower. In fact, the material was likely stolen by Russian hackers engaged in international espionage. That's not the sort of thing WikiLeaks wants to admit it is involved with.[9]

WikiLeaks's August 9 disinformation brought Rich's death to the attention of a larger number of right-wing media sites. However, still 35% of the right-wing media sphere simply ignored the story.

The next 9-month period hardly saw any notable increase in the public attention to Rich's death. There were various episodes in which different political operatives, such as the GOP lobbyist Jack Burkman and the Russian hacker(s) Guccifer 2.0, tried to exploit Rich's death to further their own political goals. However, societal attention to Rich did not return until May 2017, when Fox concocted its own version of the Rich conspiracy theory to save Trump from trouble.

Fox News's Disinformation Campaign

On May 9, 2017, Trump fired FBI director James Comey, who was investigating the links between Trump's 2016 campaign and Russia. In an attempt to prompt a special counsel investigation, Comey then leaked a memo that showed Trump asking the FBI director to drop potential charges against his former national security advisor, Michael Flynn. This series of political developments raised the question of whether Trump's firing of the FBI director constituted an obstruction of justice and prompted the FBI to open a counterintelligence inquiry into whether Trump was secretly working on behalf of Russia. Meanwhile, more than 100 lawmakers on Capitol Hill called for an independent special counsel to oversee the Russia probe, drastically raising the political stakes in the investigation that could derail Trump's presidency.

Republicans' initial reactions to Trump's firing of Comey were largely ambiguous and divided. For instance, 10 GOP senators supported Trump's action, 16 opposed it, and 21 did not express any opinions. However, when the Justice Department decided to appoint a special counsel, key Republicans, including House Speaker Paul Ryan, Senate Majority Leader Mitch McConnell, and Senate Intelligence Committee Chairman Richard Burr, voiced their support for the investigation.

As the GOP began to rally behind the appointment of the special counsel, Donald Trump was all but guaranteed to face an independent investigation. It was at that time that the Seth Rich conspiracy theory became a useful narrative to protect Trump. The Russia probe was largely based on the intelligence that Russia had interfered in the 2016 presidential election to help elect Trump. One important piece of evidence for this is that Russia hacked the DNC and delivered the emails to WikiLeaks. However, if the DNC emails were delivered to WikiLeaks by Seth Rich rather than by Russian hackers, then this evidence of Russian interference would be disproved. If enough people believed the Seth Rich conspiracy theory, then the special counsel might be pressured to shift his focus away from Russia and Trump.

According to documentary evidence such as phone calls, emails, and text messages, Fox News's story about Seth Rich's death in May 2017 was politically motivated and carefully timed to protect Trump. In March 2017, Ed Butowsky, a friend of Trump and then-Fox News contributor, hired a private investigator named Rod Wheeler to investigate Rich's death. In April, Wheeler and Butowsky met then-White House spokesperson Sean Spicer to keep the Trump administration abreast of their ongoing investigation. One day after Trump fired James Comey, Butowsky and Fox News employee Malia Zimmerman allegedly notified Rod Wheeler that they had identified an FBI source who confirmed the email exchange between Rich and WikiLeaks.[10] On May 14, Butowsky told Wheeler that Trump had just read their article and wanted it published immediately. In an email Butowsky sent to Fox News producers and hosts on May 15, he stated that "one of the big conclusions we need to draw from this is that the Russians did not hack our computer systems and ste[a]l emails and there was no collusion [between] Trump and the Russians."[11]

Disinformation about Rich was first released in five articles by Fox News across two platforms: Fox 5 DC, a Fox-owned and -operated TV station; and foxnews.com. On May 15, Fox 5 DC published the first article, titled "Family's Private Investigator: There Is Evidence Seth Rich Had Contact with WikiLeaks Prior to Death." This article claimed that evidence linked Rich to WikiLeaks. It also implied that the DNC, the D.C. police department, and the D.C. mayor were all involved in a coverup. Early on the morning of May 16, foxnews.com published a second article that echoed many of the claims in the first article. A few hours later, a third article from foxnews.com was published and promoted the claim from an anonymous source that 44,053 emails were transferred from Rich to WikiLeaks's MacFadyen.[12] This article was later quoted in a fourth article from Fox 5 DC in the early afternoon.[13] By the time Fox published its fifth article, titled "Family of Slain DNC Staffer Seth Rich Blasts Detective Over Report of WikiLeaks Link," in the late afternoon, the FBI, the D.C. mayor, the police department, and Rich's family had all denied the allegations in Fox News's previous reports. However, this fifth article continued to push the same message that Seth Rich was linked to WikiLeaks. It omitted the first sentence of the police department's statement[14] to create the appearance that the police department still considered Rich's link to WikiLeaks an unsettled issue.

It is worth noting that it was Fox News's supposedly "news" division that first published the Seth Rich disinformation stories. In the following days, these stories were repeated by many on-air guests and hosts during both Fox News's "straight news" programs and its opinion programs. By May 23, it became clear that Fox News's "anonymous" sources for its Rich stories did not exist. On that day, Fox News put out a retraction statement claiming that the stories did not meet its high editorial standards. However, Fox News host Sean Hannity continued to pursue the story even after the retraction.

Fox News's disinformation quickly spread to the rest of the right-wing media sphere. Among the 41 right-wing media sites that first reacted to the Fox News story, 40 repeated, amplified, linked to, or reposted at least one of Fox's disinformation stories without offering any established facts from the police department, the D.C. mayor, or the DNC.[15] These included established media outlets, such as the *Washington Times* and Real Clear Politics, that had not fallen prey to WikiLeaks' disinformation campaign in August 2016. Yet, following Fox News's disinformation stories that were masked as news, many right-wing media organizations turned into a lie machine.

Comparing Fox's disinformation campaign to the two earlier phases of the evolving Seth Rich conspiracy theory in 2016 reveals its superior effectiveness. The first phase, a social-media-driven process (July 10–August 8, 2016), gradually spread the conspiracy across approximately 30% of the right-wing media sphere. The second phase, a WikiLeaks-led process (beginning August 9, 2016), elicited divided

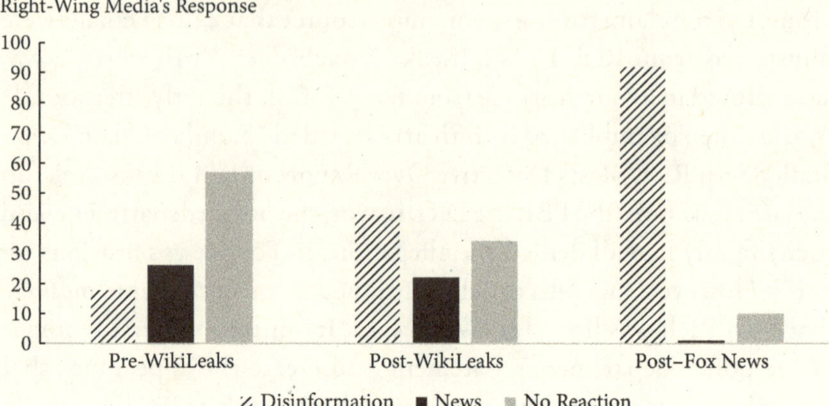

FIGURE 5.6 Right-wing media's reactions to the Seth Rich conspiracy theory during three time periods.

responses from various right-wing media outlets. In contrast, Fox's disinformation campaign demonstrated a far greater ability to mobilize right-wing media into a unified political machine. Figure 5.6 visually contrasts right-wing media's responses to the Seth Rich conspiracy theory across these three periods. The y-axis shows the percentage of media outlets in the right-wing media sphere. On the x-axis, right-wing media that repeated or amplified the Seth Rich conspiracy theory were labeled as disinformation, those that focused on established facts were labeled as news, and those that did not react were labeled as no reaction.

It is unlikely that the owners and managers of various right-wing media outlets convened in a backroom and collectively decided to promote the Rich conspiracy theory. If there was no coordination, what then connected these different right-wing media sites into a coherent political machine that amplified Fox News's disinformation?

Media-Led Political Organizing

The answer could simply be that the conspiracy theory diffused from the center of the network—namely, Fox News (including Fox 5 DC)—to the rest of the right-wing media sphere. Right-wing media outlets pay attention to each other's work regularly. Talk radio hosts, for example, regularly read articles from right-wing digital sites during breaks or as they prepare their shows; Fox News hosts also listened to talk radio during their commutes.[16] When Fox published the Seth Rich conspiracy theory, other right-wing media took notice and likely saw the political value of promoting it. Figure 5.7 shows the hyperlink network of right-wing media that spread the Seth Rich conspiracy theory between May 15 and 23. Node label size is based on the number of unique links a media outlet received from other right-wing media between May 15 and May 23.

As Figure 5.7 shows, the hyperlink network of the Rich conspiracy theory was highly centralized—with the Freeman centralization score at 0.87.[17] This means that the network is highly organized around its most central nodes: Fox News and Fox 5 DC. With almost all the

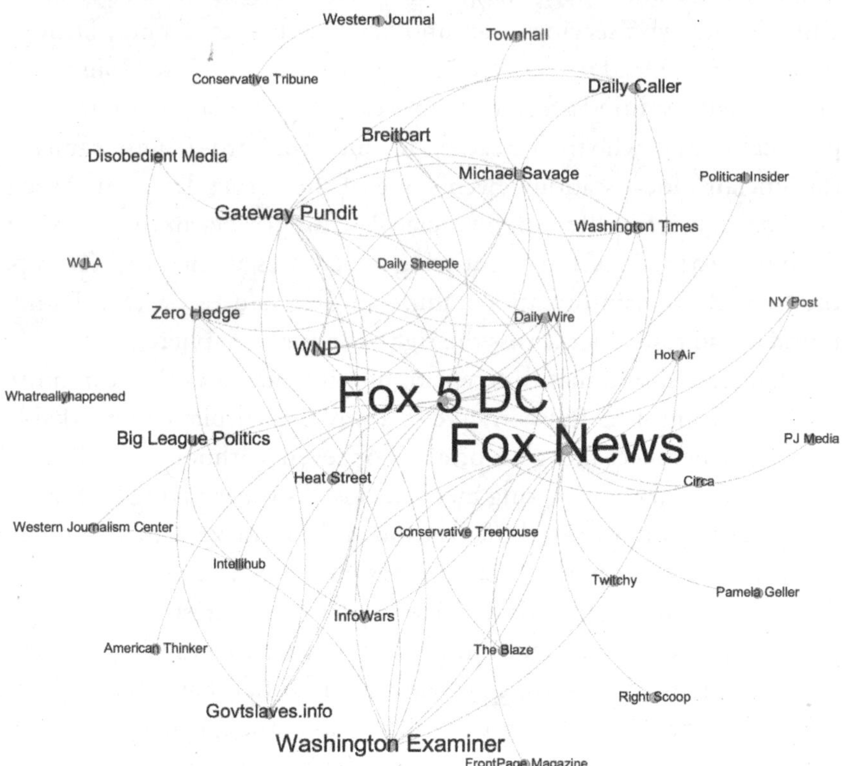

FIGURE 5.7 Hyperlink network of right-wing media that spread the Seth Rich conspiracy theory (5/15-5/23).

Source: Media Cloud

hyperlinks pointing toward Fox and Fox 5 DC, these two media outlets commanded attention from most right-wing media outlets.

Moreover, the right-wing media outlets that paid attention to Fox likely saw the value in repeating the Seth Rich conspiracy theory. Although it is difficult to ascertain what motivated each right-wing media outlet to spread the Seth Rich disinformation story, it stands to reason that most shared the political agenda with Fox News—namely, protecting Trump from the Russia probe. By May 2017, President Trump had already consolidated his support from various right-wing media outlets.[18] After Trump won the 2016 election, many right-wing media outlets not only began promoting the president regularly but also deepened their ties with the Trump administration. At the time of Fox News's disinformation campaign, Breitbart's former CEO, Steve Bannon, was working for Trump in the White House; Newsmax's CEO, Chris Ruddy, was serving as an unofficial advisor to Trump; Drudge Report's Matt Drudge was a frequent visitor to the White House; and Sinclair had just hired a former Trump campaign spokesman as its chief political analyst, who then created the "must-run" pro-Trump segments for Sinclair's local stations. Even some of the "never-Trumpers," such as Washington Free Beacon financier Paul Singer, began to align with Trump in 2017.[19] As most right-wing media sites aligned with Trump, the Seth Rich disinformation campaign designed to protect Trump found broad resonance across the right-wing media sphere.

Chapter 5 shows that different right-wing media outlets can unite behind a disinformation narrative in a way that displays a remarkable level of coherence and goal orientation even without central command or formal coordinating mechanisms. As the evolving Seth Rich conspiracy theory shows, the activation of the right-wing media sphere as a cohesive political machine depends on a critical condition: an external threat endangers a widely shared partisan interest—in this case, protecting a sitting Republican president from investigation. In the event of a crisis, if a leading right-wing media outlet that commands attention takes the lead to concoct and spread a strategic narrative, then the right-wing media sphere will likely rally behind that narrative.

Fox's Seth Rich disinformation campaign was only one case of media-led political organizing. Its salience, longevity, and scale may differ from other cases due to its unique political context and the influence of the media driving the narrative. WikiLeaks's Seth Rich disinformation story was essentially a media-led disinformation campaign too. However, where WikiLeaks failed to activate a majority of right-wing media into a coherent lie machine, Fox News succeeded. When WikiLeaks promoted the disinformation story to give itself political cover for colluding with Russia, many right-wing media outlets reacted critically. However, when Fox News pushed out its Seth Rich disinformation stories in May 2017, none of the right-wing media outlets that had previously cast doubt on WikiLeaks's motives questioned Fox News's motives or alerted their readers to Fox News's history of deliberately misleading the public.

We should remember that Fox News's disinformation campaign occurred when GOP elites largely acquiesced to the decision to appoint a special counsel for the Russia probe. It also likely benefited from a combination of favorable conditions such as the established familiarity of the Seth Rich conspiracy theory within the right-wing media sphere and the urgency of dealing with an external threat that endangered a common partisan interest. However, Fox News's campaign also fell apart quickly because it was immediately debunked by government authorities, Rich's family, and the mainstream media and because its own private investigator who was cited in the story backtracked on his statement shortly thereafter. Nevertheless, Fox News's Seth Rich disinformation campaign shows that the right-wing media sphere, in addition to following the lead of GOP elites, can follow Fox News and turn into a powerful political weapon.

6

Conclusion

ON SEPTEMBER 24, 2020, RUPERT Murdoch reached out to Trump's son-in-law Jared Kushner with a candid critique: "Know you are spending less on TV than Biden. However, my people tell me his ads are a lot better creatively than yours. Just passing it on [sic]." Kushner replied the following day, assuring Murdoch that the Trump campaign had "some new creative out this week." Later, Murdoch responded that the new Trump ad was "an improvement." He didn't stop there, though; he forwarded Kushner an email from a Fox employee containing a link to a Biden campaign ad before it was broadcast on Fox.[1]

The exact details of the Biden campaign ad remain unclear, but since Fox's audience is largely partisan toward the Republicans, it is likely that the ad was an attack ad aimed at reducing support among Trump's base.

Studies on negative campaigns show that responding quickly and forcefully to attack ads is crucial for winning elections.[2] Failing to do so can be disastrous for political candidates, as demonstrated by the Democratic presidential candidate Michael Dukakis's muted response to the infamous Willie Horton ads in the 1988 presidential election. Dukakis later expressed regret that he was not prepared to handle the attack ads and lacked a well-thought-out strategy

Weapons of Mass Deception. Yunkang Yang, Oxford University Press. © Yunkang Yang (2025).
DOI: 10.1093/9780197820339.003.0007

to counter them.[3] Sharing confidential information about Biden's ads with Kushner, Murdoch gave the Trump campaign a significant advantage by allowing them to anticipate the attacks and prepare a well-crafted response in advance. This advantage was something that Dukakis could only have dreamed of three decades ago.

Murdoch's action once again highlights Fox's role as a political organization working toward specific political objectives. It also underscores the consequences of not recognizing this crucial point. Murdoch was able to gain insights into the Biden campaign and convey them to Kushner only because the Biden team treated Fox like any other news organization that airs campaign ads. Had the Biden campaign understood that Fox was operating as a political organization, it would probably have thought twice about advertising on Fox.

So the problem is not that Fox engaged in political activities. If billionaires such as Rupert Murdoch want to promote their political agendas in a transparent way, that is their prerogative. The problem lies in our collective failure to recognize that right-wing media like Fox often function as political organizations. The goal of this book is to shed light on this overlooked issue, presenting the most comprehensive evidence to date.

In Chapter 1, I analyzed Federal Election Commission (FEC) filings spanning the 2016, 2018, 2020, and 2022 elections. The evidence is undeniable: Outlets like Newsmax, the Daily Wire, the Daily Caller, and others have consistently received payments from Republican political action committees (PACs) and super PACs for activities such as fundraising and voter outreach during these election cycles. These activities go far beyond the reporting and editorializing typically associated with news organizations. They are, unequivocally, political organizing activities. Chapter 1 demonstrates that right-wing media function as political organizations precisely because they engage in these overt acts of political mobilization.

In Chapter 2, I analyzed millions of online articles published by 30 major outlets during Trump's first term in office. The findings reveal a troubling pattern: Disinformation was consistently a key feature of high-engagement articles between 2017 and 2020. Through a qualitative analysis of four key disinformation case studies, I examined how right-wing media and political elites weaponized journalistic norms and practices for political purposes. Chapter 2 demonstrates that right-wing media can function as political organizations through the act of reporting. By producing and amplifying falsehoods—whether intentionally or inadvertently—they can mobilize audience attention toward specific political objectives.

Chapters 3, 4, and 5 explore how right-wing media outlets interact with one another. Owned by different right-wing billionaires, they do not always share the same political objectives. Chapter 3 reveals that ideological disagreements over policy can lead to open conflicts between outlets. However, as demonstrated in Chapter 4 and 5, when their collective interests are at stake, right-wing media can coalesce around a strategic narrative. In such pivotal moments, they follow the lead of Republican elites or a dominant right-wing media outlet, uniting into a formidable political machine capable of responding coherently to a political crisis.

I conclude this book by addressing three questions that may arise from its findings. The first question is: Do the mainstream or left-wing media outlets also engage in partisan activities that cross the line between politics and journalism, functioning as political organizations? While a full empirical exploration of this question lies beyond the scope of this book, I did review the same FEC filings for evidence of paid campaign activities involving the mainstream and left-wing media. As I will show, these activities, as documented by FEC filings, appear to be concentrated primarily on the political right. Nevertheless, a comprehensive examination of the media's role in political organizing on the left is essential—though that would be a task for another book.

The second question arises because some readers may draw parallels between this book's findings and the 19th-century partisan press and wonder whether today's right-wing media mirror the partisan newspapers once run by party loyalists. My answer is no. Most of the prominent right-wing media outlets examined in this book are owned or managed by right-wing ideologues, not GOP loyalists. Unlike the 19th-century partisan newspapers, which were accountable to political parties and, by extension, the party's electorate, these right-wing media outlets answer primarily to their rich patrons. This distinction has profound implications for American democracy—specifically, who holds the power to shape the narratives that influence voters' perceptions of reality.

The third question is: What can be done to hold right-wing media that function as political organizations accountable? Here I offer two ideas. The first involves leveraging existing institutional tools, such as filing complaints with the FEC, to penalize activities that qualify as in-kind campaign contributions. While much of the political organizing work by right-wing media is either paid, which is ethically questionable but not classified as campaign contributions, or speech, which enjoys broad protection under the Press Clause of the First Amendment, this approach could at least deter them from engaging in unpaid campaign activities, such as "catch-and-kill" operations. The second idea is to regulate the dual-class or multiclass share structures of publicly traded right-wing media companies, ensuring they are more accountable to investors rather than being beholden to their founders. It is true that many right-wing media outlets are privately held, but some, like Newsmax, have plans of filing for an initial public offering (IPO) in the United States.[4] Reforming dual-class share structures could help make such outlets less susceptible to the political influence of their owners, fostering greater transparency and accountability.

Media's Engagement in Election Campaigns

In 2022, journalist Bob Woodward expressed concerns about perceived media bias to Senator Lindsey Graham. Graham replied by saying, "Don't you worry about your business; people have already written it off as another form of politics."[5]

Graham's remark echoed the sentiments of Matthew Boyle, who, as noted in the introduction, declared that "journalistic integrity is dead." The underlying logic of Boyle's remarks is that since the mainstream media is seen as a tool for advancing partisan agendas, it is acceptable for right-wing media to operate like a political organization—even to the point of waging information warfare at the expense of journalistic integrity.

Research has shown that such criticisms are a strategic effort to undermine the credibility of the press in the minds of voters.[6] The claim that the legacy press has a partisan bias lacks empirical support. While some professional journalists might vote for Democrats or adopt liberal stances on certain policy issues, no compelling evidence suggests that journalists' own ideological or partisan bias has shaped news media coverage.[7]

Unlike right-wing media outlets funded by ideological billionaires who often influence editorial decisions, legacy media firms are shaped by a different set of forces. Market pressures from advertisers, the professional imperative to maintain credibility, and the logistical challenges of gathering timely and accurate information all play a significant role in shaping the news coverage.[8] These factors limit the influence of journalists' personal ideological preferences on their reporting.

As media scholar Tien Tsung Lee noted, studies examining legacy media content found no significant or consistent partisan bias.[9] Research that claims to identify liberal bias in mainstream news coverage suffers from methodological flaws.[10] Scholars have shown that audiences' perceptions of liberal bias are more strongly linked to their ideological and partisan leanings than to any actual bias in the content itself.[11]

I analyzed the same FEC filings for potential evidence of paid campaign activities involving the *Washington Post*, the *New York Times*, and other mainstream outlets. I focused on 19 major English-language mainstream media organizations[12] identified by the Pew Research Center as sources of political news for at least 5% of Democrats, 5% of Republicans, or 5% of all U.S. adults.[13] Eleven organizations received 6,470 payments worth $3.8 million in total from 294 campaign organizations between 2015 and 2022. Figure 6.1 shows aggregated payment amount to each of the 11 media organizations.

Only six mainstream media organizations had a total payment amount exceeding $5,000 between 2015 and 2022: the *New York Times*, the *Washington Post*, CNN, CBS, the *Wall Street Journal*, and Politico. Figure 6.2 shows the percentage breakdown of the payment categories for each of these six media organizations.

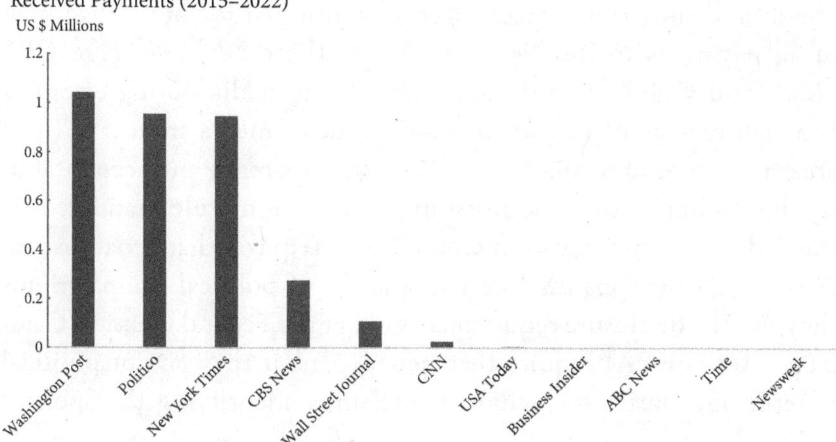

FIGURE 6.1 Total payments from campaign organizations between 2015 and 2022.

Source: FEC

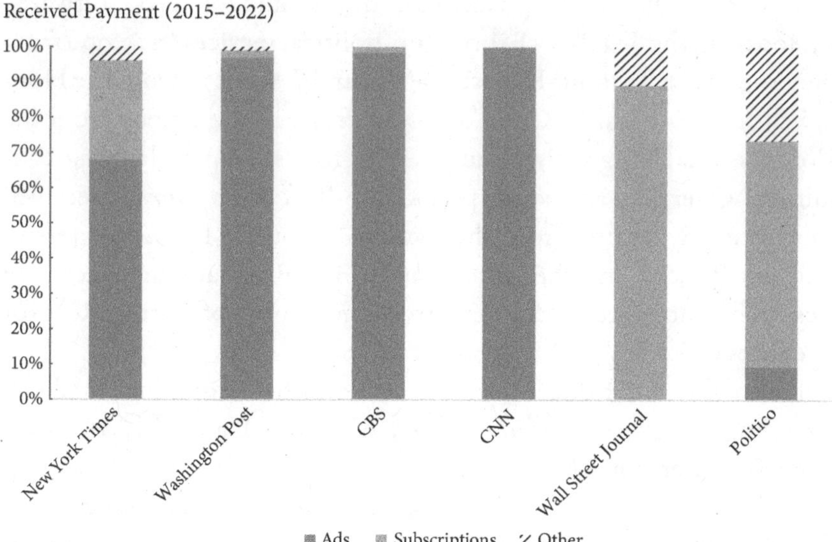

FIGURE 6.2 Payment categories for six mainstream media organizations.

Ads and subscription fees together accounted for more than 95% of all payments to the *New York Times*, the *Washington Post*, CBS News, and CNN. Placing campaign ads on media during elections is a well-regulated practice in the U.S. news media industry. There are certain federal regulations to ensure transparency and accountability. For example, the "sponsorship identification" rule mandated by the Federal Communication Commission requires that broadcast radio and TV stations disclose the sponsor of political campaign ads they air. The disclosure requirements under the Federal Election Campaign Act (FECA) require that newspapers, if they accept political advertising, must also include a disclaimer identifying the sponsor of the ad.

However, Politico and the *Wall Street Journal* also received significant payments in the "other" campaign-related category. During the seven years reviewed, Politico received approximately $13,000 from Priorities USA Action for "database," $15,000 from the DNC for "digital acquisition," $10,000 from Our Black Party for "media monitoring," $16,210 from the Tea Party Patriots Citizens Fund for "PAC software," $5,800 from the Tea Party Express for "political services," $17,000 from the Progressive Turnout Project for "research," $46,575 from the Honeywell International PAC for "website services," and $7,000 from the Congressional Progressive Caucus PAC for "strategic planning consulting." Over the same study period, the *Wall Street Journal* received approximately $3,000 from the Lyndon Larouche PAC, Progressive Turnout Project, and the Conservative First PAC, among others, for "research," and it received $1,027 from the Friends of Dennis Ross for "websites expenses."

I also did the same search for major liberal opinion media—including the *Nation*, *Mother Jones*, AlterNet, Daily Kos, the *New Republic*, Intercept, *American Prospect*, the Raw Story, and Salon—between 2015 and 2022. I found no record of payment. To the extent that it is documented by the FEC, the phenomenon of media organizations engaging in campaign activities during elections appears to be concentrated on the political right. In other words, there is an asymmetry of media-campaign collaboration on the ideological spectrum in America.

Not a Return to the 19th-Century Partisan Press

The book's framework of right-wing media as political organizations perhaps harkens back to the 19th-century partisan press, where major newspapers essentially functioned as an extension of political parties. In the mid-19th century, 95% of newspapers were partisan.[14] At the height of the Jacksonian era between the 1820s and 1830s, newspaper men, according to historian Carl Fish, "were the most important single class of party workers."[15] Serving as de facto state directors of political parties or political lieutenants, they were singularly tasked with voter outreach.[16] These newspaper men did much more than just edit newspapers. They organized rallies, drafted party platforms, recruited candidates, issued campaign extras, served on party committees, and, among other activities, worked to advance the goals of political parties.[17] According to historian Gerald Baldasty, newspaper editors formed the nucleus of political organization in the 19th century.[18]

An important factor driving the integration of newspapers into the party apparatus was endemic financial instability in the news business. Even the most successful newspapers in the United States at that time struggled with low profit margins.[19] Because private sources of income such as advertising and subscription were tenuous, newspaper editors relied heavily on party patronage for financial stability. The political party, if in power, often rewarded its newspaper editors lucrative printing contracts at both the state and federal level; some editors also received salaries as they were offered political appointments.[20]

Heavily subsidized by political parties, editors were expected to demonstrate their loyalty. Their fervent defense of their respective parties took the form of bombastic attacks against the opposing party, with some instances even escalating to physical confrontations.[21] Truthfulness, objectivity, and balance were seldom expected in their reporting. Many of these editors were partisan zealots themselves, and even those who were not might have been quite wary of taking unorthodox positions against their party for fear of losing the patronage.[22] Editors who showed disloyalty or failed to meet party expectations were swiftly replaced or had their financial support cut off.[23] The system of party patronage effectively ensured that partisan newspapers remained steadfastly aligned with their respective party platform.

With the current heightened levels of political polarization and partisanship, some scholars express concerns that right-wing media, such as Fox News, mirror the 19th-century partisan press that prioritized partisan allegiance over truth. For example, political scientists Tim Groeling and Matthew Baum considered 19th-century partisan newspapers the precursors of Fox News,[24] and Harvard researchers Yochai Benkler and his colleagues described Fox News and conservative talk radio shows as "functioning in effect as a party press" for the GOP during the 2020 election.[25]

My book challenges the notion that today's right-wing media are merely a continuation of the 19th-century partisan press. While partisan press was directly subsidized by political parties and acted as their mouthpiece, right-wing media are privately funded by wealthy individuals. Compared with party patronage, privatized political patronage poses a distinct risk to American democracy—namely, that it may perpetuate minority rule because of the lack of democratic accountability.

In a two-party electoral system like that of the United States, a media outlet financed by a major political party is likely constrained by the need to adopt majority positions on issues to secure a majority of votes. Therefore, party patronage should discourage the media outlet from deviating from the party's established platform. The 19th-century partisan press was directly accountable to the party and, by extension, to the party's constituents. Electoral accountability ensured that the media outlet reflected the party's interests and the preferences of its supporters.

However, the situation differs when a media outlet is controlled by a billionaire. Unlike a party-owned media outlet, a billionaire-owned media organization is not subject to any forms of democratic accountability. This lack of accountability grants the billionaire significant freedom to dictate the outlet's editorial stances and issue positions, irrespective of whether they align with the will or interests of most voters.

On a host of issues such as abortion, gun safety laws, and climate change, billionaire-owned right-wing media have consistently advocated extremist positions that diverge significantly from the views held by most American voters. To advance their own ideological agendas, they have challenged GOP incumbents in primaries,[26] obstructed Republican legislative agendas,[27] pressured President Bush to withdraw his Supreme Court nomination,[28] and called for the resignation of Republican officials.[29] Much as right-wing media can echo and repeat Republican talking points, they have also increasingly captured the GOP, pressuring Republican elites to adopt their agendas and messaging.[30] This form of privatized political patronage represents a model of minority rule,[31] where rich ideologues hold tremendous power to shape voters' perceptions of reality.

Holding Right-Wing Media Accountable

In February 2018, Free Speech For People (FSFP) filed a complaint with the FEC, alleging that American Media Inc.—the owner of the *National Enquirer*—violated FECA.[32] The complaint centered on a $150,000 payment made by American Media to Karen McDougal (also known as Stormy Daniels) to bury her story about an alleged affair with Donald Trump. FSFP argued that this payment was intended to influence the 2016 presidential election by suppressing potentially damaging information about then-candidate Trump, thus constituting an in-kind contribution[33] in violation of FECA.

FECA prohibits corporations from making direct contributions to federal candidates and their campaign committees. However, it gives media an exemption, allowing news organizations to freely report on candidates without being classified as contributors or campaign spenders. The statutory media exemption states that campaign expenditure does not include "any news story, commentary, or editorial distributed through the facilities of any broadcasting station, newspaper, magazine, or other periodical publication, unless such facilities are owned or controlled by any political party, political committee, or candidate."[34]

American Media's "catch-and-kill" practice was not a press activity. It was not intended to publish a news story, commentary, or editorial, and therefore should not qualify for protection under the press exemption. Acting as an extension of the Trump 2016 campaign, American Media, as FSFP argued, should be subject to FECA's regulations on campaign contributions and expenditures.

Civil society groups like FSFP have increasingly played an important role in holding right-wing media outlets accountable. In 2023, when Murdoch's email regarding Biden's campaign ad was publicly disclosed, the watchdog group Media Matters filed a complaint with the FEC, alleging that Murdoch's action constituted an illegal corporate in-kind contribution to the Trump campaign.[35]

Neither the American Media nor the Fox case has resulted in penalties. In the American Media case, the FEC delayed its investigation for two years. After FSFP sued the agency for inaction, a district court dismissed the lawsuit on technical grounds in 2020. In the Fox case, although the Office of the General Counsel of FEC found that Fox violated FECA, the chairman of the FEC, Sean Cooksey, ultimately declined to investigate in 2024. He argued that the information Murdoch provided to Jared Kushner did not meet the definition of "something of value" under campaign contribution rules. More important, he emphasized a broad interpretation of exempted press activities, asserting that "Fox Corporation is, first and foremost, a media organization whose press activities and editorial decision-making are broadly protected."[36]

Despite these challenges, filing complaints with the FEC remains a vital tool for holding right-wing media accountable. Alongside ongoing efforts to monitor the political organizing activities of right-wing media, civil society groups should advocate for clearer boundaries of press exemptions. At the same time, the FEC must strengthen its enforcement mechanisms to ensure timely and effective investigations.

My second suggestion is to regulate the dual-class or multiclass share structures of publicly traded right-wing media companies like Fox. Dual-class share structures, which date back to the early 20th century, create two types of shares with differing voting rights. This mechanism allows business owners to attract external investment while retaining control of the company, even with a minority ownership stake.

Dual-class shares are prevalent across various sectors, with media companies like Fox and tech companies like Meta utilizing this structure to consolidate decision-making power.

Fox Corporation has two classes of shares: Class A and Class B. Holders of Class A shares have voting rights only in very limited circumstances, while holders of Class B shares retain most of the voting power. As of 2024, the Murdoch Family Trust owns less than 1% of Class A shares but controls 43.39% of Class B shares. This concentration of Class B shares grants the Murdoch family significant power over the company. For instance, amending or repealing Fox's bylaws requires the approval of at least 65% of Class B shares. Similarly, calling a special stockholders' meeting requires a written request from holders of at least 20% of Class B shares, unless initiated by a majority of the board or the board's chair.[37] This structure effectively ensures the Murdoch family's dominance in decision-making at Fox.

Eliminating the dual-class share structure at Fox Corporation would significantly weaken the Murdoch family's control over the company and increase its accountability to the majority of its stockholders. Without this structure, activist investors would find it easier to propose acquisitions or instigate changes in company leadership. While it is unrealistic to expect Fox Corporation to voluntarily dismantle this structure, the stock exchange NASDAQ, where Fox is listed, and the Securities and Exchange Commission (SEC) can play a pivotal role in addressing this issue. In 1940, for example, the New York Stock Exchange prohibited listed companies from issuing non-voting stock and limited superior-voting stock to no more than 18.5% of all outstanding common shares. Similarly, in 1988, the SEC adopted a rule banning most forms of dual-class shares, though this was overturned by the Court of Appeals for the District of Columbia in 1990.[38]

Reforming dual-class share structures will undoubtedly face resistance from companies that benefit from them, but history demonstrates that meaningful change is possible. Moreover, Congress has the authority to enact legislation to restrict or regulate the use of dual-class shares across publicly traded companies. Achieving this goal would likely require coordinated efforts among regulators, legislators, and industry stakeholders, but such collaboration could pave the way for a more accountable corporate governance structure for publicly traded right-wing media outlets like Fox.

There are other ways to hold right-wing media accountable, such as defamation lawsuits. Each tool in the accountability toolbox serves a unique purpose. Filing a complaint with the FEC is most effective when right-wing media's political organizing activities constitute in-kind campaign contributions. Eliminating dual-class share structures applies specifically to publicly traded companies. Defamation lawsuits are particularly impactful when the defamed parties are private citizens, as demonstrated by the lawsuit filed by two election workers in Georgia against the Gateway Pundit, or private companies, as seen in the Dominion vs. Fox lawsuit. To hold right-wing media accountable, it is important to adopt a comprehensive approach that leverages all these tools.

Looking Ahead

When I began researching for this book in 2017, I sensed that right-wing media were doing more than merely expressing bias in their content—they were breaking fundamental journalistic norms. So, I set out with a clear goal in mind: to expose these violations and prove to scholars that right-wing media are not merely biased news outlets but something far more consequential. As I delved into their actions during Trump's first term in office, I uncovered extensive evidence that some of the most prominent outlets were operating, by design, as political organizations. Their transgressions in editorial processes weren't accidental or misguided; they were deliberate. Their involvement in political organizing wasn't an isolated phenomenon; it was pervasive across all top right-wing media outlets. However, what transpired during the 2020 election cycle went beyond anything I had expected—many right-wing media outlets engaged in the antidemocratic behavior of fueling an insurrection to overturn a free and fair election.

In the immediate aftermath of the insurrection, the right-wing media sphere experienced a brief moment of fracturing. Rupert Murdoch, who reportedly expressed discomfort with Trump's election denialism,[39] wrote to a former Fox executive: "We want to make Trump a non-person."[40] In the following months, Fox News distanced itself from Trump, notably by refusing to cover nearly all of his rallies during the first half of 2022.[41] Instead, the network heavily promoted Florida Governor Ron DeSantis, whose rising popularity in the polls positioned him as a viable alternative to Trump for the 2024 presidential race. In contrast, Newsmax took a different approach. Its CEO, Christopher Ruddy, reaffirmed the network's pro-Trump stance, declaring that Newsmax had an editorial policy of supporting Trump in 2020.[42] His commitment remained evident in late 2021 and early 2022, as Newsmax extensively covered Trump's rallies in Texas and Arizona.

Just as it seemed that the tide within the right-wing media sphere might be turning against Trump, the FBI executed a search warrant at Mar-a-Lago in the summer of 2022 as part of an investigation into his handling of classified documents. The event triggered a swift and unified response from most right-wing media outlets, which coalesced around a singular narrative: The search was a politically motivated witch-hunt. For example, Fox's then-host Tucker Carlson called it a power grab, talk radio host Buck Sexton called it a preemptive coup, and The Blaze commentator Steve Crowder described it as tyrannical.[43]

The framing of the Mar-a-Lago search as a political witch-hunt reinvigorated right-wing media's support for Trump, rallying his base and shifting the narrative back in his favor. The narrative persisted well into 2023, as Trump faced a series of indictments while campaigning to be the Republican nominee. Each indictment kept Trump in the headlines and was cast as further proof of a coordinated effort to undermine him. The news about Trump's indictment not only amplified Trump's visibility but also reinforced his dominance within the right-wing media sphere, solidifying his position as the standard-bearer of the Republican Party once again.

In the near future—for example, during Trump's second term—the patterns documented in my book are likely to persist. While the political and ideological landscape on the right may evolve, right-wing media will rally to Trump's defense whenever he is in trouble—whether by deflecting attention from scandals or shielding him from investigations. At the same time, they will continue engaging in ideological battles among themselves, pushing competing agendas, and championing different candidates to shape the future leadership of the GOP.

Worryingly, the privatized political patronage that has sustained the right-wing media sector for decades shows no signs of waning. Emerging right-wing oligarchs, such as Elon Musk, have shown a clear interest in acquiring media enterprises to expand their political influence. America appears to be drifting toward a regime where authoritarian leaders control the machinery of government, while their oligarch partners dominate much of the media landscape. This alliance of power and wealth is extremely difficult to challenge.

APPENDIX

Chapter 1

Table A.1.1 Sum of Payments from PACs and Super PACs to Right-Wing Media (2015–2022)

Media	Amount	PACs and Super PACs
The Blaze and Blaze Media	$19,599	Peter Meijer for Congress Anthony Bouchard for Congress Libertarian National Committee, Inc. Bold Conservatives PAC
Breitbart	$366,385	Scott Walker Inc Make America Number 1 American Legacy Political Action Committee Conservative, Authentic, Responsive Leadership for You and for AmericaWomen Vote Smart Bold Conservatives PAC NRSCDan Crenshaw for Congress

Continued

Table A.1.1 *Continued*

Media	Amount	PACs and Super PACs
		Make America Great Again Inc.
		Club for Growth Action
Daily Caller	$210,463	Republican National Committee
		Conservative Trust of America
		Bold Conservatives PAC
		Lyndon Larouche Political Action Committee
		NRSC
Daily Wire	$1,205,880	Cathy McMorris Rodgers for Congress
		Dan Crenshaw for Congress
		Friends for Kathy Barnette
		Huck PAC
		Jan Morgan for US Senate
		Jeff Fortenberry for United States Congress
		New Journey PAC, Inc.
		NRCC
		Republican National Committee
		Weber for Congress
Fox News	$259,146	AB PAC
		Alexis Johnson for Congress
		Biden for President
		Brady for Congress
		Cindy Hyde-Smith for US Senate
		DNC Services Corp./Dem. Nat'l Committee
		Friends of Heidi St. John
		Gary Palmer for Congress
		Lindsey Graham 2016
		Paullange2215
		Pompeo for Kansas, Inc.
		Republican National Committee
		RGA Right Direction PAC
Conservative Review	$6,500	The 2016 Committee

Media	Amount	PACs and Super PACs
Liftable Media (Western Journal)	$91,727	America Fighting Back PAC
		Bergmann for Congress 2018
		Business-Industry Political Action Committee
		Jackson for Congress
		Republican Party of Texas
		Team Huizenga
National Review	$3814	Alex Mooney for Congress
		Carly for President
		Mooney for Congress 2016
		Nikki Haley for President Inc.
		NRSC
		Paul King for Congress Campaign Committee
		Republican National Committee
		Save America Now PAC
		Texans for Lamar Smith
Newsmax	$449,609	Anthony Bouchard for Congress
		Bold Conservatives PAC
		Campaign to Support the President
		Carly for President
		Casey for Congress
		Conservative Trust of America
		Conservative Warchest PAC
		Conservative, Authentic, Responsive Leadership for You and for America
		Diehl for US Senate
		Donald J. Trump for President, Inc.
		Friends for Kathy Barnette
		Garland Tucker for Senate
		Great America PAC
		Gun Owners of America, Inc. Political Victory Fund
		Huck PAC
		Joe Pinion for US Senate Inc
		John Bolton PAC
		Melissa Martz Campaign Account CD 18

Continued

Table A.1.1 *Continued*

Media	Amount	PACs and Super PACs
		New Journey PAC, Inc.
		NRCC
		Right to Rise USA
		Root for the Wall PAC
		Support American Leaders PAC
		Trump Save America Joint Fundraising Committee
		Ward for Senate
New York Post	$8,813	Citizens Against Plutocracy
		Emily's List
		Espaillat for Congress 2016
		Friends for Gregory Meeks
		Friends of Schumer
		Gillibrand for Senate
		Suozzi for Congress
Townhall	$47,511	Elise for Congress
		FreedomWorks for America
		NRCC
		Republican National Committee
		Ted Cruz for Senate
		Trip Pittman for US Senate
Washington Examiner	$2,955	Hagan for Congress
		DCCC
		Tim Scott for Senate
		Nikki Haley for President Inc.
Washington Times	$21,807	American Legacy Political Action Committee
		Carly for President
		Donald J. Trump for President 2024, Inc.
		Fairfax County Republican Committee (Federal)
		Freedom for All PAC
		Laura Loomer for Congress Inc

Media	Amount	PACs and Super PACs
		Nikki Haley for President Inc.
		Republican National Committee
		Save America
		Texans for Lamar Smith
WND	$35,266	Bold Conservatives PAC
		Cruz for President
		Friends for Kathy Barnette
		Laura Loomer for Congress Inc
		Perkins for Oregon
		Volunteers for Nehlen

Chapter 2

List Construction

The right-wing media list was built on four existing lists compiled by media scholars and practitioners. The first three existing lists came from the study of the 2016 presidential election coverage by Faris et al. (2017). Faris and his colleagues analyzed right-wing media's election coverage in 2016 and identified the top 10 most-linked right-wing media sites on the open web, the top 10 most-shared right-wing media on Facebook, and the top 10 most-retweeted right-wing media on Twitter.

Faris et al. (2017)'s classification of media partisanship was based on the retweet patterns of people who either retweeted Hillary Clinton or Donald Trump in the 2016 election. While we expect that the retweeters of right-wing media sites on average are more likely to retweet Trump than Clinton, not every site that drew more Trump retweeters was right-wing media. To mitigate this potential classification problem, I validated the partisanship of right-wing media by referencing Media Bias Fact Check (MBFC) and BuzzFeed News's 2016 list of right-wing media.[1]

Given that Faris et al. (2017)'s top right-wing media lists were based on social media shares and open web links, I added PJ Media's top conservative media list to include online traffic as a third indicator of right-wing media's online prominence. PJ Media compiled a list of top conservative media sites based on averaged web traffic rankings from Alexa, Quantcast, and SimilarWeb in 2017, three web traffic tracking companies.[2]

To increase the sample size and integrate the book's theoretical framework with the case studies, I also added prominent right-wing media outlets from each case study to the top right-wing media list. For each case, I identified the top 10 most-linked right-wing media that were not included in previous lists. This means that I kept adding new media sites until I identified the 10th new right-wing media for each case. I also used

MBFC and BuzzFeed's partisan media list for the identification of partisanship. Table A.2.1 shows the total number of articles published by each right-wing media outlet, along with Facebook interactions, between 2017 and 2020, as well as the source of my data. The number of stories and Facebook engagement data came from NewsWhip, a social media analytic firm that tracks user engagement with stories published by 500,000 online publishers.

Data Collection

First, I collected the article URLs of 41 non-local right-wing media outlets through a subscription with NewsWhip in 2021.[13] Besides article links, NewsWhip provided article publication time, headline, excerpt, authorship, and Facebook engagement data (i.e., likes, shares, comments, and six reaction categories). Next, I built customized Python web scrapers based on existing packages, such as BeautifulSoup and Newspaper3k, and collected the full text of each article between 2017 and 2020. Most article content was retrievable through the original article URLs at the time of data collection. In cases where media outlets changed the original article URLs as a result of archiving, additional steps were taken to retrieve archived articles (i.e., from the Internet Archive). URLs that pointed to other forms of media content such as videos and podcasts were discarded.

Thirty-two non-local right-wing media outlets consistently produced text-based article content between 2017 and 2020. At the time of data collection, I was able to retrieve the full text of more than 99% of all articles for Fox News, the Daily Wire, Breitbart, the *New York Post*, the Daily Caller, The Blaze, the *Washington Times*, the Washington Free Beacon, PJ Media, the Federalist, the Gateway Pundit, WorldNetDaily (WND), the *National Review*, the Political Insider, Real Clear Politics, Newsmax,

Table A.2.1 46 Major Right-wing Media (2017–2020)

Media	# Stories	# FB Interactions	Source
Fox News	293,665	1,723,688,614	Faris et al., 2017
Breitbart	659,217	886,360,367	Faris et al., 2017
Daily Caller	170,273	505,814,719	Faris et al., 2017
Free Beacon	28,537	67,919,130	Faris et al., 2017
Conservative Tribune[3]	N/A	N/A	Faris et al., 2017
Western Journal	69,117	535,903,519	Faris et al., 2017

Media	# Stories	# FB Interactions	Source
WND	65,474	86,586,941	PJ Media
Gateway Pundit	44,486	91,534,034	Faris et al., 2017
Zero Hedge	84280	37,884,615	PJ Media
Infowars	54,688	28,590,341	PJ Media
The Blaze	41,532	353,305,303	PJ Media
Daily Wire	51,202	1,369,140,920	PJ Media
Political Insider	17,093	81,009,765	Faris et al., 2017
Right Scoop	16,312	13,157,819	Faris et al., 2017
New York Post	242,991	726,583,350	Faris et al., 2017
Washington Examiner	136,782	199,199,279	Faris et al., 2017
Washington Times	798,246	293,496,120	Faris et al., 2017
Truth Feed[4]	10,513	39,176,102	Faris et al., 2017
Ending the Fed[5]	N/A	N/A	Faris et al., 2017
Heat Street[6]	4,150	3,751,981	Chapter 5
McMasterLeaks[7]	N/A	N/A	Chapter 3
Circa[8]	15,826	8,879,843	Chapter 3
Conservative Review	30,490	26,039,801	Chapter 3
WJLA	73,607	70,845,048	Chapter 5
Fox 5 DC	44,359	74,230,065	Chapter 5
Michael Savage	607	443,278	Chapter 5
FrontPage Magazine	10,822	11,340,715	Chapter 3
Twitchy	45,702	30,938,917	Chapter 4
Conservative Treehouse	13,565	8,503,624	Chapter 4
Big League Politics	12,076	7,499,643	Chapter 5
Disobedient Media	377	197,443	Chapter 5
American Thinker	30,744	33,451,526	Chapter 4

Continued

Media	# Stories	# FB Interactions	Source
Federalist	19,157	94,143,206	Chapter 4
Hot Air	29,484	22,431,981	Chapter 4
American Spectator	9,253	5,001,928	Chapter 3
Intellihub	3,496	1,153,272	Chapter 5
Govtslaves[9]	1,376	37,509	Chapter 5
Townhall	247,139	89,281,482	Chapter 4
Daily Sheeple	6,460	1,162,524	Chapter 5
PJ Media	138,585	144,933,521	Chapter 5
NewsMax	191,132	34,022,392	Chapter 3
Pamela Geller	18,442	39,465,227	Chapter 3
Real Clear Politics	87,402	49,070,807	Chapter 4
Your News Wire	15,668	58,854,902	Chapter 4
National Review	45,483	83,302,311	Chapter 3
Weekly Standard[10]	8,590	2,302,234	Chapter 3
thelaststand.com[11]	N/A	N/A	Chapter 5
What Really Happened[12]	N/A	N/A	Chapter 5

American Thinker, Hot Air, Right Scoop, Big League Politics, and the *American Spectator* (spectator.org) between 2017 and 2020. For Western Journal, the full text of its articles between 2018 and 2020 was retrieved. For the *Washington Examiner*, the full text of 42% of its articles in 2017, 49% in 2018, 92% in 2019, and 99% in 2020 was collected. For townhall.com, the full text of 13% of its articles in 2017, 16% in 2018, 97% in 2019, and 98% in 2020 was retrieved. For Your News Wire (rebranded as News Punch in 2018), the full text of all but 2017 articles was retrieved. For pamelageller.com (renamed as gellerreport.com), the full text of 79% of its articles in 2017, 99% in 2018, 99% in 2019, and 94% in 2020 was retrieved. For Zero Hedge, the full text of 3% of its articles in total was retrieved. For Twitchy, the full text of all but 2018 articles was collected. For Infowars, the full text of all but the second half of 2020 was retrieved. For FrontPage Magazine, the full text of 47% of its articles in 2017, 76% in 2018, 98% in 2019, and 99% in 2020 was collected. For Conservative Treehouse, the full text of 84% of its articles in 2017 and 99% of its 2018, 2019, and 2020 articles was collected. Conservative Review's article full text was not retrievable, possibly due to IP address blocking.

Four media outlets ceased operation during the four-year period, including the *Weekly Standard*, Truth Feed, Heat Street, and Circa. For the *Weekly Standard*, the full text of 62% of its 2017 articles and 67% of its 2018 articles was retrieved. Truth Feed, Heat Street, and Circa's full text was not retrievable. The full text of the remaining right-wing media on my list, including the Daily Sheeple, intellihub.com, michaelsavage.com, govtslaves.com, and disobedient media was not retrievable.

Structural Topic Modeling

A structural topic model (STM) is used to discover topics automatically and estimate their relationship with variables. As a variant of latent Dirichlet allocation (LDA) models, STM defines a topic as a mixture of words, where each word has a probability of belonging to a topic, and assumes that each document is a mixture of topics (Roberts et al., 2015). LDA models assume a data-generating process for each document: First, a distribution over topics is drawn from a common Dirichlet prior; then, each word in the document is drawn according to the topic distribution (Grimmer & Stewart, 2013).

There is no well-established definition of "topics" in communication research (Günther & Domahidi, 2017). Some studies use topic models to identify broad issue areas such as poverty, climate change, and gun violence (Barbera et al., 2019); others used topic models to identify subtopics or specific themes within an issue (Farrell, 2016a, 2016b). In Chapter 2, I use STM to identify distinct news events rather than broad topic areas.

Compared with basic LDA models, STM has three core differences: Topics can be correlated, each document has its own prior topic distribution influenced by covariates (topic prevalence), and words within each topic can be influenced by covariates (topic content) (Farrell, 2016b). I use STM mainly because it enables document metadata such as the date of publication and the name of media outlets to influence the discovery of topics. The inclusion of the date is especially useful given that the coverage of news events is usually influenced by news cycles. The inclusion of the name of the media outlets is also important because various right-wing media may differ in terms of their coverage of news events.

Creating the High-Engagement Sample

Thirty right-wing media outlets that consistently produced content between 2017 and 2020 were first selected.[14] Then, sampling was conducted for each media outlet on a weekly basis: For each media outlet, top articles were sampled to cover 80% of total Facebook engagement each week. Table A.2.2 shows the number of articles in the sample with the total number of articles in parentheses.

Once sampled, top articles across right-wing media outlets were combined into a single corpus for every six-month period, resulting in eight corpora. The following STM analyses were conducted on each corpus.

Preprocessing Texts

Each word from article headlines and excerpts[15] was stemmed and lowercased. Punctuation and stopwords were removed using the STM package in R. In addition, for each corpus, words that appeared in fewer than 10 article headlines and excerpts were removed to reduce noise.[16]

Estimating the Structural Topic Model

Following Roberts et al. (2019), I included the name of the media outlet as well as the publication date as two document-level covariates to influence topic prevalence. Publication date was coded as a "day" variable that ranges from 0 to 180 for each corpus. In addition, the "day" variable was transformed through a b-spline to allow for nonlinear effects.

The granularity of topics depends on the number of topics specified in the model. The more topics there are, the more specific the topics are.

Table A.2.2 High-Engagement Articles Between 2017 and 2020—Numbers in Parentheses Indicate Total Articles

Media	2017	2018	2019	2020
American Thinker	1762 (7,792)	1,536 (77,08)	1,412 (7,400)	1,214 (7,844)
Big League Politics	175 (578)	600 (2,207)	1,256 (4,904)	1,140 (4,387)
Breitbart	7,242 (174,477)	6,940 (187,820)	7,125 (166,941)	7,696 (129,979)
Daily Caller	5,053 (37,409)	3,686 (40,253)	3,682 (30,817)	3,168 (61,794)
Daily Wire	3,599 (12,124)	4,497 (13,477)	3,811 (12,281)	4,353 (13,320)

Media	2017	2018	2019	2020
Fox News	4,378 (75,804)	4,507 (72,254)	4,995 (73,261)	5356 (72,346)
Free Beacon	2,003 (10,075)	1,046 (8,202)	881 (6,202)	684 (4,058)
FrontPage Magazine	994 (3,573)	785 (3,453)	526 (2,720)	215 (1,076)
Hot Air	1,747 (7,598)	1,597 (7,028)	1,396 (7,294)	1,245 (7,564)
Infowars	2,163 (16,138)	2,554 (16,057)	3,891 (11,366)	3,220 (11,127)
National Review	1,237 (9,201)	1,233 (12,515)	1,345 (9,377)	1,169 (14,390)
NewsMax	2,221 (53,834)	2,209 (39,988)	1,379 (44,607)	939 (52,703)
New York Post	4,661 (53,478)	2,960 (58,989)	2,914 (62,833)	3,134 (67,691)
Pamela Geller	2,348 (5,611)	199 (3,957)	1,698 (3,903)	2,217 (4,971)
PJ Media	1,212 (31,872)	585 (30,710)	842 (35,511)	1,213 (40,492)
Real Clear Politics	1,124 (21,605)	758 (21,591)	684 (21,957)	399 (22,249)
American Spectator	454 (2,364)	545 (2,234)	582 (2,038)	382 (2,617)
The Blaze	2,473 (11,511)	2,194 (10,657)	1,924 (9,322)	2,865 (10,042)
The Conservative Treehouse	607 (3,929)	727 (3,231)	668 (3,155)	477 (3,250)
Federalist	799 (4,173)	642 (4,511)	816 (4,536)	772 (5,937)
Gateway Pundit	3,341 (10,801)	4314 (11,826)	3888 (9,640)	4330 (12,255)
Political Insider	1,507 (4,391)	1,386 (3,872)	1,490 (4,169)	1,819 (4,661)

Continued

Media	2017	2018	2019	2020
The Right Scoop	852 (4,776)	582 (4,110)	536 (3,723)	390 (3,703)
Townhall	3,106 (125,433)	3,015 (90,560)	2,938 (14,714)	2,831 (16,432)
Washington Examiner	3,875 (33,019)	3,141 (35,049)	2,877 (31,879)	3,149 (36,835)
Washington Times	2,706 (219,559)	2,631 (203,801)	2,417 (211,655)	1,268 (163,231)
Western Journal (Western Journalism)	2,262 (8,056)	5,174 (19,218)	4,559 (28,764)	2,899 (13,079)
WND	1,865 (17,444)	1,130 (15,877)	1,061 (15,670)	1,937 (16,483)
Your Newswire	509 (4,708)	440 (3,835)	1065 (3,415)	897 (3,710)
Zero Hedge	4,054 (21,731)	2,302 (20,095)	3,507 (20,683)	4,720 (21,771)
Total	70,329 (993,064)	63,915 (955,085)	66,165 (864,719)	66098 (829,997)

While too many topics might lead to similar entities that cannot be differentiated meaningfully, too few topics might result in broad entities that should be separated (Maier et al., 2018). Hence, it requires the researcher to qualitatively assess the coherence and interpretability of a model to determine the appropriate number of topics.

For this study, a 100-topic model for each six-month period yielded semantically coherent and easily interpretable results. When going above 100 topics, the model started to include unnecessary details, rendering some topics uninterpretable. When going below 100 topics, the model began to blend different news events into a single topic, making certain topics less coherent.

To provide additional evidence, I ran two other models—one with 50 topics and the other with 150 topics—to compare against the final 100-topic model in the July–December 2020 corpus as an example. Table A.2.3, Table A.2.4, and Table A.2.5 show the results of a 50-topic model, a 100-topic model, and a 150-topic model, respectively.

It is clear that the 50-topic model blended protests in Seattle and Portland into a single topic (topic 4 in Table A.2.3); in addition, the first and second topic are both too broad to interpret. By comparison, the 150-topic model suffers from too much granularity: The topic model included specific names of media outlets such as the Daily Wire and Geller Report into the topics that are not useful, making the topics difficult to interpret.

Validating Top Topics in Each Corpus

Once the number of topics was determined, I applied STM to each corpus. To validate the substantive meaning of topics, I used findThoughts

Table A.2.3 Top Words Associated with the Top Five Topics in a 50-Topic Model on the July–December 2020 Corpus

Topic	Top Words
1	trump, presid, donald, poli, first, lead, trump's, voter, say, melania
2	american, like, will, warn, look, now, one, make, great, do
3	vote, elect, state, ballot, voter, pennsylvania, county, georgia, count, michigan
4	police, protest, portland, citi, riot, antifa, rioter, violence, violent, seattle
5	coronavirus, mask, covid, vaccine, wear, pandemic, covid-, fauci, health, say

Table A.2.4 Top Words Associated with the Top Five Topics in a 100-Topic Model on the July–December 2020 Corpus

Topic	Top Words
1	covid-, coronavirus, vaccine, fauci, covid, health, say, doctor, anthony, pandemic
2	hunter, biden, investigation, fbi, report, email, laptop, special, probe, criminal
3	trump, win, lead, president, poll, elect, biden, will, victory, vote
4	portland, riot, protest, rioter, antifa, violence, night, violent, burn, federal
5	state, elect, pennsylvania, result, georgia, secretary, unit, texas, lawsuit, recount

Table A.2.5 Top Words Associated with the Top Five Topics in a 150-Topic Model on the July–December 2020 Corpus

Topic	Top words
1	trump, presid, donald, daily, wire, vote, say, will, said
2	news, american, report, geller, spectator, usa, democrat, polit, watch, politics
3	biden, hunter, investigation, report, email, joe, justice, laptop, son, senate
4	portland, antifa, rioter, protest, riot, violence, night, federal, burn, police
5	vaccine, covid, coronavirus, covid-, health, doctor, hydroxychloroquine, say, effect, drug

and plotQuote functions in the STM R package to read the top words associated with each topic and a sample of 20 documents associated with each topic. I manually evaluated the semantic coherence and interpretability each of the top 10 topics for each corpus. Table A.2.6 shows the top words associated with the most prominent topics for each corpus.

Table A.2.6 Top Words Associated with the Top Topics for Each Corpus (2017–2020)

Corpus	Topic	Top Five Words
01–06/2017	Trump-related discourse	trump, happen, break, make, big, thing
01–06/2017	Trump's tweets	trump, president, tweet, twitter, president
01–06/2017	Trump's executive order	trump, president, order, executive, sign
01–06/2017	Trump Tower wiretapping	obama, spy, wiretap, administration, trump
01–06/2017	Repeal Obamacare	republican, bill, obamacare, gop, repeal
07–12/2017	Trump-related discourse	trump, president, donald, say, said

Corpus	Topic	Top Five Words
07–12/2017	Mueller probe	mueller, special, russia, robert, counsel
07–12/2017	FBI and Clinton	fbi, department, email, clinton, justice
07–12/2017	CNN and Trump	cnn, tweet, trump, media, fake
07–12/2017	Senate and Obamacare	senate, obamacare, republican, repeal, bill
01–06/2018	Trump-related discourse	trump, president, donald, said, call
01–06/2018	Parkland shooting	school, student, high, shoot, parkland
01–06/2018	FBI and Clinton	fbi, clinton, mccabe, report, comey
01–06/2018	Election	democrats, poll, republican, election, voter
01–06/2018	Nunes memo	nunes, fisa, memo, intelligence, house
07–12/2018	Trump-related discourse	trump, said, president, call, donald
07–12/2018	Liberals and leftists	liberals, left, care, political, american
07–12/2018	Supreme Court hearings	kavanaugh, brett, hearing, democrats, court
07–12/2018	Kavanaugh controversy	kavanaugh, brett, sexual, assault, misconduct
07–12/2018	Jobs and economy	job, percent, year, number, rate
01–06/2019	Trump-related discourse	trump, president, donald, said, say
01–06/2019	Illegal immigrants	border, migrant, mexico, illegal, patrol
01–06/2019	Alabama abortion bill	abortion, bill, sign, state, alabama

Continued

Table A.2.6 *Continued*

Corpus	Topic	Top Five Words
01–06/2019	Jussie Smollett	jussie, smollett, chicago, hate, crime
01–06/2019	State of the Union address	union, state, address, pelosi, trump
07–12/2019	Trump-related discourse	trump, president, said, donald, support
07–12/2019	House impeachment vote	impeach, trump, house, democrat, pelosi
07–12/2019	Ukraine and Biden	biden, joe, hunter, vice, ukraine
07–12/2019	House Intelligence Committee	schiff, adam, committee, chairman, intelligence
07–12/2019	Illegal immigrants	illegal, immigrants, alien, charge, ice
01–06/2020	Trump-related discourse	trump, president, said, take, donald
01–06/2020	Mainstream media	media, know, think, reality, people
01–06/2020	Senate impeachment trial	senate, impeach, trial, vote, mcconnell
01–06/2020	Government response to Covid-19	coronavirus, outbreak, test, spread, response
01–06/2020	Covid-19 and HCQ	coronavirus, hydroxychloroquine, treatment, drug, hospital
07–12/2020	Covid-19 vaccine	covid, vaccine, fauci, health, say
07–12/2020	Hunter Biden laptop	hunter, biden, investigation, fbi, laptop
07–12/2020	Voter fraud and recount	state, recount, pennsylvania, texas, lawsuit
07–12/2020	Portland protest	portland, riot, protest, antifa, violence
07–12/2020	Election	trump, win, lead, biden, poll

Table A.2.7 Article Counts in Four Disinformation Topics (2017–2020)

Media	Trump Tower Wiretapping	Nunes Memo	Ukraine & Biden	HCQ & Covid-19
Breitbart	18	33	43	14
Newsmax	16	17	6	2
Gateway Pundit	12	88	29	46
WND	10	9	7	10
Zero Hedge	9	24	18	5
Daily Wire	9	16	8	11
Conservative Treehouse	8	25	3	4
Daily Caller	7	34	21	3
Pamela Geller (Geller Report)	7	0	2	11
Political Insider	7	15	5	3
Infowars	7	15	15	11
Real Clear Politics	7	14	5	0
New York Post	6	3	5	10
Fox News	6	22	21	8
Townhall	5	24	16	12
American Thinker	5	6	4	8
PJ Media	5	8	2	3
Washington Times	4	12	8	5
Your News Wire (News Punch)	4	0	3	1
National Review	4	10	7	1
Washington Examiner	3	49	16	11
Hot Air	3	10	6	5

Continued

Table A.2.7 *Continued*

Media	Trump Tower Wiretapping	Nunes Memo	Ukraine & Biden	HCQ & Covid-19
Right Scoop	3	8	6	2
Federalist	3	10	4	1
The Blaze	2	17	12	8
Western Journal	2	1	14	4
Spectator	1	6	0	2
Free Beacon	1	3	4	1
Big League Politics	1	3	1	1
FrontPage Magazine	0	3	0	0

Table A.2.8 False or Unverified Narratives in the Ukraine–Biden Conspiracy Theory

Narrative	Source	Covered By
1. Shokin was investigating Burisma when he was fired (or he was told to back off from the probe).	Viktor Shokin, John Solomon	*National Review*, *New York Post*, Fox News, Daily Wire, *Washington Examiner*, Conservative Treehouse, *National Review*
2. Joe Biden was paid $900,000 by Burisma.	Andriy Derkach, Rudy Giuliani	Infowars, Zero Hedge, Townhall, Gateway Pundit, *New York Post*, WND, Western Journal, News Max

Narrative	Source	Covered By
3. Hunter Biden was paid $83,000 per month to serve on the board of Burisma.	Unnamed sources, Reuters	Fox News, Breitbart, *National Review*
4. Joe Biden engaged in corrupt activities—namely, pressuring Ukraine to fire Viktor Shokin for investigation into Burisma.	John Solomon, the Trump 2020 campaign	WND, Townhall, Gateway Pundit, Political Insider, Federalist, PJ Media, Hot Air, American Thinker
5. The head of Burisma has been indicted over money laundering for Biden.	Zero Hedge	Zero Hedge, Gateway Pundit, Infowars
6. Hunter Biden and his partners received $16.5 million obtained by criminal means.	Andriy Derkach	Western Journal, Right Scoop, The Blaze, News Punch, Geller Report
7. The whistleblower in Trump's first impeachment trial was partisan or working for Biden.	Trump, Mark Levin	Western Journal
8. Picture shows Joe and Hunter Biden were golfing with Burisma CEO or executive.	Fox News	Fox News, Townhall, Infowars, Daily Caller

Continued

Table A.2.8 *Continued*

Narrative	Source	Covered By
9. Hunter and Joe Biden were involved in money laundering in Ukraine.	Rudy Giuliani	*Washington Times*

Factcheck sources:
Narrative 1
https://www.politifact.com/article/2019/oct/02/fact-checking-rudy-giulianis-claims-about-joe-bide/
https://www.politifact.com/factchecks/2019/may/07/viral-image/fact-checking-joe-biden-hunter-biden-and-ukraine/
https://www.politifact.com/article/2019/nov/19/who-john-solomon-heres-what-we-know-about-journali/
Narrative 2 and 9
https://www.politifa
ct.com/factchecks/2021/mar/19/facebook-posts/no-evidence-burisma-admitted-paying-joe-biden
-9000/
Narrative 3
https://www.reuters.com/article/us-hunter-biden-ukraine/what-hunter-biden-did
-on-the-board-of-ukrainian-energy-company-burisma-idUSKBN1WX1P7
https://www.politifact.com/article/2022/jan/27/boebert-lacks-proof-claim-hunter-bidens-burisma-pa/
Narrative 4
https://
www.nytimes.com/2019/10/29/business/media/fact-check-biden-ukraine-burisma-china-hunter.html
Narrative 5
https://www.factcheck.org/2019/11/viral-headlines-wrongly-report-indictment-in-ukraine/
Narrative 6
https://www.factcheck.org/2020/10/trump-revives-false-narrative-on-biden-an
d-ukraine/
Narrative 7
https://www.nytimes.com/2019/10/29/business/media/fact-check-biden-ukr
aine-burisma-china-hunter.html
Narrative 8
https://www.reuters.com/article/uk-factcheck-joe-hunt
er-biden-golf-buris/fact-checkjoe-and-hunter-biden-not-pictured-golfing-with-burisma-ceo-idUSKBN27F306

Table A.2.9 Twenty-One Major Mainstream Media Outlets (2017–2020)[17]

Media	# Stories	# Facebook Interactions
Washington Post	3,1267	1,025,637,605
New York Times	423,350	1,526,591,596
CNN	244,708	1,955,432,842
NBC	136,792	1,322,060,782
CBS	117,070	591,311,253
ABC	375,307	660,374,739
USA Today	471,527	674,529,360
Los Angeles Times	233,681	254,215,220
Politico	80091	219419129
Business Insider	327647	584,059,502
BuzzFeed	193,765	431,412,317
MSNBC	78,043	453,676,213
Wall Street Journal	173,924	185,746,427
NPR	107,120	776598,495
PBS	53,217	165,932,252
Time	66,342	189,002,048
Newsweek	133,103	416,078,592
Vox	34,247	174,992,354
HuffPost	131,877	760,758,228
The Hill	199,548	838,662,581
Guardian	407,767	1,047,768,034

Chapter 4

Table A.4.1 Coefficients for the Multilevel Logistic Regression Model

	Coefficients (SD)
(Intercept)	−0.17 (0.7)
Republican	−2.38*** (0.64)
Democrat	−0.91 (0.54)
Nonpartisan government	0.71 (0.94)
Mainstream media	−0.25 (0.42)
Right-wing media	1.33** (0.46)
Left-wing media	1.87 (1.57)
Social media user	1.01 (0.54)
NGO	−0.7 (1.09)
Involved party	0.5 (0.28)
Other	0.18 (0.33)
Opinion	3.1*** (0.74)

***$p < 0.001$, **$p < 0.01$, *$p < 0.05$

NOTES

Introduction

1. According to a court filing from Dominion Voting Systems's defamation lawsuit against the Fox News Network (Dominion v. Fox, 2023), Tucker Carlson had the following conversation with Laura Ingraham about Sidney Powell, a former Trump attorney who spread the Big Lie. Carlson: "Sidney Powell is lying by the way. I caught her. It's insane." Ingraham: "Sidney is a complete nut. No one will work with her. Ditto with Rudy." Carlson: "Our viewers are good people and they believe it." The document also revealed that Rupert Murdoch called voter fraud claims "really crazy stuff." According to Vox' reporting, Sean Hannity said he did not believe Powell's claims about voter fraud "for one second" in a deposition (Narea, 2022).
2. According to a YouGov and *The Economist* poll conducted in April 2024, 73% of Republicans said Joe Biden did not legitimately win the 2020 election. https://d3nkl3psvxxpe9.cloudfront.net/documents/econTabReport_oNJUiMQ.pdf
3. Blanco et al., 2022.
4. Research showed a clear link between the use of right-wing media and election fraud beliefs based on a two-wave panel survey conducted before and after the 2020 election (Wang et al., 2024).
5. See Benkler et al., 2018; Jamieson & Capella, 2008.
6. See Aday, 2010; Feldman et al., 2012; Groeling, 2008; Hyun & Moon, 2016.
7. See Arceneaux & Johnson, 2013; Arceneaux et al., 2024; Broockman & Kalla, 2022; Clinton & Enamorado, 2014; DellaVigna & Kaplan, 2007; Levendusky, 2013; Simonov et al., 2022.
8. Bias is a constant feature of news. Partisan journalism is known for their ideological bias. Other forms of biases such as personalization,

dramatization, and fragmentation can be found in professionally produced news content (Bennett, 2016).

9. Benkler et al. (2018) defined propaganda as "communication designed to manipulate a target population by affecting its beliefs, attitudes, or preferences in order to obtain behavior compliant with political goals of the propagandist" (p. 29).
10. Benkler et al. (2018) adopted a political economy approach to explain why "network propaganda" is mainly a phenomenon on the political right. They argued that right-wing media capitalized on "a series of technological, institutional, and political changes" (p. 319) from the 1970s to the 1990s, gaining a first-mover advantage that allowed them to capture a loyal market segment. In the 2020 book *The Disinformation Age*, edited by Lance Bennet and Steven Livingston, Yochai Benkler emphasized market as the main driving force behind right-wing media's programming strategies, though he acknowledged that "conservative billionaires and corporate interests have invested in right-wing ideology and politics" (p. 59). As Benkler (2020) summarized, "The short version of the answer is that changes in political culture created a large new market segment for media that emphasized white, Christian identity as a political identity; and that a series of regulatory and technological changes opened up enough new channels that the old strategy of programming for a population-wide median viewer, and hoping for a share of the total audience, was displaced by a strategy that provided one substantial part of the market uniquely-tailored content" (p. 51).
11. Bimber et al., 2009, p. 73.
12. Gertz, 2022.
13. Yang, 2024.
14. Chadwick, 2007.
15. Dominion v. Fox, 2023.
16. Hannity, 2017.
17. Breitbart's chief editor, Alex Marlow, admitted that even though he believed that there was "a lot of credibility" in the accusations against Moore, he directed Breitbart to discredit Moore's accusers for the sole purpose of shielding President Donald Trump from any similar accusations of sexual misconduct that might emerge in the future (Friedersdorf, 2017).
18. Jamieson & Cappella, 2008, p. 42.
19. Benkler et al., 2018.
20. Benkler et al. (2018)'s argument that right-wing media's programming strategy reflects some preexisting audience demand for identity-affirming content ignores the fact that media outlets such as Fox News actively shaped audiences' understanding of their social identity through storytelling (Nadler & Bauer, 2019). As Peck (2019) argued in his book *Fox Populism*, Fox News not only appealed to its audiences' taste but also channeled audience engagement toward specific political projects.

21. Even Donald Trump initially expressed sympathy toward Ford. But he later publicly mocked Ford in a political rally.
22. Gibson & Chiacu, 2019.
23. Wright, 2017.
24. Viguerie & Franke, 2004.
25. The Hungarian Revolution was a nationwide uprising against Soviet-imposed control. After the fall of the Hungarian government, Soviet Union forces invaded the country and brutally suppressed dissenters.
26. Oliver, 2004.
27. Penabaz, 1965 cited in Hendershot, 2011.
28. Hendershot, 2011, p. 175.
29. Hendershot, 2011; Vigueri & Franke, 2004.
30. Hemmer, 2016; Peristein, 2009.
31. Hemmer, 2016.
32. Hemmer, 2016, p. 230.
33. Viguerie & Franke, 2004, p. 127.
34. Mayer, 2017b
35. Blackwell 2015 cited in Nelson 2021.
36. Nelson, 2021.
37. Shriver 1981 cited in Liebman 1983.
38. Vaughan, 2009.
39. Rothmeyer, 1981 cited in Dibranco, 2020.
40. DiBranco, 2020.
41. DiBranco, 2020.
42. Jamieson & Cappella, 2008.
43. Yorke, 1992.
44. The penny press and later yellow journalism newspapers coexisted with the party-owned partisan press in the 19th century. They had looser ties to political parties economically but were still influenced by party machines (McGerr, 1986).
45. See Gavin, 2020; Hacker & Pierson, 2006, 2011; Hertel-Fernandez, 2019; Mayer, 2017b.
46. For example, in *The Tea Party and the Remaking of Republican Conservatism*, Skocpol and Williamson (2016) argued that conservative media functioned as a megaphone for the Tea Party movement; in *The Branding of Right-Wing Activism: The News Media and the Tea Party*, White (2018) argued that the conservative press acted as a political party rather than a news medium, organizing a conservative base around Tea Party candidates.
47. The 1947 Hutchins Commission report defines a major responsibility of the press as providing a truthful, comprehensive, and intelligent account of the day's events in a context that gives them meaning. Historian Michael Schudson studied various journalism genres across different societies and observed that journalism almost always publishes information and

commentary on contemporary affairs on a periodic basis, through a discourse taken to be important, truthful, and sincere, while addressing dispersed and anonymous audiences (Schudson, 2000).

48. Buckley, 1955.
49. Hemmer, 2016, p. 32.
50. Bauer, 2017.
51. Bauer et al., 2024.
52. Hemmer, 2016.
53. Nash, 1976, p. 149.
54. Viguerie & Franke, 2004, p. 62
55. Hemmer, 2016.
56. Kennan, 1948.
57. Freelon & Wells, 2020, p. 146.
58. Coppins, 2017.
59. Lewis, 2018.
60. Gross, 2022.
61. Osnos, 2021.
62. Bennett et al., 2008.
63. Bennett, 1990, 2015.
64. Bennett, 2017.
65. Boykoff & Boykoff, 2004; Farrell, 2016b; Mayer 2017b; Oreskes & Conway, 2011.
66. Bennett, Lawrence & Livingston, 2008.
67. Reeve, 2013b.
68. Adair, 2024.
69. Kessler et al., 2021
70. Yang & Bennett, 2021.

Chapter 1

1. Rutenberg, 2017.
2. Robert Mercer sold his stake in Breitbart to his three daughters, including Rebekah Mercer, in late 2017.
3. Mayer, 2017a.
4. Peck, 2019.
5. Jamieson et al., 2007, p. 26.
6. Jamieson & Cappella, 2008.
7. Baum & Groeling, 2008; Groeling, 2008.
8. DellaVigna & Kaplan, 2007; Guess et al., 2021; Levendusky, 2013; Smith & Searles, 2014.
9. Schudson, 2000.
10. Hananoki, 2011.
11. Green, 2011.
12. Hannity, 2020.
13. Dominion v. Fox, 2023.

14. Carlson, 2023.
15. Chadwick et al., 2018.
16. Bennett & Livingston, 2003.
17. SPJ, 2014.
18. Collins & Schecter, 2019.
19. Dominion v. Fox, 2023.
20. Tilly, 1986, pp. 390–391.
21. Bennett et al., 2014; McCarthy & Zald, 1977.
22. https://www.opensecrets.org/political-action-committees-pacs/C00575373/donors/2016
23. https://www.opensecrets.org/political-action-committees-pacs/keep-the-promise-iii/C00575423/donors/2016
24. https://x.com/slpng_giants/status/1113550715090288640 cited in Ellefson, 2019.
25. Li, Bernard & Luczak-Roesch, 2021.
26. https://x.com/slpng_giants/status/1113550715090288640 cited in Ellefson, 2019.
27. Berry & Sobieraj, 2013.
28. Munger, 2020.
29. Some right-wing media brands tried to replicate the success strategies of clickbait media. By first rewriting or making up stories and then amplifying them through deceptive coordination on Facebook (Yang et al., 2025), for a brief period of time, the Western Journal, which seldom dispatched reporters to gather news firsthand, earned as many Facebook reactions as the combined total of 10 top news organizations (Confessore & Bank, 2019). As Facebook and Google started to crack down on clickbait in 2017, Western Journal's traffic dropped precipitously.
30. Right-wing media outlets were ranked by the number of aggregated monthly unique visitors between 2018 and 2021. Traffic data came from Comscore's Media Metrix Multi-Platform Total Audience based on therighting.com's right-wing media list (therighting, 2021).
31. The online traffic data for 11/2019, 01/2020, and 06/2020 is missing on therighting.com.
32. The recipient was The Blaze's parent company, Mercury Radio Arts.
33. The recipient was the Daily Caller's affiliate Daily Caller News Foundation (DCNF).
34. DonorTrust is a special vehicle for distributing pooled contributions from rich donors whose identity are masked.
35. Newsmax owners Chris Ruddy and Richard Scaife bought out the $15 million investment in 2000.
36. Some of the funding went through Donors Trust and Donors Capital Fund, entities designed to shield donors from public disclosure requirements.
37. Staff, 2010.
38. Newsmax Media, 2002.

39. Kenner et al., 2024.
40. The Daily Wire revealed that it had about 600,000 subscribers in 2022 (Meek, 2022).
41. Fischer, 2021.
42. McKnight, 2012.
43. Wallace-Wells, 2019.
44. Turvill, 2021.
45. Chinni, 2002.
46. Borchers, 2017; Kotch, 2019.
47. Buozis & Konieczna, 2021.
48. Hemmer, 2016.
49. Bogus, 2011.
50. Hemmer, 2016.
51. Arango, 2009.
52. Byers, 2015.
53. Wallace-Wells, 2019.
54. Fang, 2012.
55. Vogel & Schreckinger, 2016.
56. Gold & Hohmann, 2017.
57. McGraw, 2021.
58. Fuller, 2014.
59. Montgomery, 2014.
60. Mayer, 2017b.
61. Mayer, 2017a.
62. See McKnight, 2012, p. 23. Some scholars and observers argued that Rupert Murdoch's behavior was more pragmatic than ideological, citing Murdoch's support of Tony Blair and Bill and Hillary Clinton as examples. The media scholar David McKnight, however, highlighted Murdoch's donations to conservative causes and his connections to right-wing think tanks. He argued that Murdoch's News Corporation, though profit-driven, pursues an ideological mission (McKnight, 2010; 2012).
63. Mayer, 2017b.
64. For a detailed account of the right-wing political infrastructure, see *Dark Money* (Mayer, 2017b), *Democracy in Chains* (MacLean, 2017), *State Capture* (Hertel-Fernandez, 2019), "The Koch Network and Republican Party Extremism" (Skocpol & Hertel-Fernandez, 2016), *The Machine* (Fang, 2012), and *Billionaires and Stealth Politics* (Page et al., 2018).
65. Project 2025 is a policy proposal published by the Heritage Foundation to promote right-wing policies if Donald Trump wins the 2024 presidential election.
66. Mayer, 2010.
67. Montgomery, 2014.
68. Fang, 2012; Mayer, 2017b; Skocpol & Williamson, 2016.
69. PBS, 2019.

70. CNN, 2021.
71. Mayer, 2017a.
72. Bardella, 2018; Darcy, 2017; Mayer 2017a.
73. Darcy, 2017.
74. Dominion vs Fox, 2023.
75. Auletta, 2007.
76. McKnight, 2012, p. 29.
77. McKnight, 2012, p. 28.
78. Wallace-wells, 2019.
79. McKnight, 2012.
80. Arango, 2009; Wallace-Wells, 2019.
81. Wallace-Wells, 2019.
82. The *Weekly Standard's* paid circulation dropped by less than 10% between 2016 and 2017 (Schwartz, 2018).
83. Beck, 2010.
84. Barr, 2010; Reeve, 2013a.
85. Vogel & McCalmont, 2011.
86. https://therighting.com/top-20/august-2024-top-20-right-wing-news-websites/
87. https://talkers.com/top-talk-audiences/
88. Corcoran, 2009.
89. Hemmer, 2016.
90. McKnight, 2012.
91. Fang, 2012.
92. Fang, 2012.
93. Mayer, 2019a.
94. Mayer, 2019a.
95. The Clinton Foundation story, which started in 2015, claimed that Hillary Clinton traded favors on State Department policy with donations to the Clinton Foundation. As Faris et al. (2017) meticulously documented, the story was based on the book *Clinton Cash*, written by Peter Schweitzer—a cofounder of the think tank Government Accountability Institute. After promoting many dubious claims in the book, Breitbart launched the movie version of *Clinton Cash* on the eve of the Democratic Convention in 2016, which was strategically timed to generate maximal attention (Faris et al., 2017).
96. The Biden–Ukraine conspiracy theory claimed that then Vice President Joe Biden abused his power to protect Burisma, a Ukraine gas company where Biden's son Hunter served as a board member. It was based on the book *Secret Empire*, which was also written by Peter Schweitzer. Soon after the book was published, right-wing media, including Breitbart, began to promote the conspiracy theory, which then led Trump to pressure Ukraine to produce more damaging information about Joe Biden. This ultimately led to Trump's first impeachment.

97. Hananoki, 2022.
98. Farhi, 2019; Rosenwald, 2019.
99. Farhi, 2019.
100. Rosenwald, 2019; Skocpol & Williamson, 2016; Stelter, 2020.
101. Political objectives and commercial goals are often deeply intertwined, especially for right-wing media outlets aiming to attract mass audiences. As discussed, building a commercially successful brand with a large following can transform audience loyalty into votes, phone calls, and donations, which can amplify the political influence of right-wing media. However, as this chapter shows, many prominent right-wing media outlets have sustained years of financial losses while pursuing political goals. We should not overemphasize profit-making as right-wing media's primary goal. In the book *Talk Radio's America*, Brian Rosenwald relegates ideological and political aims of right-wing media to secondary importance, arguing that "hosts and media executives . . . aimed to provide the most compelling entertainment product possible and thereby reap maximal profits. Any ideological or political agenda was secondary" (Rosenwald, 2019, p. 256). Similarly, Harvard professor Yochai Benkler links the origin of right-wing media propaganda to profit motives, explaining that "changes in political culture created a large new market segment for media that emphasized white, Christian identity as a political identity; and that a series of regulatory and technological changes . . . displaced [traditional programming] by a strategy that provided a substantial part of the market with uniquely tailored content" (Benkler, 2020, p. 52). While a profit-driven approach can indeed explain why some right-wing media outlets aligned with Donald Trump, it's crucial not to overgeneralize the argument or push it to the extreme—such as by asserting that Fox's media coverage was purely shaped by preexisting audience preferences. Rupert Murdoch had clear ideological and political preferences, as he actively directed media coverage to align with his political projects, including supporting the Iraq War. Overemphasizing audience demand for identity-affirming content as the primary driver of Fox's behavior downplays the influence of media elites, like Murdoch, in shaping audiences' perceptions and channeling them toward specific political agendas (Bauer & Nadler, 2019; Peck, 2019). For instance, after the 2020 election, many Fox hosts felt pressured to endorse Trump's election lies to avoid alienating their viewers. However, it was Fox—along with other right-wing media—that initially cast doubt on mail-in voting during the early stages of the 2020 election (Benkler et al., 2020), arguably setting the stage for Trump and his supporters to later question the election results.

Chapter 2

1. Hettena, 2020.
2. Here is an example from the *Washington Post*'s reporting on this topic. https://www.washingtonpost.com/politics/graham-launches-probe-into-bidens-burisma-and-ukraine/2019/11/21/5a5675b4-0ca5-11ea-97ac-a7ccc8dd1ebc_story.html
3. These patterns are not unique to the Trump era. The weaponization of journalistic practices dates to the 1990s, when political operatives such as Chris Ruddy and David Brock pushed numerous conspiracy theories about Bill and Hillary Clinton. The Biden–Ukraine conspiracy theory bears striking resemblance to the decades-old Clinton Body Count conspiracy theory, which claimed the Clintons were implicated in the death of the former deputy White House counsel Vincent Foster: Both conspiracy theories were borne of opposition research that was conducted by political operatives, paid for by billionaires, and legitimized by conservative news organizations. In fact, many mainstream media outlets have also fallen prey (Faris et al., 2017; Marwick & Lewis, 2017), unwittingly aiding the spread of factually dubious narratives.
4. Hettena, 2020; Merchant, 2022.
5. Hettena, 2020; Sherman, 2014; Kotch, 2020.
6. Sullivan, 2018.
7. Confessore & Bank, 2019; Mayer, 2019a; Stelter, 2020a.
8. Brock & Rabin-Harvt, 2012.
9. Nadler et al., 2020.
10. Heft et al., 2020.
11. The Heft et al. (2020) study underestimated the number of articles published by Breitbart. The study found that Breitbart published approximately 30 articles per day between June and July 2018. Yet, using a different data source, I found that Breitbart in fact published more than 500 articles per day during that period.
12. In the current U.S. context, the ideological right is often associated with White, Christian identity and positions on issues like LGBTQ+ rights, climate change, school vouchers, gun rights, abortion, government regulation, affirmative action, and social welfare (Benkler et al., 2018; Hochschild, 2018; Mason, 2018). However, it has broadened its appeal among specific demographic groups—such as male Latino voters and young voters—by adopting a more isolationist stance on foreign policy and a populist approach to certain economic policies. Some scholars quantified media's ideological bias via analyzing the ideological preferences of their audiences (Gentzkow & Shapiro, 2011) or media content (Groseclose & Milyo, 2005); others relied on fact-checkers to classify media bias (Budak et al., 2016; Greene, 2024; Li & Bond, 2023; Yang et al., 2024).

13. The *Wall Street Journal* was not included in the analysis. Despite its right-leaning editorials and op-eds, its news reporting, according to fact checkers (e.g., Ad Fontes and Media Bias Fact Check) whose ideological bias ratings are widely used in political communication research, does not exhibit a strong ideological bias. The Drudge Report was also not included in the analysis. Historically, founder Matt Drudge occasionally published original stories on Drudge. But the website has largely functioned as a news aggregation website for many years, linking to stories from various external sources.
14. I use Securities and Exchange Commission filings, About pages on right-wing media sites, and their profiles on LinkedIn to gauge the size of their staff, including leadership, editors, writers, and reporters. Next, I collect data on journalistic standards and ethics from each right-wing media's website. These analyses were completed in 2021. Last, I use the content data from NewsWhip, a news analytic company that tracks the content of hundreds of thousands of online publishers, to quantify each right-wing media's content supply and performance on Facebook between 2017 and 2020. Data was collected in December 2021.
15. The 21 mainstream media outlets came from Pew Research's Election News Pathways Project. See https://www.journalism.org/2020/01/24/media-polarization-methodology/ for a more detailed description.
16. Ingram, 2015.
17. Conferssore & Bank, 2019; Zekeria, 2020.
18. Hindman, 2018.
19. Yang et al., 2023.
20. Hagey & Horwitz, 2019.
21. To be sure, mass readership is not the only yardstick to measure a right-wing media outlet's influence. Some conservative publications, such as the *National Review* and the *Weekly Standard*, are never meant to be read by millions of people. Their influence depends on a different social currency: the attention of Washington insiders. For them, who reads the article is more important than how many people read the article. This chapter's focus on high-engagement articles shows the pattern of popular content consumed by a readership that most likely approximates the average Republican primary voters. Chapter 3, however, focuses on a story that was likely designed to appeal to political elites in Washington. As I will show in Chapter 3, even though the topic of the story involving infighting within the Trump White House does not appear to have an appeal for mass readership, outlets like Breitbart and the Daily Caller still devoted significant coverage to the story.
22. STM is a variant of Latent Dirichlet allocation (LDA) topic models that allow covariates to influence topics (Roberts et al., 2014). Following established practices, I transformed the "Day" variable through b-spline to account for nonlinear time series effects on topics.

23. Drezner, 2018.
24. Berry & Sobieraj, 2013; Young, 2023.
25. There are also billionaires such as Charles Koch on the political right who clashed with Trump over certain ideological disagreements.
26. Stelter, 2017.
27. Wood, 2017.
28. Nakashima et al., 2017.
29. Kiely, 2017.
30. Krafft & Donavan, 2020, p. 195.
31. The *National Review* and Hot Air did track the Heat Street story but failed to question or verify its claims.
32. Kessler, 2017.
33. The memo is formally known as the Foreign Intelligence Surveillance Act Abuse at the Department of Justice and the Federal Bureau of Investigation.
34. The Steele dossier is a compilation of political opposition research on the ties between the 2016 Trump campaign and Russia compiled by the former British intelligence officer Christopher Steele. The dossier was indirectly funded by the DNC and the Clinton 2016 campaign.
35. DOJ, 2019.
36. In fact, the application contained an elaborate footnote that articulated the political context of the Steele dossier without naming the political actors explicitly.
37. Somodevilla, 2018; Spivak & Wittes, 2021.
38. Savage, 2018.
39. Spivak & Wittes, 2021.
40. Liptak et la., 2018.
41. Kessler, 2018.
42. Alba, 2019.
43. There were also many other disinformation narratives about Hunter Biden (e.g., his dealings in China) that did not focus on Ukraine or Burisma but could still be considered as part of the larger disinformation campaign targeting Biden and his family in the 2020 election.
44. Stern & Dixon, 2020.
45. O'Rourke, 2020.
46. Gallagher, 2020.
47. Chen et al., 2021; Evanega et al., 2020.
48. Yang & Bennett, 2021.

Chapter 3

1. Brock, 2005; Brock & Rabin-Havt, 2012.
2. Fang, 2012.
3. Mayer, 2019a.
4. Jamieson & Cappella, 2008.

5. Benkler et al., 2018.
6. Alberta, 2019, p. 596.
7. In 1986, Reagan signed a bill into law that made any immigrant who had entered the United States before 1982 eligible for amnesty.
8. Jamieson & Cappella, 2008, p. 42.
9. Jamieson & Cappella, 2008, p. 6.
10. Winter & Groll, 2017.
11. McMaster, 2024.
12. The anti-McMaster campaign died off after Bannon was forced out of the White House on August 18. McMaster continued to serve in the Trump administration for another nine months before he was replaced by former U.S. ambassador to the United Nations John Bolton.
13. Hemmer, 2022.
14. Keefe, 2018.
15. McMaster, 2024.
16. Benkler et al., 2018.
17. Mackey, 2016.
18. Hylton, 2017.
19. Warren, 2017.
20. Donald Trump considered Susan Rice a political opponent who sought to undermine him by unmasking the identities of his associates in a surveillance program run by U.S. intelligence agencies.
21. Warren, 2017.
22. I coded each article in terms of its stance on McMaster. For opinion pieces, I coded the article as "negative" if it criticized McMaster or called for his resignation, "positive" if it defended McMaster or criticized those involved in the campaign to oust him, and "neutral" if it included two opposing views about McMaster without drawing a conclusion of its own. For articles written in a straight news format, I coded the article as "negative" if it portrayed McMaster in an unfavorable or compromising light. I coded the article as "neutral" if it framed the controversy as a factional fight within the White House or presented materials from both sides. I coded the article as "positive" if it only used materials that praised or supported McMaster. I assigned each negative article, neutral article, and positive article a score of −1, 0, and 1, respectively, and aggregated the scores at the media level to represent each media's stance on McMaster. I considered sites with an average score above 0 as pro-McMaster sites, those at 0 as neutral sites, and those below 0 as anti-McMaster sites.
23. Ten right-wing media sites were excluded from this case study for one of the following reasons: They did not produce any relevant articles (e.g., thelaststand.com), they were defunct at the time of the controversy (e.g., endingthefed.com), or their RSS feed was not correctly collected by Media Cloud at the time of the controversy (e.g., WJLA). Data were first extracted based on the Boolean search term "McMaster" AND "National Security Advisor" AND ("firing" OR "firings" OR "fired").

Chapter 4

1. Fifteen major right-wing media sites were excluded from this case study for one of the following reasons: They did not produce any relevant articles (e.g., thelaststand.com); they were defunct at the time of the controversy (e.g., McMasterleaks.com); their RSS feeds were not correctly collected and indexed by Media Cloud at the time of the controversy (e.g., whatreallyhappened.com, Real Clear Politics, Weekly Standard); or their coverage was not in the format of articles. Data were collected based on the Boolean search terms "Ford" AND "Kavanaugh" in Media Cloud.
2. Alberta, 2019, p. 526.
3. Each article was coded in terms of whether it attacked Christine Ford. An article was considered to be engaging in personal attacks if it ridiculed Ford, questioned her motives, or portrayed her or her legal team as having ulterior motives. Articles that focused on personal attacks took various forms. Some were disinformation stories or opposition research that mimicked the format of straight news reporting. They usually adopted an impersonal tone but spread false information that was presented as factual statements or created misleading impressions by changing the context of the facts presented. Some were editorials and op-eds that mixed exaggeration, speculation, ridicule, or sarcasm with false or misleading information. An article was not considered to be engaging in personal attacks if it met the following criteria. First, if the article was written in the format of a straight news report, it must not use any materials that undermined Ford's credibility alone. This means that an article would be considered as engaging in personal attacks if it quoted only sources that attacked Christine Ford without presenting a counter viewpoint. Second, if the article was an opinion piece, to be considered as not engaging in personal attacks, it must not raise any questions about Ford's credibility, motives, or character. Yet, an article that simply pointed out the gaps in Ford's memory or argued that Ford's account lacked corroborating evidence was not considered as engaging in personal attacks.
4. All unique original sources were identified in each article. Original sources were defined as people or organizations cited as the origins of direct or indirect quotes. In cases where the author of an article cites an original source (e.g., politicians) through an intermediary (e.g., mainstream media), only the original source was identified and categorized. For instance, Twitter often served as an intermediary for right-wing media to get quotes from politicians. For original sources cited through tweets, I checked the description of the source's Twitter account and categorized the source according to his or her organizational affiliation.
5. Faris et al., 2017.
6. Because the controversy was about Kavanaugh and Ford, it is expected that right-wing media cited these two sources extensively. For this study, it was not necessary to include them in the coding scheme.

7. King et al., 1994.
8. The chi-square test on stance and format shows that these two variables are correlated. A logistic regression of "format" on 10 different types of sources shows that "format" is correlated to GOP sources and right leaning media sources. Hence, format was included as a control variable.
9. The centralization score (Freeman, 1979) measures the extent to which the network is organized around its most central point. The general procedure is to quantify the differences between the degree-based centrality scores of the most central point and those of all other points. Centralization is the ratio of the sum of differences to the maximum possible sum of differences. The score varies from 0 to 1, with 0 representing a complete graph where every node is connected to every other node, and 1 representing a star network in which only one node has a degree greater than 1. The centralization score was computed using Freeman (1979)'s degree-based centralization in R's sna package.

Chapter 5

1. Mueller, 2019.
2. Mueller, 2019.
3. Isikoff, 2019.
4. Bump, 2019; Isikoff, 2019.
5. The Boolean search terms used to extract relevant tweets about Seth Rich were "#sethrich" OR ("Seth AND Rich"). Crimson Hexagon kept the metadata for all posts captured by search strings, but the content of deleted tweets was removed from its database. More details can be found at https://www.crimsonhexagon.com. The search was conducted in October 2017. The total volume of historical tweets about Seth Rich between July 10, 2016, and August 8, 2016, was 74,169, with 16,783 deleted tweets.
6. The Boolean search terms used to extract articles about Seth Rich were "Seth AND Rich." Media Cloud took two steps to identify relevant articles: First, it searched through its inventory of articles published by right-wing media sources in the five collections that I specified (U.S. Conservative Political Blogs, U.S. Top 25 Conservative Political Blogs, Center Right, Right, and Buzzfeed Hyper-Partisan Sources) and collected those "seed articles" that met the search requirements; second, it harvested the hyperlinks in the seed articles and collected hyperlinked articles if they also met the search requirements.
7. Noble & Blake, 2016.
8. https://www.youtube.com/watch?v=Kp7FkLBRpKg
9. Sexton, 2016.
10. Bump, 2017.
11. Folkenflik, 2017.
12. The article also stated that both the Metropolitan Police and the FBI's national office declined to comment. Only at the end of the article did Fox

News include a sliver of denial from Rich's father, written as "he didn't believe his son would leak emails."

13. The story also included a series of denials—the D.C. mayor Muriel Bowser called the claim about the stand-down order preposterous, a spokesperson for the FBI's Washington field office denied that the FBI was involved in the case, and Rich's family denied that Seth Rich was linked to WikiLeaks.
14. The police statement released on May 15 reads, "The assertions put forward by Mr. Wheeler are unfounded. The Metropolitan Police Department's (MPD) Homicide Branch is actively investigating Mr. Rich's murder and we continue to work with the family to bring closure to this case as we do with all homicide investigations. If there are any individuals who feel they have information, we urge them to call us at 202-727-9099 or text us at 50,411. The department is offering a reward of up to $25,000 for information on this case that leads to the arrest and conviction of the person or persons responsible." When citing the statement, Fox News omitted the first sentence.
15. Between May 15 and May 23, five sites—the Daily Wire, the Daily Caller, Hot Air, the Right Scoop, and the *Washington Examiner*—later cast doubt on Fox's story after initially repeating the falsehood.
16. Rosenwald, 2019.
17. Fox News and Fox 5 DC were combined into the single organizational entity Fox in the network analysis.
18. Berger, 2018.
19. Severns, 2018.

Chapter 6

1. https://www.fec.gov/files/legal/murs/8117/8117_18.pdf
2. Craig et al., 2014; Jamieson, 1992.
3. Benson, 2012.
4. Reuters, 2024.
5. Bob Woodward made the comment in an interview with TOV journalist Steve Paikin in February 2023. https://www.youtube.com/watch?v=5yBHNpKTIEE&t=2362s
6. Domke et al., 1999.
7. Gans, 1979; Tuchman, 1978.
8. Sparrow, 2006.
9. Lee, 2005.
10. Nyhan, 2012.
11. Lee, 2005.
12. These outlets are CNN, NBC News, ABC News, CBS News, MSNBC News, NPR, the *New York Times*, the *Washington Post*, PBS, the *Wall Street Journal*, *USA Today*, Politico, Huffington Post, *Time*, *The Hill*, *Newsweek*, Vox, Business Insider, and Vice.
13. Pew Research Center, 2020.

14. Baldasty, 1992.
15. Fish, 1967, p. 123, cited in Sheppard, 2007.
16. Baldasty, 1992.
17. Baldasty, 1992; Campbell, 2019.
18. Baldasty, 1992.
19. Campbell, 2019.
20. Baldasty, 1992; Campbell, 2019.
21. Sheppard, 2007.
22. Baldasty, 1992.
23. Campbell, 2019.
24. Groeling & Baum, 2013.
25. Benkler et al., 2020.
26. Collins, 2017.
27. Rosenwald, 2019.
28. Markels, 2005.
29. Palmeri, 2017.
30. Hacker & Pierson, 2020.
31. Levitsky & Ziblatt, 2023.
32. https://freespeechforpeople.org/wp-content/uploads/2018/02/Signed-Notarized-FSFP-Complaint-v-Trump-AMI-2-16-18-1.pdf
33. "Contribution" is defined by FECA as "any gift, subscription, loan, advance, or deposit of money or anything of value made by any person for the purpose of influencing any election for federal office."
34. The press exemption, as Stanford law professor Michael McConnell argued, likely also applies to nonperiodic communications in formats not mentioned explicitly in FECA, such as the Internet, films, and books (McConnell, 2013).
35. Mueller, 2023.
36. https://www.fec.gov/files/legal/murs/8117/8117_18.pdf
37. https://www.sec.gov/Archives/edgar/data/1754301/000162828024036123/fox-20240630.htm?utm_source=chatgpt.com
38. https://crsreports.congress.gov/product/pdf/IF/IF11992/2
39. Peters, 2022.
40. Prokop, 2023.
41. Peters, 2022.
42. Chotiner, 2020.
43. Folkenflik, 2022.

Appendix

1. BuzzFeed classified the partisanship of media based on content. It manually reviewed the content and the About pages of some 600 partisan sites and found that more than 400 right-wing media either self-identified as right-wing or conservative media or published content that reflected a right-wing slant (Silverman et al., 2017). MBFC adopted a similar

approach, categorizing not only the partisanship of media outlets but also their facticity.

2. PJ Media's ranking was based on the average rankings from Alexa, which ranks websites by a combined measure of unique visitors and page views, Quantcast, which ranks websites by the number of U.S. monthly visits, and SimilarWeb, which ranks websites by the number of monthly visits (Bolyard, 2017).
3. Conservative Tribune was acquired by Western Journal in 2015.
4. Truth Feed became defunct in 2018.
5. Ending the Fed became defunct in 2017.
6. Heat Street became defunct in 2018.
7. McMaster Leaks became defunct in 2017.
8. Circa became defunct in 2019.
9. Govtslaves.com became defunct in 2019.
10. *Weekly Standard* was shuttered in 2018.
11. Thelaststand.com became defunct in 2017.
12. Whatreallyhappened.com was not tracked by NewsWhip.
13. Five media outlets—whatreallyhappened.com, thelaststand.com, Daily Sheeple, govtslaves.com, and disobedient media—were not tracked by NewsWhip at the time of data collection.
14. Conservative Review was excluded because its articles' full text was not retrievable. Twitchy was excluded because most of its articles were not written in a standard news or opinion article format.
15. Excerpts were one- or two-sentence summaries of the article provided by the publishers to NewsWhip.
16. Setting the word threshold reduced the number of terms in each corpus to the range between 5,000 and 8,000, which allowed me to use the default initialization method "spectral" in the STM package. The "spectral" initialization method generally performs well on corpora with fewer than 10,000 terms. All models were initialized using "spectral."
17. Vice and the BBC were removed because of their non-English content.

BIBLIOGRAPHY

Adair, B. (2024). *The Beyond the Big Lie: The epidemic of political lying, why Republicans do it more, and how it could burn down our democracy*. Simon & Schuster.

Aday, S. (2010). Chasing the bad news: An analysis of 2005 Iraq and Afghanistan war coverage on NBC and Fox News Channel. *Journal of communication, 60*(1), 144–164.

Adolph, C. (2016). *simcf: Counterfactuals and confidence intervals for estimated regression models.* (R package version 0.2.17.)

Alba, D. (2019, October 29). Debunking 4 viral rumors about the Bidens and Ukraine. *The New York Times.*

Alberta, T. (2019). *American carnage: On the frontlines of the Republican civil war and the rise of President Trump.* Harper.

Arango, T. (2009, August 2). New owner for a magazine as political tastes change. *The New York Times.*

Arceneaux, K., & Johnson, M. (2013). *Changing minds or changing channels?: Partisan news in an age of choice.* University of Chicago Press.

Arceneaux, K., Dunaway, J., Johnson, M., & Wielen, R. (2024). *The house that Fox News built?* Cambridge University Press.

Auletta, K. (2007, June 25). Promises, promises. *The New Yorker.*

Azari, J. R. (2016). How the news media helped to nominate Trump. *Political Communication, 33*(4), 677–680.

Baldasty, G. J. (1992). *The commercialization of news in the nineteenth century.* University of Wisconsin Press.

Barberá, P., Casas, A., Nagler, J., Egan, P. J., Bonneau, R., Jost, J. T., & Tucker, J. A. (2019). Who leads? Who follows? Measuring issue attention and agenda setting by legislators and the mass public using social media data. *American Political Science Review, 113*(4), 883–901.

Bardella, K. (2018, January 10). Inside Steve Bannon's Fight Club. *The New York Times*.

Barr, A. (2010). *Beck links up with FreedomWorks*. Politico.

Bauer, A. J. (2017). *Before "fair and balanced": Conservative media activism and the rise of the new right* (PhD dissertation). New York University.

Bauer, A. J., & Nadler, A. (2019). Taking conservative news seriously. In A. Nadler & A. J. Bauer (Eds.), *News on the right: Studying conservative news cultures* (pp. 1–16). Oxford University Press.

Bauer, A. J., Juarez Miro, C., & Giraldo, I. (2024). Introduction—The curse of relevance: Challenges facing right-wing studies. *Journal of Right-Wing Studies, 2*(1), 1–15.

Baum, M. A., & Groeling, T. (2008). New media and the polarization of American political discourse. *Political Communication, 25*(4), 345–365.

Beck, G. (2010, May 18). *FreedomWorks* [Video]. YouTube. https://www.youtube.com/watch?v=EU8nfVt77So

Benkler, Y., Faris, R., & Roberts, H. (2018). *Network propaganda: Manipulation, disinformation, and radicalization in American politics*. Oxford University Press.

Benkler, Y. (2020) A political economy of the origins of asymmetric propaganda in American media. In L. Bennett & S. Livingston (Eds.), *The disinformation age: Politics, technology, and disruptive communication in the United States* (pp. 43–66), Cambridge University Press.

Benkler, Y., Tilton, C., Etling, B., Roberts, H., Clark, J., Faris, R., . . . & Schmitt, C. (2020). *Mail-in voter fraud: Anatomy of a disinformation campaign*. The Berkman Klein Center for Internet & Society. https://papers.ssrn.com/sol3/papers.cfm?abstract_id=3703701

Bennett, W. L. (2016). *News: The politics of illusion*. University of Chicago Press.

Bennett, W. L., Segerberg, A., & Walker, S. (2014). Organization in the crowd: Peer production in large-scale networked protests. *Information, Communication & Society, 17*(2), 232–260.

Bennett, W. L., & Livingston, S. (2003). Editors' introduction: A semi-independent press: Government control and journalistic autonomy in the political construction of news. *Political Communication, 20*(4), 359–362.

Bennett, W. L. (2015). Indexing theory. *The International Encyclopedia of Political Communication*, 1–5.

Bennett, W. L. (2017). Press-government relations in a changing media environment. In K. Kenski & K. H. Jamieson (Eds.), *The Oxford Handbook of Political Communication* (pp. 249–262). Oxford University Press.

Bennett, W. L. (1990). Toward a theory of press-state. *Journal of Communication, 40*(2), 103–127.

Bennett, W. L., Lawrence, R. G., & Livingston, S. (2008). *When the press fails: Political power and the news media from Iraq to Katrina.* University of Chicago Press.

Benson, E., (2012). Dukakis's regret. *New York Magazine.*

Berger, J. (2018, October 29). Trump is the glue that binds the far right. *The Atlantic.*

Berry, J. M., & Sobieraj, S. (2013). *The outrage industry: Political opinion media and the new incivility.* Oxford University Press.

Bimber, B., Cynthia, S., & Flanagin, A. (2009). Technological change and the shifting nature of political organizations. In A. Chadwick & P. Howard (Eds.), *Routledge handbook of internet politics* (pp.72–85). Routledge.

Blackwell, M. (2015). *The real nature of politics.* Leadership Institute.

Blanco, A., Wolfe, D., & Gardner, A. (2022, November 7). Tracking which 2020 election deniers are winning, losing in the midterms. *The Washington Post.*

Boczkowski, P. J., & Papacharissi, Z. (Eds.). (2018). *Trump and the media.* MIT Press.

Bolyard, P. (2017, December 27). Top 50 conservative websites for 2017. *PJ Media.* https://pjmedia.com/news-and-politics/paula-bolyard/2017/12/27/50-top-conservative-websites-in-2017-n55260

Bogus, C. (2011). *William F. Buckley Jr. and the rise of American conservatism.* Bloomsbury.

Borchers, C. (2017, June 2). Charity doubles as a profit stream at the Daily Caller News Foundation. *The Washington Post.*

Boykoff, M. T., & Boykoff, J. M. (2004). Balance as bias: Global warming and the US prestige press. *Global Environmental Change, 14*(2), 125–136.

Brock, D. (2005). *The Republican noise machine: Right-wing media and how it corrupts democracy.* Three Rivers Press (CA).

Brock, D., & Rabin-Havt, A. (2012). *The Fox effect: How Roger Ailes turned a network into a propaganda machine.* Anchor.

Broockman, D., & Kalla, J. (2022). The impacts of selective partisan media exposure: A field experiment with Fox News viewers. *OSF Preprints,* doi.org/10.31219/osf.io/jrw26.

Buckley, W. (1955). National Review statement of intentions. In G. Schneider (Ed.), *Conservatism in American since 1930* (pp. 195–200). New York University.

Budak, C., Goel, S., & Rao, J. M. (2016). Fair and balanced? Quantifying media bias through crowdsourced content analysis. *Public Opinion Quarterly, 80*(S1), 250–271.

Bump, P. (2017, August 1). A timeline of the explosive lawsuit alleging a White House link in the Seth Rich conspiracy. *The Washington Post.*

Bump, P. (2019, July 9). Don't blame the Seth Rich conspiracy on Russians. Blame Americans. *The Washington Post.*

Buozis, M., & Konieczna, M. (2021). Conservative news nonprofits: Claiming legitimacy without transparency. *Journalism*, *24*(6), 1211–1231.

Byers, D. (2015, March 31). *National Review goes nonprofit.* Politico.

Campbell, S. (2019). *The bank war and the partisan press.* University of Kansas Press.

Carlson, T. (2023, March 14). Tucker Carlson Tonight [Transcript]. *Fox News Channel.* Retrieved May 9, 2023, from Factiva database (Dow Jones).

Carlson, M., Robinson, S., & Lewis, S. C. (2021). *News after trump: Journalism's crisis of relevance in a changed media culture.* Oxford University Press.

Chadwick, A. (2007). Digital network repertoires and organizational hybridity. *Political Communication*, *24*(3), 283–301.

Chadwick, A., Vaccari, C., & O'Loughlin, B. (2018). Do tabloids poison the well of social media? Explaining democratically dysfunctional news sharing. *New Media & Society*, *20*(11), 4255–4274.

Chen, E., Chang, H., Rao, A., Lerman, K., Cowan, G., & Ferrara, E. (2021). Covid-19 misinformation and the 2020 US presidential election. *The Harvard Kennedy School Misinformation Review*, *1*(7), 1–17.

Chinni, D. (2002). The Other paper: The Washington Times's role. *Columbia Journalism Review*, https://web.archive.org/web/20060419012416/https://www.cjr.org/issues/2002/5/wash-chinni.asp.

Chotiner, I. (2020, November 24). Why NewsMax support Trump's false voter-fraud claims. *The New Yorker.*

Clinton, J. D., & Enamorado, T. (2014). The national news media's effect on Congress: How Fox News affected elites in Congress. *The Journal of Politics*, *76*(4), 928–943.

CNN. (2021, June 16). *CNN special report: Assault on democracy.* https://cnnpressroom.blogs.cnn.com/2021/06/16/cnn-special-report-assault-on-democracy-the-roots-of-trumps-insurrection/

Collins, B., & Schecter, A. (2019, November 19). Stephen Miller planted anti-Rubio stories in Breitbart during 2016 campaign, leaked emails show. *NBC News.*

Collins, E. (2017, September 29). Steve Bannon's Breitbart is going to war against GOP incumbents. *USA Today.*

Coppins, M. (2017). What if the right-wing media wins? *Columbia Journalism Review.* https://www.cjr.org/special_report/right-wing-media-breitbart-fox-bannon-carlson-hannity-coulter-trump.php

Confessore, N., & Bank, J. (2019, August 21). In the Trump era, a family's fight with Google and Facebook over disinformation. *The New York Times.*

Corcoran, M. (2009, September 1). The Weekly Standard's war. *Fairness & Accuracy in Reporting.*

Craig, S. C., Rippere, P. S., & Grayson, M. S. (2014). Attack and response in political campaigns: An experimental study in two parts. *Political Communication, 31*(4), 647–674.

Darcy, O. (2017, September 19). Bannon orders Breitbart to step up negative coverage of Trump-backed candidate. *CNN.*

DellaVigna, S., & Kaplan, E. (2007). The Fox News effect: Media bias and voting. *The Quarterly Journal of Economics, 122*(3), 1187–1234.

Dibranco, A. (2020). Conservative news and movement infrastructure. In A. Nadler & A. J. Bauer (Eds.), *News on the right: Studying Conservative News Cultures* (157–173). Oxford University Press.

DOJ (2019). *Review of four FISA applications and other aspects of the FBI's Crossfire Hurricane investigation.* Office of the Inspector General, U.S. Department of Justice.

Dominion, Inc., and Dominion Voting Systems Corporation v. Fox News Network, LLC, N21C-03-257 EMD (2023). https://int.nyt.com/data/documenttools/redacted-documents-in-dominion-fox-news-case/dca5e3880422426f/full.pdf

Domke, D., Watts, M. D., Shah, D. V., & Fan, D. P. (1999). The politics of conservative elites and the "liberal media" argument. *Journal of Communication, 49*(4), 35–58.

Drezner, D. (2018, January 17). The Fox News effect. *The Washington Post.*

Ellefson, L. (2019, August 7). Breitbart's audience has dropped 72% since Trump took office—as other right-wing sites have gained. *The Wrap.*

Evanega, S., Lynas, M., Adams, J., Smolenyak, K., & Insights, C. G. (2020). Coronavirus misinformation: Quantifying sources and themes in the Covid-19 "infodemic." *JMIR Preprints, 19*(10), 1–13.

Fang, L. (2012). *The Machine: A field guide to the resurgent right.* New Press.

Farhi, P. (2019, December 3). Fox News personalities continue to stump for GOP candidates. *The Washington Post.*

Faris, R., Roberts, H., Etling, B., Bourassa, N., Zuckerman, E., & Benkler, Y. (2017). Partisanship, propaganda, and disinformation: Online media and the 2016 US presidential election. *Berkman Klein Center Research Publication,* https://papers.ssrn.com/sol3/Delivery.cfm?abstractid=3019414.

Farrell, J. (2016a). Network structure and influence of the climate change counter-movement. *Nature Climate Change, 6*(4), 370–374.

Farrell, J. (2016b). Corporate funding and ideological polarization about climate change. *Proceedings of the National Academy of Sciences, 113*(1), 92–97.

Feldman, L., Maibach, E. W., Roser-Renouf, C., & Leiserowitz, A. (2012). Climate on cable: The nature and impact of global warming coverage on Fox News, CNN, and MSNBC. *The International Journal of Press/Politics, 17*(1), 3–31.

Fish, C. R. (1967). *The civil service and the patronage.* Russell & Russell.

Fischer, S. (2021, January 19). The Daily Wire is profitable, and eyeing entertainment. *Axios.*

Folkenflik, D. (2017, August 1). Behind Fox News' baseless Seth Rich story: The untold tale. *NPR.*

Folkenflik, D. (2022, August 9). Analysis: Fox and right-wing media snap to Trump's defense after FBI search. *NPR.*

Freelon, D., & Wells, C. (2020). Disinformation as political communication. *Political Communication, 37*(2), 145–156.

Freeman, L. C. (1979). Centrality in social networks I: Conceptual clarification. *Social Networks, 1*, 215–239.

Friedersdorf, C. (2017, December 29). Breitbart's astonishing confession. *The Atlantic.*

Fuller, J. (2014, April 4). Meet the wealthy donor who's trying to get Republicans to support gay marriage. *The Washington Post.*

Gallagher, F. (2020, April 22). Tracking hydroxychloroquine misinformation: How an unproven Covid-19 treatment ended up being endorsed by Trump. *ABC News.*

Gans, H. (1979). *Deciding what's news.* Vintage Books.

Gavin, D. (2020). Party domination and base mobilization: Donald Trump and Republican party building in a polarized era. *The Forum: A Journal of Applied Research in Contemporary Politics, 18*(2), 135–168.

Gelman, A., & Hill, J. (2006). *Data analysis using regression and multilevel/hierarchical models.* Cambridge University Press.

Gentzkow, M., & Shapiro, J. M. (2011). Ideological segregation online and offline. *The Quarterly Journal of Economics, 126*(4), 1799–1839.

Gertz, M. (2022, May 16). Fox News is the Republican Party. Here are over 400 examples proving it. *Media Matters.*

Gibson, G., & Chiacu, D. (2019, April 18). Trump curses Mueller appointment: This is the end of my presidency. *Reuters.*

Gold, M., & Hohmann, J. (2017, January 29). Koch network condemns Trump ban on refugees and immigrants. *The Washington Post.*

Green, M. (2011, October 31). Behind Sean Hannity's desk. *GQ.*

Greene, K. T. (2024). Partisan differences in the sharing of low-quality news sources by US political elites. *Political Communication, 41*(3), 373–392.

Grimmer, J., & Stewart, B. M. (2013). Text as data: The promise and pitfalls of automatic content analysis methods for political texts. *Political Analysis, 21*(3), 267–297.

Groeling, T. (2008). Who's the fairest of them all? An empirical test for partisan bias on ABC, CBS, NBC, and Fox News. *Presidential Studies Quarterly, 38*(4), 631–657.

Groeling, T., & Baum, M. (2013). Partisan news before Fox: Newspaper partisanship and partisan polarization, 1881–1972. In *APSA 2013 Annual Meeting Paper, American Political Science Association 2013 Annual Meeting.* https://www.hks.harvard.edu/publications/partisan-news-fox-newspaper-partisanship-and-partisan-polarization-1881-1972

Groseclose, T., & Milyo, J. (2005). A measure of media bias. *The Quarterly Journal of Economics, 120*(4), 1191–1237.

Gross, T. (2022, January 6). How Dan Bongino is building a right-wing media infrastructure in time for 2024. *NPR.*

Guess, A. M., Barberá, P., Munzert, S., & Yang, J. (2021). The consequences of online partisan media. *Proceedings of the National Academy of Sciences, 118*(14), 1–8.

Günther, E., & Domahidi, E. (2017). What communication scholars write about: An analysis of 80 years of research in high-impact journals. *International Journal of Communication, 11,* 3051–3071.

Hacker, J. S., & Pierson, P. (2006). *Off center: The Republican revolution and the erosion of American democracy.* Yale University Press.

Hacker, J. S., & Pierson, P. (2011). *Winner-take-all politics: How Washington made the rich richer—and turned its back on the middle class.* Simon & Schuster.

Hacker, J. S., & Pierson, P. (2020). *Let them eat tweets: How the right rules in an age of extreme inequality.* Liveright Publishing.

Hagey, K., & Horwitz, J. (2019, September 15). Facebook tried to make its platform a healthier place. It got angrier instead. *The Wall Street Journal.*

Hananoki, E. (2011, March 29). Cruise ship confession: Top Fox News executive admits lying on-air about Obamas. *Media Matters.*

Hananoki, E. (2022, May 16). Fox News' personalities have participated in more than 100 Republican events since 2017. *Media Matters.*

Hannity, S. (2017, November 14). Hannity [Transcript]. *Fox News Channel.* Retrieved March 9, 2023, from Factiva database (Dow Jones).

Hannity, S. (2020, November 5). Hannity [Transcript]. *Fox News Channel.* Retrieved March 9, 2023, from Factiva database (Dow Jones).

Hart, R. P. (2020). *Trump and us: What he says and why people listen.* Cambridge University Press.

Heft, A., Mayerhöffer, E., Reinhardt, S., & Knüpfer, C. (2020). Beyond Breitbart: Comparing right-wing digital news infrastructures in six western democracies. *Policy & Internet, 12*(1), 20–45.

Hemmer, N. (2016). *Messengers of the right.* University of Pennsylvania Press.

Hemmer, N. (2022). *Partisans: The conservative revolutionaries who remade American politics in the 1990s*. Basic Books.

Hendershot, H. (2011). *What is fair on the air?* University of Chicago Press.

Hettena, S. (2020, March 9). Is Zero Hedge a Russian Trojan Horse? *The New Republic*.

Hertel-Fernandez, A. (2019). *State capture: How conservative activists, big businesses, and wealthy donors reshaped the American states—and the nation*. Oxford University Press.

Hindman, M. (2018). *The Internet trap: How the digital economy builds monopolies and undermines democracy*. Princeton University Press.

Hochschild, A. (2018). *Strangers in their own land*. The New Press.

Hylton, W. (2017, August 16). Down the Breitbart hole. *The New York Times*.

Hyun, K. D., & Moon, S. J. (2016). Agenda setting in the partisan TV news context: Attribute agenda setting and polarized evaluation of presidential candidates among viewers of NBC, CNN, and Fox News. *Journalism & Mass Communication Quarterly*, *93*(3), 509–529.

Ingram, M. (2015, August 18). Facebook has taken over from Google as a traffic source for news. *Fortune*.

Isikoff, M. (2019, July 9). Exclusive: The true origins of the Seth Rich conspiracy theory. *Yahoo News*.

Jamieson, K. H., (1992). *Dirty politics: Deception, distraction, and democracy*. Oxford University Press.

Jamieson, K. H., Hardy, B. W., & Romer, D. (2007). The effectiveness of the press in serving the needs of American democracy. In K. H. Jamieson (Ed.), Institutions of American democracy: A republic divided (pp. 21–51). Oxford University Press.

Jamieson, K. H., & Cappella, J. N. (2008). *Echo chamber: Rush Limbaugh and the conservative media establishment*. Oxford University Press.

Keefe, P. (2018, April 23). McMaster and commander. *The New Yorker*.

Kennan, G. (1948). *The inauguration of organized political warfare* (Policy Planning Staff Memorandum). The U.S. State Department.

Kenner, D., Ellison, S., & O'Connell, J. (2024, March 26). Qatari royal invested about $50 million in pro-Trump network Newsmax. *The Washington Post*.

Kessler, G. (2017, March 5). Trump's "evidence" for Obama wiretap claims relies on sketchy, anonymously sourced reports. *The Washington Post*.

Kessler, G. (2018, February 9). Did Hillary Clinton collude with the Russians to get "dirt" on Trump to feed it to the FBI? *The Washington Post*.

Kessler, G. Rizzo, S., & Kelly, M. (2021, January 24). Trump's false or misleading claims total 30,573 over 4 years. *The Washington Post*.

Kiely, E. (2017) Revisiting Trump's wiretap tweets. *Factcheck.org*.

King, G., Keohane, R. O., & Verba, S. (1994). *Designing social inquiry: Scientific inference in qualitative research*. Princeton University Press.

Kotch, A. (2020, December 9). Who funds the Federalist? Finally, we know. *The Center for Media and Democracy*. https://www.exposedbycmd.org/2020/12/09/who-funds-the-federalist-finally-we-know/

Kotch, A. (2019, March 13). Charles Koch continues to bankroll the Tucker Carlson–founded Daily Caller. *Sludge*.

Krafft, P. M., & Donovan, J. (2020). Disinformation by design: The use of evidence collages and platform filtering in a media manipulation campaign. *Political Communication*, *37*(2), 194–214.

Lawrence, R. G., & Boydstun, A. E. (2017). What we should really be asking about media attention to Trump. *Political Communication*, *34*(1), 150–153.

Lee, T. T. (2005). The liberal media myth revisited: An examination of factors influencing perceptions of media bias. *Journal of Broadcasting & Electronic Media*, *49*(1), 43–64.

Levendusky, M. (2013). *How partisan media polarize America*. University of Chicago Press.

Levitsky, S., & Ziblatt, D. (2023). *Tyranny of the minority: Why American democracy reached the breaking point*. Penguin Random House.

Lewis, M. (2018, February 9). Has anyone seen the president? *Bloomberg*.

Li, Y., Bernard, J., & Luczak-Roesch, M. (2021). Beyond clicktivism: What makes digitally native activism effective? An exploration of the Sleeping Giants movement. *Social media + Society*, *7*(3), 1–22.

Li, Y., & Bond, R. M. (2023). Examining semantic (dis) similarity in news through news organizations' ideological similarity, similarity in truthfulness, and public engagement on social media: A network approach. *Human Communication Research*, *49*(1), 47–60.

Liebman, R. (1983). Mobilizing the moral majority. In R. Libebman & R. Wuthnow (Eds.), *The new Christian right: Mobilization and legitimation* (pp. 1–15). Aldine Publishing Company.

Liptak, K., Collins, K., Murray, S., & Merica, D. (2018, February 2) Trump moves towards releasing the memo he hopes will undermine Russia probe. *CNN*.

Mackey, R. (2016, November 16). Steve Bannon made Breitbart a space for pro-Israel writers and anti-Semitic readers. *The Intercept*.

MacLean, N. (2017). *Democracy in chains: The deep history of the radical right's stealth plan for America*. Penguin.

Maier, D., Waldherr, A., Miltner, P., Wiedemann, G., Niekler, A., Keinert, A., . . . & Adam, S. (2018). Applying LDA topic modeling in communication research: Toward a valid and reliable methodology. *Communication Methods and Measures*, *12*(2–3), 93–118.

Markels, A. (2005, October 27). Why Miers withdrew as Supreme Court nominee. *NPR.*

Marwick, A. E., & Lewis, R. (2017). Media manipulation and disinformation online. *Data & Society Research Institute* 359, 1146–1151.

Mason, L. (2018). *Uncivil agreement: How politics became our identity.* University of Chicago Press.

Mayer, J. (2010, August 23). Covert operations. *The New Yorker.*

Mayer, J. (2017a, March 17). The reclusive hedge-fund tycoon behind the Trump presidency. *The New Yorker.*

Mayer, J. (2017b). *Dark money: The hidden history of the billionaires behind the rise of the radical right.* Anchor.

Mayer, J. (2019a, March 11). The making of the Fox News White House. *The New Yorker.*

Mayer, J. (2019b, October 4). The invention of the conspiracy theory on Biden and Ukraine. *The New Yorker.*

McCarthy, J. D., & Zald, M. N. (1977). Resource mobilization and social movements: A partial theory. *American Journal of Sociology, 82*(6), 1212–1241.

McConnell, M. W. (2013). Reconsidering Citizens United as a Press Clause case. *Yale Law Journal, 123*, 412–458.

McGerr, M. (1986). *The decline of popular politics: The American North, 1865–1928.* Oxford University Press.

McGraw, M. (August 16, 2021). The GOP waves white flag in the same-sex marriage wars. *Politico.*

McMaster, H. R. (2024). *At war with our selves: My tour of duty in the Trump White House.* HarperCollins Publishers.

McKnight, D. (2010). Rupert Murdoch's News Corporation: A media institution with a mission. *Historical Journal of Film, Radio and Television, 30*(3), 303–316.

McKnight, D. (2012). *Murdoch's politics: How one man's thirst for wealth and power shapes our world.* Pluto Press.

Meek, A. (2022, April 9). The Daily Wire, for the first time, reveals the size of its paid subscriber base. *Forbes.*

Merchant, N (2022, February 15). U.S. accuses Zero Hedge of spreading Russian propaganda. *The Associated Press.*

Montgomery, P. (2014, June 13). Meet the billionaire brothers you never heard of who fund the religious right. *The American Prospect.*

Mueller, R. S. (2019). *The Mueller report: Report on the investigation into Russian interference in the 2016 presidential election.* U.S. Department of Justice.

Mueller, J. (2023, March 5). FEC complaints filed over allegations Murdoch gave Kushner unaired Biden political ads. *The Hill.*

Munger, K. (2020). All the news that's fit to click: The economics of clickbait media. *Political Communication*, *37*(3), 376–397.

Nadler, A., Bauer, A. J., & Konieczna, M. (2020). Conservative newswork: A report on the values and practices of online journalists on the right. *Columbia Journalism Review*.

Nadler, A., & Bauer, A.J. (2019). *News on the right: Studying conservative news cultures*. Oxford University Press.

Nakashima, E., Barrett, D., & Entous, A. (2017, April 11). FBI obtained FISA warrant to monitor former Trump adviser Carter Page. *The Washington Post*.

Narea, N. (2022, December 22). Sean Hannity's damming deposition in the Fox News defamation lawsuit, explained. *Vox*.

Nash, H. (1976). *The conservative intellectual movement in America since 1945*. Basic Books.

Nelson, A. (2021). *Shadow network: Media, money, and the secret hub of the radical right*. Bloomsbury Publishing.

Newsmax Media. (2002). *Registration statement under the Securities Act of 1933*. Securities and Exchange Commission.

Noble, A., & Blake, A. (2016, August 9) WikiLeaks offers $20,000 for information about murder of Seth Conrad Rich, DNC staffer. *The Washington Times*.

Nyhan, B. (2012). Does the US media have a liberal bias?: A discussion of Tim Groseclose's left turn: How liberal media bias distorts the American mind. *Perspectives on Politics*, *10*(3), 767–771.

Oliver, M. (2004, November 30). Rev. Billy James Hargis, 79: Pastor targeted communism. *Los Angeles Times*.

Oreskes, N., & Conway, E. M. (2011). *Merchants of doubt: How a handful of scientists obscured the truth on issues from tobacco smoke to global warming*. Bloomsbury Publishing USA.

O'Rourke, C. (2020). No, this photo doesn't show Joe and Hunter Biden with Burisma CEO. *PolitiFact*. The Poynter Institute.

Osnos, E. (2021, December 2021). Dan Bongino and the big business of returning Trump to power. *The New Yorker*.

Page, B. I., Seawright, J., & Lacombe, M. J. (2018). *Billionaires and stealth politics*. University of Chicago Press.

Palmeri, T. (2017, August 11) Breitbart's war on McMaster bites Bannon. *Politico*.

PBS. (2019, October 22). *Zero tolerance: Kurt Bardella interview* [Video]. YouTube https://www.youtube.com/watch?v=E_KuPGzwhgM

Peck, R. (2019). *Fox populism: Branding conservatism as working class*. Cambridge University Press.

Penabaz, F. (1965). Crusading preacher from the West: The story of Billy James Hargis. Christian Crusade.

Peristein, R. (2009). *Before the store: Barry Goldwater and the unmaking of the American consensus.* Bold Type Books.

Peters, J. (2022, July 29). Fox News, once home to Trump, now often ignores him. *The New York Times.*

Pew Research Center. (2020). Americans are divided by party in the sources they turn to for political news. *Pew Research Center.*

Prokop, A. (2023, February 28). "Make Trump a non person": Rupert Murdoch's Ron DeSantis pivot, explained by a legal filing. *Vox.*

Reeve, E. (2013a, January 4). Dick Armey sticks his FreedomWorks payback to Glenn Beck. *The Atlantic.*

Reeve, E. (2013b, May 29). Why fact-checkers find more GOP lies. *The Atlantic.*

Reuters (2024, September 5). Cable news channel Newsmax confidentially files for US IPO. *Reuters.*

Roberts, M. E., Stewart, B. M., Tingley, D., Lucas, C., Leder-Luis, J., Gadarian, S. K., . . . & Rand, D. G. (2014). Structural topic models for open-ended survey responses. *American Journal of Political Science, 58*(4), 1064–1082.

Roberts, M. E., Stewart, B. M., & Tingley, D. (2019). Stm: An R package for structural topic models. *Journal of Statistical Software, 91*, 1–40.

Rosenwald, B. (2019). *Talk radio's America: How an industry took over a political party that took over the United States.* Harvard University Press.

Rothmeyer, K. (1981). Citizen Scaife. *Columbia Journalism Review.*

Rutenberg, J. (2017, August 20). Behind the bluster of Steve Bannon's #war cry. *The New York Times.*

Savage, C. (2018, January 30). The real aim of the Nunes Memo is the Mueller investigation. *The New York Times.*

Schudson, M. (2000). The domain of journalism studies around the globe. *Journalism, 1*(1), 55–59.

Schwartz, J. (2018, December 14). The Weekly Standard, conservative outlet that criticized Trump, to shut down. *Politico.*

Severns, M. (2018, June 8). Trump leans to love mega donors. *Politico.*

Sexton, J. (2016, August 10). Seth Rich's family to conspiracy theorists: Please stop. *Hot Air.*

Sheppard, S. (2007). *The partisan press: A history of media bias in the United States.* McFarland.

Sherman, G. (2014). *The loudest voice in the room: How the brilliant, bombastic Roger Ailes built Fox News and divided a country.* Random House.

Shriver, L. (1981). *The Bible vote: Religion and the New Right.* Pilgrim Press.

Skocopol, T., & Hertel-Fernandez, A. (2016). The Koch network and Republican party extremism. Perspectives on Politics, *14*(3), 681–699.

Skocpol, T., & Williamson, V. (2016). *The Tea Party and the remaking of Republican conservatism.* Oxford University Press.

Smith, G., & Searles, K. (2014). Who let the (attack) dogs out? New evidence for partisan media effects. *Public Opinion Quarterly*, *78*(1), 71–99.

Silverman, C., Lytvynenko, J., Vo, L., & Singer-Vine, J. (2017, August 8). Inside the partisan fight for your news feed. *BuzzFeed*.

Simonov, A., Sacher, S., Dubé, J. P., & Biswas, S. (2022). Frontiers: the persuasive effect of Fox News: Noncompliance with social distancing during the COVID-19 pandemic. *Marketing Science*, *41*(2), 230–242.

Somodevilla, C. (2018, February 02). Even if you take the Nunes memo seriously, it makes no sense. *Politico*.

Sparrow, B. H. (2006). A research agenda for an institutional media. *Political Communication*, *23*(2), 145–157.

Spivak, R., & Wittes, B. (2021, January 12). About that Presidential Medal of Freedom: Revisiting the Nunes memo. *Lawfare*. https://www.lawfareblog.com/about-presidential-medal-freedom-revisiting-nunes-memo

SPJ (2014). *SPJ code of ethics*. Society of Professional Journalists.

Staff. (2010, March 31). Christopher Ruddy. *Folio Magazine*.

Stelter, B. (2017, March 6). Birth of a conspiracy theory: How Trump's wiretap claim got started. *CNN*.

Stelter, B. (2020). *Hoax: Donald Trump, Fox News, and the dangerous distortion of truth*. Simon & Schuster.

Stern, D., & Dixon, R. (2020, February 27). Ukraine court forces probe into Biden role in firing of prosecutor Viktor Shokin. *The Washington Post*.

Sullivan, M. (2018, November 29). When Fox News staffers break ethics rules, discipline follows—or does it? *The Washington Post*.

Tilly, C. (1986). *The contentious French*. Harvard University Press.

Therighting. (2021). *Rankings of traffic to the top right-wing websites based on unique monthly visitors*. https://www.therighting.com/metrics

Tuckman, G. (1978). *Making news: A study in the construction of reality*. Free Press.

Turvill, W. (2021 February 5). Murdoch's New York Post achieves first profit "in modern times." *Press Gazette*. https://pressgazette.co.uk/news/new-york-post-profit/

Vaughan, J. (2009). *The rise and fall of the Christian Coalition*. Wipf & Stock Publishers.

Viguerie, R., & Franke, D. (2004). *America's right turn: How conservatives used new and alternative media to take over America*. Taylor Trade Publishing.

Vogel, K., & Schreckinger, B. (2016, September 7). The most powerful woman in GOP politics. *Politico*.

Vogel, K., & McCalmont, L. (2011, June 15). Top radio talkers sell endorsements. *Politico*.

Wallace-Wells, B. (2019, January 3). Who killed the Weekly Standard? *The New Yorker*.

Warren, M. (2017, August 4). The real reason McMaster let Susan Rice keep her security clearance. *The Weekly Standard.*

Wells, C., Shah, D., Lukito, J., Pelled, A., Pevehouse, J. C., & Yang, J. (2020). Trump, Twitter, and news media responsiveness: A media systems approach. *New Media & Society, 22*(4), 659–682.

Wells, C., Shah, D. V., Pevehouse, J. C., Yang, J., Pelled, A., Boehm, F., . . . & Schmidt, J. L. (2016). How Trump drove coverage to the nomination: Hybrid media campaigning. *Political Communication, 33*(4), 669–676.

White, K. (2018). *The branding of right-wing activism: The news media and the Tea Party.* Oxford University Press.

Winter, J., & Groll, El. (2017, August 10). Here's the memo that blew up the NSC. *Foreign Policy.*

Wang, Y., Jung Kim, S., Shan, Y., Sun, Y., Jiang, X., Lee, H., Borah, P., Wagner, M., & Shah, D. (2024) Slant, extremity, and diversity: How the shape of news use explains electoral judgments and confidence. *Public Opinion Quarterly, 88*(SI), 708–734.

Wood, P. (2017, January 12). Trump "compromising" claims: How and why did we get here? *BBC.*

Wright, A. (2017, May 17). Republicans jump on special prosecutor bandwagon. *Politico.*

Yang, Y., & Bennett, L. (2021). Interactive propaganda: How Fox News and Donald Trump co-produced false narratives about the Covid-19 crisis. In P. Van Aelst & J. G. Blumler (Eds.), *Political communication in the time of coronavirus* (pp. 83–100). Routledge.

Yang, Y., Davis, T., & Hindman, M. (2023). Visual misinformation on Facebook. *Journal of Communication, 73*(4), 316–328.

Yang, Y., McCabe, S., & Hindman, M. (2024). Does Russian propaganda lead or follow? Topic coverage, user engagement, and RT and Sputnik agenda influence on US media. *International Journal of Press/Politics.* https://doi.org/10.1177/19401612241271074

Yang, Y. (2024). Rethinking right-wing media in the wake of an attempted coup. In K. White, D. Kreiss, S. McGregor & R. Tromble (Eds.), *Media and January 6th* (pp.163–172). Oxford University Press.

Yang, Y., Paudel, R., McShan, J., Hindman, M., Huang, H.H. & Broniatowski, D. (2025). Coordinated link sharing on Facebook. *Scientific Reports, 15* (1): 15684.

Yorke, J. (1992, June 9). Limbaugh, Bush's house guest. *The Washington Post.*

Young, D. (2023). *Wrong: How media, politics, and identity drive our appetite for misinformation.* Johns Hopkins University Press.

Zekeria, T. (2020, June 25). The dirty secret behind Ben Shapiro's extraordinary success on Facebook. *Popular Information.* https://popular.info/p/the-dirty-secret-behind-ben-shapiros?s=r

INDEX

For the benefit of digital users, indexed terms that span two pages (e.g., 52–53) may, on occasion, appear on only one of those pages.

Note: paragraph identifiers for figures are identified with *f*; for tables with *t*.